Additional Praise for
The End of Energy Obesity

"Peter Tertzakian has succeeded once again. In *The End of Energy Obesity* he has outlined a visionary approach to meeting the serious energy and environmental challenges of the world's projected population growth, continued economic growth and increasing living standards. This book is a clarion call to policy makers, business leaders and energy consumers everywhere."

—Guy Caruso, Senior Advisor, CSIS, Washington, D.C.
(former Administrator, US Energy Information Administration)

"Peter Tertzakian is one of the great energy thinkers of our time. In this compelling book he examines the factors that will drive 21st century energy demand in both developed and developing countries, and addresses the critical energy issue of our time: How can mankind bring its ever-growing demand for energy under control?"

—Hal Kvisle, CEO, TransCanada Corporation

"Anyone interested in understanding the forces that drive conflict and instability when it comes to energy should read Peter Tertzakian's important book. He makes it clear that the road ahead is difficult but not impossible. For those interested in how to attack the energy problem today for a better future, this is a must read book."

—General John P. Abizaid (Ret.), Former Combatant Commander, U.S. Central Command and member of the SAFE Energy Security Leadership Council

"*The End of Energy Obesity* is a fresh look at a pressing problem. Peter Tertzakian has followed his best seller of *A Thousand Barrels a Second* with thought provoking writing that's a must read for those concerned about the way forward for the industrialized world."

—The Honorable Peter MacKay, Minister of Defense and Minister for the Atlantic Gateway, Government of Canada

"Peter Tertzakian has once again taken an extremely complex topic on our unsustainably high use of energy in the USA and the world and put the topic into a series of food and body analogies. His prose is fun to read and the analogies are so apt. For anyone concerned about how we go on an energy diet, this book is a must read."

—Matthew R. Simmons, Chairman, Simmons & Company, Intl, Author of *Twilight in the Desert: The Pending Saudi Oil Shock and the World Economy*

"This book explores the critical role networked IT solutions play in changing the way energy is used and delivered. The network truly becomes a platform for monitoring and managing energy consumption in a much more efficient way, and we expect the benefits to accelerate as the network becomes more pervasive. Tertzakian shows the reader how networked collaboration technologies such as TelePresence can enable powerful, face-to-face interactions while reducing our energy appetite and carbon footprint."

—John Chambers, Chairman and CEO, Cisco

"Peter Tertzakian confronts us with our addiction to energy and its unfortunate and risky implications. For a new generation of policy makers anxious to make the right decisions about the environment and economic growth, *The End of Energy Obesity* is a timely self-help guide."
—Alan McFarlane, CEO Walter Scott & Partners Ltd, Edinburgh

The End of Energy Obesity advances The Asymmetry Principle of Energy Consumption — that our collective leverage for addressing global energy supply, security, and environmental challenges lies asymmetrically with reduced energy use rather than with new energy supply. This is key to meeting prudent goals for mitigating climate change risks."
—Ernest J. Moniz, Cecil and Ida Green Professor of Physics and Engineering Systems, Director, MIT Energy Initiative

"Perhaps the most imaginative energy economist around, Tertzakian has a gift for identifying complex energy trends and rendering them readable and understandable for experts and the general public alike. This book is full of fresh ideas that open up new and promising ways of thinking about the potential rewards of energy conservation."
—Thomas Huffaker, Former U.S. Consul General, Calgary, Canada

"Once again, Peter Tertzakian takes on a very complex and contentious issue: the world's seemingly insatiable appetite for energy. He not only discusses the consequences to prosperity, environment and security, but importantly lays out fact-based and logical ideas that require change, but don't compromise our standard of living."
—Gregory B. Jansen, Managing Director, Commonfund Capital, Inc.

"The crowd looked left as Peter looked right . . . again. In this new book he eloquently argues that solutions to energy obesity lie as much in the demand side as increasingly expensive supply additions. The book highlights the importance that consumer habits in the emerging industrial superpowers, specifically China will have on the global oil balance."
—David Hewitt, China Oil and Gas Analyst, CLSA, Hong Kong

"This book raises the essential challenge of our age — how to balance our resources and lifestyles. While it focuses brilliantly on today's energy issues, providing insightful commentary and discerning solutions, there is a broader message for all to appreciate."
—Peter Gaffney, Gaffney, Cline and Associates, U.K.

"For entrepreneurs involved in developing new, clean energy technologies, Peter Tertzakian's *The End of Energy Obesity* is an essential read. The context he presents puts all energy systems into perspective, and also shows that solutions to the world's sustainability problems extend into realms that may not be obvious to most people."
—Jonathan Rhone, CEO, Nexterra Energy Corp.

"This is a visionary book. A clear wake up and road map for our energy future."
—Harley Hotchkiss, Former chairman of the National Hockey League board of Governors

"Peter Tertzakian's book is a must-read for anyone looking for a comprehensive representation of the energy-related challenges that lie ahead in the coming decades."
—Deborah Yedlin Business Columnist, Calgary Herald

The End of Energy Obesity

Breaking Today's Energy Addiction for a Prosperous and Secure Tomorrow

Peter Tertzakian

with Keith Hollihan

WILEY

John Wiley & Sons, Inc.

Published by John Wiley & Sons, Inc., Hoboken, New Jersey.
Published simultaneously in Canada.
Photo credits: PhotoDisc, Inc./Getty Images.

For general information on our other products and services or for technical support, please
contact our Customer Care Department within the United States at (800) 762-2974,
outside the United States at (317) 572-3993 or fax (317) 572-4002.

Wiley also publishes its books in a variety of electronic formats. Some content that appears
in print may not be available in electronic books. For more information about Wiley
products, visit our web site at www.wiley.com.

Library of Congress Cataloging-in-Publication Data

Tertzakian, Peter.
   The end of energy obesity : breaking today's energy addiction for a prosperous and
secure tomorrow / Peter Tertzakian with Keith Hollihan.
      p. cm.
   Includes bibliographical references and index.
   ISBN 978-0-470-43544-1 (cloth)
  1. Energy industries.   2. Energy consumption.   3. Economic development.
 4. Power resources.   I. Hollihan, Keith.   II. Title.
   HD9502.A2T472 2009
   333.79—dc22
                                                        2009007447

Printed in the United States of America.

10 9 8 7 6 5 4 3 2 1

Contents

Acknowledgments

When I started this project at the beginning of 2008, I thought writing another book would be easier than my first. Keith Hollihan—who helped me with *A Thousand Barrels a Second: The Coming Oil Break Point and the Challenges Facing an Energy Dependent World*—agreed, especially when he heard my new ideas and how I had outlined the flow. It was not easy. Writing this book was one of the most challenging undertakings of my career because it involved contrasting the rigors of quantitative economic analysis against abstract prognostications about our civilization's social condition. The latter was exciting, but daunting new territory for me. Thanks go to Keith for working on a project that took 50 percent longer to create than we first expected. His contributions as a sounding board, writer, and editor once again helped me turn what is otherwise dry subject matter into what I hope you will find accessible, thought-provoking material—and enjoyable too!

This book would not have been possible without the fresh and inquisitive mind of Beata Komierowski, a young economist who was never shy about challenging what I thought was my wisdom, but was really entrenched convictions that needed modernizing. Her edits were invaluable, and her data mining and detailed quantitative analysis can be found throughout the book.

Long-time friend Scott Fawcett, who works at Cisco, was a real champion of my ideas early on, and deserves much gratitude. By setting up numerous interviews with high tech experts around the world and giving me unfettered access to Cisco's Telepresence systems, he and other Cisco employees helped me validate what were just conjectures at the start of the project—and helped save many gallons of jet fuel!

Friend and coworker Nancy Smith was a trusted reader that tirelessly and candidly provided me with feedback, constructive advice, detailed edits, and above all, encouragement. Thanks as well to the many others, including Derek Evans, Deborah Yedlin, Peter Gaffney, Tom Huffaker, Dale Edmonston, Philip Chang, Sebastian Gault, John Stewart, Subodh Gupta and Norval Scott, who took time to read, discuss, and comment with enthusiasm.

My research group at ARC Financial has always provided me with inspiration. Thanks go to Kara Baynton, a trusted, longtime colleague who manages the group, especially when I'm off writing books. Her diligent research feeds her need to debate me—even if it's "just because"—and helps keep my thinking honest. In addition, my understanding partners at ARC are always patient with me when I undertake big projects, and this time was no exception. Through it all, my assistant Cicilia Selinger kept me organized and helped with time-consuming details like formatting.

Thanks to B.G. Dilworth of the B.G. Dilworth Agency who again gave no-nonsense advice and helped secure the publisher, John Wiley & Sons. Gratitude there goes to Debra Englander, Executive Editor, who believed in the project from the start, Kelly O'Connor who patiently waited for the manuscript to be finished, Kevin Holm who produced the book, and the many others at Wiley who made this book possible. Diagrams in the book and the cover design were diligently prepared by Edwin Herrenschmidt of nonfiction Studios, who once again didn't complain about the tight timelines given.

Finally, thanks go to my family. More than ever before, my wife Jan and my two sons Alexander and André are to be thanked for their loving patience. They have always been supportive of my pet projects, but this time their tolerance of my preoccupations went far beyond acceptable family norms. This book, like my last, is dedicated to them.

Introduction

Look around you. Nearly everything that defines our way of life requires some sort of energy-consuming device. Once upon a time, the light bulb, the automobile, and the computer were luxury items, novelties that only the wealthiest could afford and that those of lesser means did without. Today all of these items are indispensable to the way most of us live, and all consume copious amounts of energy. Even the food we eat and the clothes we wear take energy to produce and deliver, just as the buildings we live, work, and play in require energy to make and operate. Is it any wonder that our energy needs are so great? We keep adding, at an ever-increasing pace, to the list of gadgets, lifestyle choices, and services that intensify our energy addiction. Our global appetite for primary fuels keeps growing as the dual drivers of population growth and wealth creation obliges ever greater consumption on a scale that's difficult to fathom.

Over the years we've made our energy devices more efficient, only to find the irony that doing so makes us consume even more energy. We've cut back our energy use in the face of crises, only to revert to bad habits after the troubles retreat and our memories fade. We've added more renewable sources only to find that they barely make a dent in the dominance of fossil fuels. We've introduced policies only to find that they often treat the symptom and not the cause of our energy borne issues.

Now we are *energy obese*. How are we, the 6.9 billion inhabitants of this planet, going to reduce our energy appetite and change our diet of fuels for a healthier, more prosperous and secure tomorrow?

■ ■ ■

Starting around 2002, when oil prices began rising, we began to feel economic, psychological, and environmental anxiety about our ability to sustain (let alone grow) the sources of energy we need. My previous book, *A Thousand Barrels a Second: The Coming Oil Break Point and the Challenges Facing an Energy Dependent World* (McGraw-Hill, 2006), showed how societies have historically responded to the pressure that builds when a vital energy source like oil comes under siege from the forces of scarcity, demographics, environment, and politics.

In that book, I argued that we weren't technically running out of oil, but that the world's needs had grown so great and so widespread, that we would soon be confronted with an energy "break point"—a historically infrequent, disruptive event that forces change in the way societies obtain and use their energy resources. The points I made in early 2006 rang true in the first half of 2008 when surging oil prices, geopolitical anxieties, and climate change concerns made us acutely aware of our vulnerability to fundamental energy issues, and pushed us to the brink of a break point. But then the pressure on energy supplies eased as the U.S. housing bubble burst, banks went into meltdown, and the entire global economy shifted into low gear.

The financial crisis that started in the second half of 2008 was an event so severe that by reversing our economic growth it also sharply reduced our energy demand. As a consequence of less money in our pockets, thinned out investment portfolios, and joblessness and foreclosures hitting close to home, energy suffered the same lower demand as every other good and service. This extended period of tight credit and contracting wealth demonstrated the least palatable, but most direct way to cut our energy needs: a rapid cut back in spending throughout society. In four short months, energy commodity prices fell to a fraction of where they were compared to the summer of 2008. Oil's fall was especially precipitous; its price dropped to one-fifth its peak and gasoline at U.S. pumps went from over $4.00 a gallon to $1.50—the lowest price in five years.

Fundamentally, nothing in the character of how energy was delivered to us, or used by us, had changed in the latter half of 2008. Our cars were still overwhelmingly addicted to gasoline. Our lights went on the same way after Lehman Brothers collapsed as before. Our consumption habits rooted in suburban commuting and inefficient electrical power generation hadn't been reengineered overnight. Emerging economies still held the desire to develop rapidly. Geopolitical animosities between oil exporters and big importers spanning multiple generations remained unreconciled. Instead, what had changed was sudden erosion in people's willingness and ability to consume, which in turn reduced the global demand on energy across the board.

While a return to lower oil prices was a welcome by-product of the slower economy, unfortunately history shows that the return of cheap energy always gives a false sense of security and lulls us back into apathy just when visionary action is needed most. As this book goes to publication in early 2009, it's difficult to say when economic health will be restored to the world. But when normal growth does resume—and it will—it is a certainty that the energy problems put on hold in late 2008 will resurface, becoming larger and more intractable than ever before.

■ ■ ■

In Part I of this book, we will explore the direct connection between economic growth, improved quality of life, and greater energy consumption. That's a relationship I call the First Principle of Energy Consumption, which describes an imperative that has characterized successful societies since the dawn of civilization several thousand years ago. Unfortunately, looking to the future, in a world in which the balance of energy commodities can easily be tipped, it's also a relationship that is no longer sustainable.

In Part II, we'll look closely at the roster of conventional solutions that are considered whenever an energy crisis becomes dire. I'll explain where those options fail to meet our current needs. Despite much talk about renewable energy sources, "clean tech" devices, offshore drilling, efficiency gains, carbon taxes, and so on, the solutions to our looming energy issues largely lie elsewhere. The sheer scale of our seven billion-person global village means that we can no longer easily meet our world's craving for cheap, clean, and secure energy just by following old paradigm approaches such as tapping new supplies, legislating partial policies, or instituting slow advances in conventional and alternative energy technologies. Hard science and engineering can and will help us figure out how to rebalance our needs in the face of the next break point, but the root cause of our energy problems must be addressed by considering the social dynamics of consumption as well.

In Part III, we will encounter a number of new, even radical ideas about energy. As we assess the convergence of circumstances that are likely to reshape the way we think about energy, we'll learn about new uses for the energy-consuming technology we already have; new innovations in the store of fossil fuels available to us; and new, alternative ways of living, playing, and working that use less energy. It is in this last area, in particular, that we will begin to see an energy solution with tremendous leverage. Instead of finding more barrels of oil and turning our arable land from food production to fuel production, the most promising energy innovation will come from developing creative ways to lower energy use while actually improving our lifestyles. For the first time in history, a convergence of circumstances and the availability of pivotal solutions can combine to break the relationship between increasing prosperity and increasing energy consumption.

A New Vocabulary

To improve the accessibility of my thoughts and arguments, I will present a new vocabulary, and thus, a new way of thinking about energy-related problems and solutions. In modern society, energy is as pervasive and as necessary as the food we eat, and the linguistic parallels between the two are strong. Accordingly, and given the many similarities between our demand for food calories and our demand for energy, I'll be talking a lot in this book about *energy appetite*. That's the term I use for describing how much energy we consume. I'll refer to appetite from a world perspective, then compare nations and, most importantly, bring that appetite metric down to the individual level. I'll show you in graphic terms how much our energy appetite has grown over the last century after the introduction into society of wondrous inventions like the light bulb, automobile, and central heating.

I'll also use the term *energy obesity*. In North America, an abundance of cheap, unhealthy food and sedentary lifestyle has led to an obesity epidemic. Ironically, obesity is rapidly becoming a concern in developing countries too, where Western-style foods have suddenly become plentiful and upward-mobility has become possible. Health professionals recognize that too many cheap, empty calories in our diet contribute to the problem of obesity, as do mind-set, genetic and family history, and lifestyle and behavior choices. But whatever the causes, the results are yielding serious social problems such as high health care costs, loss in productivity, and reduced quality of life for millions of people.

That metaphor holds true in the world of energy, too. Over the last decade, specifically in North America, our energy appetite has soared to such an extent that we are now energy obese. You'll be able to see the figures, make the comparisons, and draw your own conclusions, but I feel confident my observations and inferences will be as obvious to you as they are to me. Like cheap junk food, long-term availability of cheap energy has allowed industrialized countries, especially the United States and Canada, to become accustomed to a lifestyle of overconsumption. We traded in our fuel efficient cars for gas-guzzling SUVs; we moved into larger houses, farther away from where we work; and our lifestyles depend on central heat and air conditioning, year-round access to fresh fruits and vegetables, and cheap foreign-made consumer items. Any energy we may have saved with technological advances in efficiency, we promptly consumed without a second thought. Having grown up following the norms of this society over the past half century, I admit to being as blameworthy as the next person in perpetuating energy obesity.

Such choices felt positive and natural at the time—but they have come at a cost. Like physical obesity, where illnesses like diabetes and heart disease show us the alarming severity of the condition, energy obesity can also be understood in part by looking at the problems that result. Susceptibility to volatile energy costs, increasing vulnerability to energy security, and the harmful impact on the environment are some of the more obvious symptoms. Those conditions have been building for years, and in the summer of 2008, before the onset of the credit crisis, we saw the symptoms become dramatically more acute as every energy commodity rose in price, energy security escalated to the top of political agendas, and the issue of fossil fuels and climate change became prominent in the public conversation.

Lacking magic bullets and miracles, we found ourselves facing difficult choices until the financial crisis temporarily destroyed energy demand. In the time that has been made available to us before that demand begins to surge again we must summon our reserves of innovation and discipline. The good news is that we can solve all of our energy-related problems by focusing on the one fundamental challenge that is often overlooked: reducing the quantity of energy we actually consume. If we focus on reducing energy appetite rather than putting so much emphasis on searching for oil in extreme parts of the world, relying on incomplete energy policies, making dubious trade-offs between food and fuel, or curbing, trading, and burying carbon emissions, we won't continue fooling ourselves (like the dieter who swears off cake and cookies and binges on ice cream as a reward for good behavior).

This is an area in which we can all have a profound impact. Energy is a global issue and it can seem as though decisions about it are made in insulated realms well beyond the ordinary person's influence—in the halls of government, the mega-corporation, or the Organization of the Petroleum Exporting Countries (OPEC) cartel. Ultimately, however, energy is consumed at the level of you and me; collectively we are the ones who make billion-dollar decisions about energy in the way we heat our homes, light our cities, and how far we drive our cars. We also make billion-dollar decisions about energy indirectly through what products we buy, where they are manufactured, and how we use them, as well as where we live, how we work, and what we do in our spare time.

We must develop, then, a healthier and more conscientious awareness of the energy we consume. This comes from understanding, first of all, that having an energy appetite is not bad but positive. It is through the use of energy that we enjoy the comforts and advances of modern life. Indeed, developing nations understand this notion acutely, which is why countries like China and India are focused so resolutely on expanding their energy holdings and locking up future reserves.

Here my food metaphor remains apt. People who don't get enough calories over time are usually unhealthy, just as those who eat too many calories over time are typically afflicted with a different set of health problems. In the same way, nations that don't have access to enough energy and those that consume too much face different problems. Overeating is a result of both cognitive and emotional malfunctioning. The intellect does not recognize when the body's hunger has been adequately satiated. In other words, the problem lies not necessarily with the appetite being too large, but with the mind's poor judgment in recognizing the point when one's eating has become excessive and unhealthy. Energy obesity involves a similar disconnect between mind-set and lifestyle. We must expose and understand that disconnect to make the right changes in our energy-intense societies.

Ending energy obesity means understanding the characteristics of our energy appetite, choosing good sources of energy over bad ones, reducing the waste of unused energy, optimizing our diet through a healthier selection of fuels, and limiting the power of our addictions by reducing our overreliance on detrimental energy sources. But ending energy obesity cannot entail ending our pursuit of a higher standard of living. Just as food cannot be simply taken away without dire consequences, so the lifeline we have to energy consumption should be acknowledged and appreciated. In order to end energy obesity, we must look to new technologies that use less energy, improve our lifestyle, and offer irresistible value to energy obese consumers, businesses, and nations around the globe.

By the end of this book, you'll learn how nations grow their energy appetites and diets; appreciate the sheer scale of our energy consumption; recognize what's lean and what's obese; have a better feel for what's idealistic and what's pragmatic; understand where the greatest opportunities for ending energy obesity lie; and you'll have a futuristic look at the amazing ways your life will change positively in the next decade. After all, just like the old adage, "you are what you eat," it's synonymous to say "how you live shapes your energy appetite."

But I'm getting ahead of myself. For now, let me show you how we have arrived at our current circumstances, why conventional strategies for resolving our energy problems are insufficient, and where we possess real leverage for making meaningful change.

The End of Energy Obesity

Part I

THE MAKING OF OUR ENERGY APPETITE

Chapter 1

After the Banquet

It seems fitting that Henry Ford and Thomas Edison—the two men most associated with growing our energy appetite—met at a banquet. The occasion was the concluding ceremony of the Seventeenth Annual Association of Edison Illuminating Companies, held in August 1896 at Manhattan Beach on Coney Island.

Henry Ford was 33 years old and had been working at Detroit Edison for five years, but he was already chief engineer for a company that supplied electricity to 1,000 residents and 8,000 streetlights in the Detroit area. Thomas Edison, 16 years Ford's elder, was the ambitious younger man's lifelong idol. Ford was part of the generation Edison inspired when he gained worldwide fame in 1882 for building an electric power plant and illuminating the buildings of lower Manhattan. With his industrial research laboratory at Menlo Park, his bold predictions about the future, and his many imaginative inventions, Edison made great feats of science and engineering seem both exciting and attainable. For Ford, as a young man experimenting in his spare time with gasoline-powered engines in the barn behind his house, it meant a lot when he read in

3

a newspaper the year before that Edison had proclaimed the horseless carriage "the coming wonder"[1] and predicted that cities would one day be filled with them. That's how Ford saw the future, too, and he was awestruck as he sat at the far end of Edison's head table at their company's yearly send-off dinner.

Edison was hard of hearing, and temperamentally disinclined to large gatherings, but he was always interested in keeping tabs on the work of his most promising engineers. As knives and forks clinked against plates, the conversation turned to the problem of batteries for electric cars. Edison leaned forward to listen. Today, most of us think of the electric car as a possible future alternative to the traditional gasoline-powered automobile. In Edison's day, there were a number of options—including steam, the internal combustion engine, and electricity—all battling to become the accepted standard for propelling motorized vehicles. In fact, battery power was the more popular consumer choice at the time—and it was certainly the standard that was in the best interest of the men at Edison's table, who were all in the electricity business. But Edison held serious doubts about its prospects, understanding clearly that the electric car would be forever limited by the short distance the vehicle could travel before needing to recharge.

Down the length of the table, the men discussed the latest developments in battery technology with enthusiasm and confidence, as though trying to impress Edison with the progress being made. Of course, batteries were the answer—electricity, after all, was the wonder source. But Edison dismissed some of the notions and ignored others, his own interest in the conversation waning. To spark things up again, Henry Ford's boss, a man named Alexander Dow, mentioned offhandedly that his young chief engineer was on the other side of the fence, technologically speaking. Ford was a proponent of the gasoline-powered car. It was a ridiculous idea, and Dow described an amusing scene to accompany it. Ford was fond of driving his wife and son in a four-wheeled quadricycle of his own invention up to the walls of the Detroit Edison Company. Dow had been drawn to the window to see it, annoyed by the idea that his best engineer was wasting his time on such a diversion, accomplishing little more, he believed, than scaring horses with a loud engine and forcing pedestrians off the road.

Instead of joining the other men in their tone of good-humored dismissiveness, Edison began asking Ford pointed questions about his hobby. While the senior engineers and businessmen lost interest and mused about the meal and the convention, Edison and Ford were soon sitting side-by-side, deep in conversation.

Ford sketched out his engineering ideas on scrap paper and Edison pressed him on the nuances of cylinders and pistons. The questions and answers went on at length until even a curious listener might have turned attention elsewhere. Then Edison sat back in appreciation and banged his fist on the table. "Young man, that's the thing!" he said enthusiastically. "You have it. Keep at it. Electric cars must keep near to power stations. The storage battery is too heavy. Steam cars won't do either, for they have a boiler and fire. Your car is self-contained, carries its own power plant, no fire, no boiler, no smoke, and no steam. You have the thing. Keep at it!"[2]

Ford was ecstatic. To get that kind of affirmation from the man who had done more than any other to invent the modern world was a thrilling moment in his young life. Edison's words inspired Ford three years later to shore up his own entrepreneurial courage and leave the security and prestige of his position at Detroit Edison and found the Detroit Automobile Company. There he would begin development on a series of cars, tirelessly tinkering with a vision in mind, each new vehicle solving more problems and getting closer to the achievement of the first ever mass-produced car, the Model T.

Edison's prophecy came to pass. Ford's motorized vehicles were the coming wonder. Twenty or so years after their first meeting, Ford's success, wealth, and fame would outstrip Edison's (who Ford admitted, with regret, was the world's worst businessman). But Ford never stopped revering Edison and wondering at the impact of his ideas. The two men eventually renewed their acquaintance and became good friends. Ford funded some of Edison's later work and built a shrine for him in his museum in Dearborn, Michigan. Every year, the two men took a car camping trip with whichever president was leading the nation at the time. They called themselves the Vagabonds and took pride in how dirty they got while exploring the great outdoors.

By then, automobiles were everywhere, as were light bulbs and power lines, those innovations spreading outward in a spiral of change and economic growth, the ramifications of which we're still experiencing today. The way we work, live, and consume goods has never been the same since. As I aim to show you, our energy appetite also expanded as a result of those two men in ways that even the great Edison couldn't imagine. The meal shared by Edison and Ford at that banquet in Coney Island was just the beginning of America's, and indeed the world's, never-ending energy feast. To power the modern societies Edison and Ford made possible, immense quantities of oil, coal, natural gas, and uranium have been consumed over the century that followed.

The problem we face today is what to do now that the great banquet is over.

The First Principle of Energy Consumption

Innovations like electricity and the automobile change our lives. Because they bring us many advantages, we want them and readily accept the changes they bring to our lifestyles and behaviors in comfort, efficiency, and productivity. Our economy grows and our standard of living improves as a direct result of these life-altering inventions. We consume more energy, too. In fact, the relationship between economic growth, an improved standard of living, and an expanded energy appetite is so strong and so consistent throughout history that I call it the *First Principle of Energy Consumption*.

Simply put, this principle means that the better off you are, the more energy you use. History bears this principle out. During the early agrarian age 6,000 years ago, human beings increased their energy appetite when they first yoked the ox and used its power to till fields and draw water from wells. The ox was just as much an energy-consuming device as an automobile or a vacuum cleaner. For the early farmer, the increase in productivity that resulted made oxen a compelling alternative to doing the same work by hand. After all, human muscle provides about 35 watts of power, a mere one-twentieth the power of a large animal. All the farmer needed to do to generate this extra power was to supply the ox with hay—the biofuel of the day.

At the same time, however, as the benefits of this power source were realized and reliance on oxen increased, so did the farmer's dependence on energy. In order to get more work out of the ox, the farmer needed to grow more hay. Of course, if the farmer didn't see a net benefit from his efforts, there wouldn't be any reason to increase his appetite for energy. But the work supplied by the ox, even taking into account the extra work required to grow and harvest the hay, produced a surplus of energy that could be devoted toward improving quality of life. The farmer won time to till more fields and produce more food, raise a larger family, build a better house, see to religious concerns, manage the affairs of government, contribute to communal defense, tell stories, sing songs, make crafts and produce art, or have surplus to pay to be entertained by those who did.

Consider something closer to our times. You may not have heard of Gaius Sergius Orata before, but he was the Edison or Ford of his time. A Roman merchant and engineer with bright ideas, entrepreneurial inclinations, and a gift for getting things done, Orata invented the *hypocaust* about 2,100 years ago.

Orata's hypocaust—from the Latin word meaning "heat from below"—was a kind of centralized home heating system for the typical Roman villa. In order to build it, the foundation of the villa was constructed with small pillars to create a crawl space beneath the stone floors. Outside the house, a slave was needed to tend twigs and logs in an attached, subsurface fire place, and the resulting hot air was then channeled through the crawl space, heating the cold stone floors and providing the family inside with climate controlled comfort all winter long.

Orata's innovation was received with open arms by the Roman world. Prior to this, living through cold, damp European winters was not easy, especially in the north. Houses were drafty and lacked fireplaces, so people wore wraps or heavy clothes and shifted their activities to whichever rooms were being warmed by the sun. The only artificial heat came from small charcoal braziers— metal containers with legs and handles that could be moved from room to room. Though primitive, such devices were a cheap and relatively effective system, and are still in use in parts of Italy today.

When the hypocaust came along, it offered a significant upgrade over the smoky charcoal brazier. Soon, it became a popular addition to homes and Orata became wealthy buying estates, retrofitting them for his hypocaust, and selling them to those eager for the quality of life improvements afforded by his innovation. Indeed, Orata's idea caught on in unanticipated ways. Roman builders soon began engineering systems that funneled hot air through hollow channels between stone walls as well as below the floors. Later, Orata's system was adapted to heating water in communal bathing facilities. The famous Roman bath was the result, a tangible symbol of the luxury and quality of life the people of that ancient empire enjoyed.

It's easy to appreciate why the Romans would readily adopt Orata's new technology. Imagine your own life without central heating in the winter—indeed, without stoves, electric lighting or a car—and picture how eagerly you might snap those advantages up as soon as they became available. When we think about such devices, however, we rarely consider the fuel or energy required to make them work and we don't calculate or project how much our energy appetite will grow as a result. Instead, we long for the luxury or the convenience, and only worry about the fuel when it becomes too costly or inconvenient to obtain.

Charcoal was the primary fuel used for heating and cooking in ancient Rome, as it was in Europe until well after the Industrial Revolution. Charcoal is the result of wood burned in the absence of oxygen. As a fuel, it has many advantages—it is relatively smokeless and odorless; it is very portable, easy to ignite, and burns for a long time. The wood required to heat hypocausts is less efficient than charcoal and, on its own merits, would seem to be a step backward. But the charcoal brazier had its limitations and the hypocaust had plenty of compelling advantages. The hypocaust was fueled by great quantities of wood, replenished and fed, of course, by the attendant slaves. As wealthy Romans began to appreciate their improved quality of life, the innovation spread. More hypocausts, more luxury, and more wood were needed. The logical conclusion? The use of the hypocaust in more and more houses and community baths was directly responsible for the deforestation of land wherever the innovation took hold. In order to feed the growing Roman energy appetite, the great forests of Europe literally went up in smoke.

The hypocaust is just one example of how advanced societies achieve a higher standard of living through increased consumption of energy. Once we have become accustomed to the advantages of a new energy-consuming technology like the hypocaust, or in our case the light bulb or the automobile, we do not voluntarily choose to give them up. In fact, from the time humans first learned to use fire in a controlled manner, with each standard of living improvement throughout history, our appetite for energy has grown ever larger.

Breaking that 6,000-year super trend—the empirical law that I call the First Principle of Energy Consumption—is what this book is about. Can we, the world community, figure out for the first time in our history how to keep improving our standard of living while actually cutting back on the amount of energy we consume? I believe we can, but first we must understand the complexities behind the evolution of our dependence on energy.

The Way We Live

There's nothing simple or easy about curbing energy appetite. Without energy and energy-consuming devices, our modern life is unthinkable. Every i-Phone and laptop, every gas station and subway, every cup of coffee and bowl of cereal—every commodity we use, consume, or enjoy embodies the energy needed to produce it, deliver it to our hands, and turn it on. Think of a time in your life when the power went out or you ran out of gas—how helpless and disconnected that made you feel. The car engine, the refrigerator, the battery on the telephone were immediately revealed to be essentials that you took for granted until their power source was removed. Just imagine the chaos it would bring if these essentials were unavailable for any length of time.

One such time was the massive blackout that started at 4:11 P.M. on August 14, 2003 when a power plant in Cleveland, Ohio, went offline. The blackout spread in a chain reaction across much of northeast North America, as the regional electricity grid effectively short-circuited itself. Suddenly, fifty million people were given a hands-on lesson in how wired our world is, even in a supposedly wireless age, and how pervasively energy is integrated into the way we live.

In New York City, the birthplace of the electric grid, the abrupt power failure was particularly jarring. This wasn't another 9-11, but the disruption and confusion that ensued had people thinking it was. On Wall Street, computer terminals and television screens went dark without warning, as they did all over the city. Subways came to a sudden halt, and 400,000 passengers found themselves stuck beneath the ground. In office towers, elevators stopped working, trapping employees inside, air conditioning units and fans went dead, and many thousands of workers began the trek down long, dark stairwells, lighting their way with the low glow of their cell phone screens. The streets filled up as department stores and shops and train stations emptied. It was a brutally hot afternoon, and there was no place to get cool. Vendors, sensing the opportunity, immediately began selling their bottled water and ice cream with extra zeal.

Using our Blackberries and cell phones, we've grown accustomed to being in contact with anyone, anywhere, at any time. When the power went out, that infrastructure of instant communication collapsed as circuits got overloaded and area cell towers ceased to function. Those trying to reach their loved ones and coworkers formed long lines at the pay phones still in operation. The electronic billboards that bathe Times Square in a constant neon light were dark, the endless flow of information and advertising cut like a ribbon. Anyone with a portable radio drew listeners around them as people were eager to get news about what had happened, even as they were puzzled by what to do next and how to get home.

Without subways and commuter trains, the mass transportation system was nonexistent. Taxis and buses could not begin to handle the overflow. The tunnels were closed for safety and security so the only way out of Manhattan, suddenly an island again, was to walk across the bridges. Tens of thousands began the trek in the heat, slinging jackets over shoulders, opening shirt collars, kicking off uncomfortable shoes. The exodus was another reminder of 9-11, but this time the mood was calm and peaceful, even jovial, as everyone marveled at the city emptying out one step at a time. In the boroughs, travel by car was an adventure in chaos and a lesson in social adaptability. Some 11,600 traffic signals were out of order. Inevitably, at least one civilian took charge at every major intersection, standing tall in the middle of the traffic, directing the cars to go forward or wait, accepting bottles of water or baseball caps from grateful drivers passing by, enjoying the cheers and thanks.

Grocery stores, corner delis, and restaurants needed to sell their perishable goods or throw them out. Home refrigerators needed to be emptied, too. Prices on food plummeted even as the cost of batteries, flashlights, candles, bottled water, and portable radios went up. But anyone without cash in their wallet before the power went out couldn't buy what the stores and street vendors were selling. Cash registers didn't work, credit cards couldn't be used, and ATMs were sealed as tightly as Egyptian tombs. You couldn't even fill your car with gas, since the pumps, run by electricity, were also out of order.

And yet for one night the city got by. The mood was upbeat, the troubles few. Bars and public squares became gathering spots as spontaneous parties and barbeques broke out. Most people relaxed on their stoops, gathered with neighbors on the sidewalk, or leaned out their windows to get air. For once, you could see the stars twinkling brightly in the sky, but the darkness at street level was stunningly thick and disorienting. Here and there generators hummed—and certainly in the hospitals, babies were still being born, operations taking place, patients being cared for—but even the most iconic landmarks, like the Chrysler Building and the Empire State Building, were utterly dark.

For many, it was that image of the New York City skyline at night that seemed most strange. The strings of lights across the bridges, the sparkling buildings, the amassed collection of all that commerce, finance, culture, and humanity: everything had gone black. It would be several days before power was fully restored to the city, as block by block the lights and air conditioners and refrigerators came back to life. It was a short-lived energy fast that changed not a bit the long-term appetite for energy in the United States. Within a week, New York and the rest of the country were back to business as usual.

Breaking the First Principle

The bright lights of New York may provide the iconic image of a modern metropolitan skyline, but on the other side of the world in Asia, new types of cities saw an unprecedented burst in growth and wealth over the past decade. Shanghai—the New York or London of the rapidly industrializing third world—is a modern marvel, with striking architecture, rapid economic growth, and an exhilarating pace of life. Billboards, traffic jams, and skyscrapers are ubiquitous. Air conditioners, high tech lighting, refrigerators, large screen TVs, computers, and cell phones are the norm. As a result, residents of Shanghai have experienced a dramatic increase in energy appetite over the past few years. To feed that hunger, giant hydroelectric dams have been built, valleys and villages flooded, and thick power cables strung across the countryside on immense steel towers. Throughout China, with government policies and economic growth steering the change, urban lifestyles are expanding and wealth is growing as a once dormant fifth of the world's population has begun buying the cars, modern living spaces, and refrigerators we all take for granted. The scale of that shift and the impact on our global energy appetite cannot be overlooked.

Elsewhere in the world, whether in Bangalore, Toronto, or Mexico City, energy appetite has surged as twenty-five years of strong economic growth and increased trade and development have deepened and spread. Up until the financial crisis of 2008, in the West, we were feeling the pressures of this global energy demand more acutely than in past decades because the collective economies of China, India, and the other aggressively industrializing countries were suddenly competing on the same field for fuels like crude oil, natural gas, and coal. In the intensified scramble for limited resources, energy supplies were tightening, prices were being driven up, and the possibilities of geopolitical conflict were growing, even as we further stressed the world's ecosystem by exploiting and burning fossil fuels. But how do we tell the developing world that it is okay for us to have grown obese on consuming all of the world's cheap energy, but it would be better if they remained malnourished and underfed? In our comfortable society of plenty in the west, we may overlook the underlying importance of energy to the way we live, but nations like China and India understand that an appetite for energy *is the fundamental means of achieving the "American Dream,"* a dream they now wish to share in themselves. Regardless of the financial crisis, they want what we have, and they know that they need reliable, plentiful energy to get and maintain it.

Today, whenever we debate the many energy problems we face, it's easy to lose sight of the great benefits that have come about because of our growing dependence on fossil fuels. As a society, we have become increasingly addicted to energy because we thoroughly enjoy the standard of living that energy-consuming devices and services make possible. In previous eras, our appetite for energy was relatively low, but so was our quality of life. In the medieval age, most people survived at a subsistence level through the labor of their own hands, while kings and lords lived off the labor of others—much like early farmers lived off the work of oxen and Romans lived off slave labor. The industrial revolution increased our energy appetite dramatically as a higher standard of living reached more and more people. Even those we think of as moving from the idyllic countryside to overcrowded cities and awful factory conditions did so not because they were forced into slavery, but because the industrializing cities, however grim, still represented a step up from where they came from. Energy-consuming devices like the air conditioner, the light bulb, and the car serve us like slaves and make kings of us all. But what do we do now that our energy appetite has grown so large that it threatens our energy supply, our environment, and our political stability?

The answer is that we must reduce our overall energy consumption while still improving our quality of life, not only in the comfort of the richest nations on earth, but around the world, where standards of living are just beginning to rise. Admiral Hyman Rickover, the father of the American nuclear navy and an adviser to President Carter during the energy crisis of the 1970s, observed that, "A reduction of per capita energy consumption has always in the past led to a decline in civilization and a reversion to a more primitive way of life."[3] And he's right. If we were to sufficiently ration, conserve, or cut our energy appetite today in order to bring a measure of balance to our consumption levels, the impact on our economy would be immediately painful and harmful to our standard of living. You need only think of long lines for gasoline in the United States or the impact of the coal miners' strike in the United Kingdom in the 1970s to recall societies that were under stress, economically challenged, and jarred out of a comfortable lifestyle because their supplies of important sources of energy were curtailed. In comparison, those events were only short-term periods of discomfort compared to the potential challenges we are likely to be facing in the not-too-distant future.

Few of us today, no matter what our political or economic values, would eagerly embrace a decline in our standard of living and an adoption of a more primitive way of life through a major reduction in energy appetite. And what politician would risk their political future on a platform that mandated, regulated, or inhibited lifestyles we have come to think of as part of our birthright? Since President Nixon imposed a 55 mph speed limit and President Carter wore a sweater on national television to argue for the imperative of conservation, few have had the courage to try. It's far easier for our leaders to win elections on the promise of economic growth without acknowledging the corollary of their promise: that it requires an ever-increasing amount of energy to sustain that growth.

Edison and Ford did not create our energy appetite when they met at the banquet in Coney Island; they just catalyzed a new and particularly steep phase of its growth. Our problem is not energy. We need energy, and always have and always will. Our problem is that our current lifestyle is predicated on an overconsumption of cheap energy calories beyond what is healthy or sustainable for the rest of the world. Additionally, our options for getting more out of the energy sources we currently depend on, or obtaining new, secure sources as reliable substitutes to sustain the way we live, are more limited than most of us realize.

Meaningful changes in the world of energy take decades, if not centuries, to realize. Even so, most of the discussion among experts, policy makers, and concerned citizens is about changing the nature of our energy diet—by substituting traditional energy sources with new or improved alternatives such as solar power, biofuels, or wind—or on converting more energy into useful work through improvements in efficiency. Although these are efforts worthy of scientific and entrepreneurial endeavor and undeniably part of the overall solution, even revolutionary success in such areas will not be enough to give everyone on this planet sufficient cheap, clean, and secure energy to satisfy our growing global appetite, especially over the next few decades. The reality of our energy needs—the hard numbers, the objective analysis, the global perspective—requires that we break out of the paradigm in which we are currently looking for answers and start seeking solutions elsewhere.

At the same time, nobody wants to think about taking a step back in quality of life, particularly when that change is being forced on them. For 6,000 years, energy consumption and growth in energy demand have gone hand-in-hand as part of *the First Principle*. So how do we break *the First Principle* and reduce our appetite for energy while still growing our economy and improving our standard of living?

I believe that new generations of Fords, Edisons, and Oratas will save the day. Indeed, their inventions, innovations, and progress in developing new technology are already shifting our lives in ways few of us have yet to grasp. Before this book ends, I will tell you what those converging technologies and social changes are and explain how they are shaping a world in which energy appetite can actually be reduced. Luckily, it's not a grim or depressing picture of a diminished standard of living and a stagnant economy. Instead, it's a brand-new reality that we will embrace because the new lifestyles, comforts, and entertainments, as well as more efficient and productive ways of working, will improve our lives.

To glimpse that future, imagine a lifestyle, not twenty years from now but less than ten, which doesn't center on working in a tall office building far away from your home. No more long commutes or traffic jams. No more cultural isolation in a distant suburb. Instead, you go to work on foot or in a light natural gas or electricity-powered car to the corporate headquarters in your neighborhood. Actually, it's not just *your* corporate headquarters; it serves many of your neighbors, most of whom work for a different company or in a different occupation. You like going there because it's a hub of activity. There are coffee shops, restaurants, stores, fitness centers, medical clinics, a post office, and bank outlets on that block. Inside the building, you greet familiar faces and enter a room. You enter alone but once inside people surround you. Some of those people notice you coming in and look up from their work to greet you. It's taken you some time to get used to the fact that none of these colleagues are actually present in the room. Instead, what you're seeing is their vivid and clear images projected on the telepresence wallpaper. Similarly, the communication between you and them is instantaneous, so you can not only see them but speak to them in real time as well. Occasionally, you get a visit from one of your customers or partners, and the scenery changes to allow for private consultation. You might also replace the colleagues on your display with a calm nature scene or family photos when you take a break.

Your work awaits, and you get down to it. The morning's schedule is packed with meetings, and you marvel at the fact that a few years ago every one of those events would have required a separate airplane trip. You still remember how arduous and frustrating such trips can be. These days, you only travel by plane when you want to go on vacation or make essential in-person contact; the congestion, frustration, and long waits at airports have been reduced a great deal. At lunch, you have time to see your family or friends because everyone is nearby. After work, there's a special occasion and you hurry home. It's your oldest daughter's birthday. She's away at college and has no time to come home for the weekend, but she nevertheless joins the family at the dining room table for the birthday celebration. Everyone sings and the dog, always confused by who's really there and who's not, wags his tail excitedly. The dinner table conversation is about school, work, the upcoming Superbowl, and a vacation you're planning for Mexico. Your youngest daughter tells everyone about her recent exams. She goes to the neighborhood school and sits in a class-room with her friends, but a few of her more exciting electives are with teachers from other parts of the world. That still amazes you, but she finds telepresence kind of boring, actually. She much prefers the online gath-erings in which she meets friends in their avatar forms. Sometimes they go shopping or watch a movie that way. You don't approve of the risqué way she dresses her avatar, but that's what being a teenager is all about.

On Saturday morning, you and your wife go for a hike in the countryside with the dog. When you get back, your water heater has left a message on the household message board that it's using too much electricity. You'd noticed the increase in home energy consumption a few days ago because the orb on your kitchen counter was glowing a pale yellow rather than green. Now you've confirmed the reason. You've found a copy of an automatic e-mail your home energy computer sent to an electrician identifying the problem. A simple confirmation will have him come to your house on Monday and have the appliance repaired. It's getting late in the afternoon, so your wife squeezes in a workout in the basement fitness room. The avatar instructor chides her jokingly for missing a few days. That evening, you join two other neighborhood couples at a restaurant and then go to the neighborhood concert hall where Yo Yo Ma is playing. He's not actually at your neighborhood performance center, he's playing at Lincoln Center in New York, but the three-dimensional image on the stage and pristine quality of the acoustics make the experience essentially the same as an in-person appearance, at a much lower ticket cost. The standing ovation surprises you because suddenly the view is blocked by people who are actually attending the event in New York.

Over coffee you talk about the music. The concert was great, but you're more excited about the big game tomorrow. You've got three cameras reserved at the Superbowl in Miami. It will be like following the action from the 50 yard line. You'd been skeptical about paying extra for the service when it first came out two years before, but once you'd experienced sports filling up the entire wall of your family room with a picture so clear you can see sweat on skin, it was impossible to go back to simple TV. Besides, the prices and energy consumption rates have come down so much, it only made sense to switch.

Does all of that sound unlikely—a fantasy of science fiction? I'm not claiming I know the exact look and feel of our world five or ten years from now, but I do know the coming changes are that dramatic, or more. It's possible, looking back at other major shifts in energy consumption over the past 250 years, to predict the way today's technologies and social and market forces might align. Consider the shift in lifestyle that someone living before Edison and Ford would have experienced when things like the light bulb, car, and airplane arrived. Would they have believed it if you'd told them what was going to happen? In a few short decades, American cities were converted from whale lamps and horse drawn carriages to telephones and family cars. More to the point, think of the changes you've experienced in your own life in the last 10 years. The way you shop, communicate, meet people, listen to music, find your way when you're lost, entertain yourself, and do business have all been utterly transformed. When was the last time you made a call from a pay phone? Do you even think twice about shopping online anymore? Have you used your computer to call or Skype someone for free, even though they're halfway around the world? People born in the last twenty years barely know what it's like to communicate without e-mail, hold a physical plane ticket in their hand, or "dial" a phone. The changes in our own lifetimes have been radical, and there will be a lot more where that came from.

Technology is not the sole answer to our energy problems. Social and policy changes will need to contribute to the overall solution, as will improvements in our current energy infrastructure. I'll address all those challenges and possibilities in the chapters to come. But technology combined with enthusiastic consumer demand for new lifestyles will be the real difference maker. Right now, we're blindly focused on searching for answers within the old paradigm of energy, and it's a vision that really needs to shift. Our efforts to find new forms of energy, alternative sources for the energy we already consume, and different ways of reducing waste and carbon emissions are all vital, but they are insufficient for handling the magnitude of the problems we face. Instead, we need to embrace habits, lifestyles, mind-sets, and technologies that might seem on the fringe now, but will soon become part of the new way we live.

Chapter 2

Whetting the Energy Appetite

I t's a complicated business explaining pivotal shifts in human history. Some books focus on culture or ideology or social organization to define an era; others examine economics, demographics, or military conflicts. In this book, I look at history through a different lens: shifts in society's energy appetite. To explain why we consume more energy now than ever before, first I need to tell you about how and why certain types of machines and devices have been pivotal in changing the way we live. Through this understanding, we can position ourselves to contemplate the later chapters in this book, when we think about what new kinds of devices may be able to work their magic in reverse: leveling or reducing energy consumption while increasing standard of living.

The origin of our energy appetite was the discovery of fire. A 2008 archaeological discovery along the Dead Sea rift now suggests that our fire-making ability dates as far back as 790,000 years. Safe to say, we've come a long way since the days of our prehistoric hominid ancestors with the bony eyebrows and sloped foreheads.

Now we take making fire for granted. For example, let's say you wanted to set alight this book. Doing so wouldn't be difficult, depending on your whereabouts. If you're at home, you could turn on your gas or electric stove, or light up your gas fireplace or barbecue. If you're outside, a passing smoker would likely offer a match or cigarette lighter to get things going.

But for the first 790 millennia of our energy history, all the way up until the mid-1800s, making fire was a tedious process that required tools, skill, and patience. Few these days other than contestants on the TV reality show *Survivor* have even attempted to master the technique of making a fire the old-fashioned way. First, you'll need to acquire a piece of flintstone and steel—call ahead before you get in the car to your local hardware store. Then you must repeatedly strike the piece of flint with the piece of steel, aiming the sparks this produces into a small receptacle called a tinderbox (no doubt available wherever flint and steel are sold). Inside the tinderbox, a piece of charred cloth or other inflammable material would be set alight by the sparks, and the resulting low-burning ember could then be used to ignite wooden splints, adding larger and larger pieces of wood, leaves, or other dried material until the fire is large enough for heating and cooking purposes.

With practice, as well as good materials, you could have a fire going in seconds. Luckily for us, in 1827 John Walker, an English chemist, discovered a way of treating small pieces of wood with chemicals that made them burn when friction was applied. The new disposable devices—sold as "Lucifer matches"—were a compelling alternative to the old tinderbox method, being both easier to light and more convenient to carry.

Even though the first matches were far from perfect—they reacted violently when struck, and smelled awful—they caught on quickly, especially after Charles Sauria, a French chemist, added white phosphorus to the match tip in 1830 to remove the stench. His innovation caused a surge in demand not only for matches, but also for cigarettes, which were now much easier to light.

Sauria's matches weren't ideal either. White phosphorus is highly poisonous, and it caused chronic toothache and jaw abscesses among smokers and match factory workers alike. Some 20 years later, two

Swedish brothers, Johan and Carl Lundström, concocted a new formula that used nontoxic red phosphorus, giving birth to the "safety match" as we know it today.

The impact that this innovation had on Sweden—then a largely agricultural country—was enormous. The Lundström's company began to produce millions of matchboxes per year—all consuming large quantities of Swedish timber—while rival firms sprang up across Scandinavia, creating fierce competition for markets and resources. One company, Swedish Match, became one of the largest business empires in the world, holding interests from forestry to film companies to a controlling stake in Deutsche Bank, before falling apart after the Great Depression.

A match, though seemingly insignificant as a tiny splint of wood, was a pivotal device that put an end to flint and charred cloth, and made it much easier for consumers to burn greater quantities of wood, coal, candle wax, and combustible fuels. The match was the wall-switch of its day: a quick and easy flick of the fingers to put energy to work for society's comfort.

1776: A Pivotal Year

Throughout history, people have been quick to adopt devices that eased process or workload, always leading to their consumption of greater quantities of energy. Take the year 1776, for example. In that momentous year, the United States of America declared its independence and began the Revolutionary War; Adam Smith published his magnum opus on capitalism, *The Wealth of Nations*; and James Watt perfected the steam engine. Together, these three coincidental events converged to drive changes in technology, spurring economic growth and increasing consumerism for the next 200 years.

Just one year later, construction began on a cast-iron bridge set to span the deep and idyllic Severn Gorge nestled in the midlands of England. Known ever since as the Iron Bridge, this project was an expensive investment and a daunting engineering challenge—the first bridge ever to be built of anything other than stone or wood. And yet the imperative for the original bridge built from complex metal castings was simple: The Iron Bridge gave the early industrialists of the village

Figure 2.1   The Iron Bridge spanning the River Severn near Coalbrookdale, England

of Coalbrookdale easier access to the supplies of coal and iron ore found on the other side of the River Severn, the longest river in Great Britain. With increased coal supplies, the Coalbrookdale factories were able to manufacture more goods, which they then shipped all over the world (see Figure 2.1).

The building of the Iron Bridge is commonly associated with the beginning of the Industrial Revolution, marking a critical point in our application and expansion of manufacturing know-how. From this one undertaking, we learned how to cast iron into big things and turn those big things into the ways and means of our modern age. Craftsmanship was scaled up to replicable science and technology; guilds gave way to industry; and craftsmen who had access to capital became industrialists.

As the Industrial Revolution gathered steam, craftsmen needed increasing amounts of coal to fire their kilns, forges, and foundries. Although England was rich in coal deposits, supplies had already become more difficult to access since earlier miners had exploited the deposits near the surface of the earth. With coal near the surface scarce, ever-deeper mines had to be dug to keep up with demand. Complicating what was already a dangerous business, subterranean mine shafts inevitably filled with water, which had to be pumped out to keep the coal coming.

Like farmers 6,000 years before them, coal miners began by using animals to power their pumping system. But as mine shafts got deeper, horses were no longer strong enough to get the job done. In the early 1700s, Thomas Newcomen developed a steam engine in an attempt to replace animal with mechanical horsepower. The Newcomen Steam Engine was impressive, but it didn't solve the coal miners' problems because it required as much coal to operate as it helped retrieve from the mines. Buying a Newcomen Steam Engine was a break-even proposition at best, never mind the costs of repair and upkeep.

Fifty years later, James Watt put his mind to the problem and developed his own steam engine. This time, the coal miners were much happier with the result. The reason? Watt's engine was four times more efficient than Newcomen's in pumping water out of mine shafts. This made the steam engine a compelling substitute for a horse walking around in circles hitched to a rotating pump shaft. Once again, our ability to innovate had created a break point innovation, a device that could provide us with more fuel. In turn, with more fuel, we could carry on with the business of creating more jobs, wealth, and comfort.

Producing a Break Point Innovation

A society's energy consumption changes when an innovative new device meets market needs in a persuasive new way. We can't always predict what or which device will be successful, or what kind of mass-market product will capture the attention of millions. We can, however, analyze what went into producing what I call "break point innovations" of the past.

Few remember Watt or his steam engine in relation to coal mines or water. We think of his invention as it was applied to manufacturing and the locomotion of the giant ships and trains used in the distribution of people and manufactured goods. Watt's fame as the father of the Industrial Revolution was catalyzed by his business partner, Matthew

Boulton, a factory owner who both saw the practical applications of using the steam engine as a power source for industry, and had both the financial resources and entrepreneurial acumen to make it happen.

The great economist Joseph Schumpeter has written about the role of innovation and invention in economic growth in ways that can help explain the dynamics between Watt and Boulton. Schumpeter believed that during steady periods of economic growth, change was incremental. Competition among producers generated slight improvements in goods or processes that help drive prices down. In contrast, dramatic economic growth occurred when new inventions and their associated innovations were introduced into a staid competitive market causing "creative destruction."

Schumpeter's distinction between an invention and an innovation is important to understand. To him, invention was about newly discovered scientific principles or new advances in technology or processes. Innovation resulted when an invention was sold to a large pool of customers whose lives were thereby improved. For example, the *invention* of the transistor in 1925 was an amazing technological breakthrough based on a new understanding of scientific principles. *Innovation* happened when transistor technology was applied to radios (and later, televisions and computers) and sold to every modern household.

Moreover, break point innovations create entirely new markets, change lifestyles, and generate tremendous profits. Because of the profits associated with such creative destruction, other innovators are drawn into the game, improving the invention further, transforming it into new products, and creating segmented markets. The churn of entrepreneurial activity around break point innovations brings about immense changes in society as it grows the economy and improves our standard of living at an accelerated pace.

From Schumpeter's perspective, Watt was the inventor, Boulton was the innovator, and the steam engine was definitely a break point innovation. As the innovator, Boulton worked vigorously to spread Watt's steam engine technology throughout the world. Selling a Boulton and Watt steam engine was a challenge, as the initial investment was greater than most factory owners could manage, so Boulton developed elaborate financing plans to encourage them to take the plunge. Once an owner installed a steam engine, the productivity gains allowed him to outperform the competition. In turn, those competitors either made a decision to get their own steam engine or got squeezed out of business.

Of course, the technology didn't stand still. During the 20 years following the filing of his original patent, Watt developed a steam engine that could generate rotating motion instead of up and down movement, expanding the kind of useful work the device could provide. A decade later, innovators in Great Britain and the United States independently developed the idea of high pressure or "strong" steam, increasing the engine's power while reducing its size. With that, the steam engine, originally adopted by industry for coal mining, was applied to transportation. One of the first successful innovators in this realm was Robert Fulton, who ordered a Boulton and Watt steam engine and built it into a steamboat to ferry passengers along the Hudson River between New York City and Albany. Steam engine locomotives followed, and track was laid all over Europe and North America to serve the transportation of people and goods, generating the biggest financial boom in history.

In less than a hundred years, Watt's invention and Boulton's innovation was being used in ways they never imagined, from powering giant foundries and textile mills to ships, trains, cars, tractors, and even printing presses and clocks. The efficiency of work was increased, a wide variety of goods were produced, everything and everyone could be transported more speedily than before, consumer demand for those goods and services grew exponentially, and the rise in standard of living was spectacular. As we shall see, in keeping with the First Principle of Energy Consumption, the steam engine's effects on the world's energy appetite was impressive, too.

Compelling Qualities

Society changes rapidly when a break point innovation and its derivatives multiply through the market. People start working and living differently. The success of the introduction generates its own momentum and consumers, entrepreneurs, and businesses find new ways to apply the technology. This creates a proliferation of new ideas and approaches, all springing from the same technology that can lead to more devices and more mass adoption, generating a vortex of greater energy consumption, better lifestyle, and faster economic growth.

However, to be compelling enough for mass adoption, an innovation needs to pass certain thresholds. It must offer consumers superior utility over status quo alternatives. For example, Newcomen's engine could do the job, but never made economic sense for mine owners. On the other hand, Watt's more efficient steam engine became a must-have device when pitted against the output of a mere horse. As a side note, it was Watt who developed the word "horsepower," which is the amount of work required to raise 33,000 pounds a vertical distance of one foot in one minute.

The word "compelling" relates to an important concept in this book. I use it to describe the level of relative utility of a new product or process as compared to the next best alternative in use. Today's inexpensive Global Positioning Satellite (GPS) receivers and navigation computers are clearly compelling substitutes for a paper map. Why? Ease of use, speed in finding and following your location, accuracy, and ability to navigate are but a few of the many superior qualities of a modern GPS unit. Additionally, the cost has now fallen to the point where people are willing to pay for the must-have benefits of owning a GPS device. Other examples of compelling product innovations are calculators over slide rules, CDs over cassette tapes, word processors over typewriters, MP3 players over CDs, and so on.

To a mine owner, there were many considerations before the workhorse was put to pasture in favor of the steam engine. Relative power, reliability, productivity, adaptability, cost, and noise were some of the many dimensions of utility that factored into the purchasing decision. Noise aside, these factors made for a compelling package that was so superior to animal power that any mine owner who didn't buy a Boulton & Watt engine could no longer compete with those who had.

Breakthrough innovations are always compelling—usually on every dimension of utility. As a result, their adoption into the mass market is rapid and unstoppable. Conversely, a device that is only marginally better than its peers on a few dimensions is unlikely to see commercial success on a grand scale, let alone change the world.

The difference between marginal and compelling is important for us to keep in mind when assessing new energy technologies. I will be talking more about this in Chapter 6, but for now consider this: is ethanol a compelling substitute for gasoline? As compelling as a calculator over a slide rule? How about solar power over natural gas? A plug-in hybrid vehicle versus one that runs on diesel? We don't have to answer these questions now. Just recognize that if we're out to change our energy appetite in a meaningful way, then we must concentrate our efforts on innovations that have compelling, transformative qualities.

In the interim, let's learn more about how two break point innovations, the light bulb and the automobile, became pivotal in reshaping both our lifestyles and our propensity for increasing our energy consumption.

Electrifying the World

Thomas Edison is often credited with inventing the light bulb. In actuality, we remember Edison today because of his genius and perseverance at making the light bulb a household necessity. In the mid-1880s, there was a great race among many inventors to develop a functional light bulb. Edison was late to the contest, and did not always realize that others were ahead of him in solving the technological problems at hand. But by being the first to develop a delivery system to bring electricity into our homes and places of work, Edison provided the light bulb with its raison d'être. Without access to electricity, no one would have felt the need to switch from arc lighting in the streets or coal gas lanterns in the home.

Edison understood that in order to create demand for the light-bulb, he would need to make it as easy as possible for consumers to abandon the lighting source they currently used and adopt what he was offering instead. The convenience of coal gas, which could be pumped underground and directly into houses and streetlamps, was his biggest challenge, so he designed his lighting system with that in mind. He built a central power station on Pearl Street in lower Manhattan, and installed the largest generators ever operated. With telegraph and telephone cables criss-crossing overhead, new lines and dead lines draping over one another in an unsafe tangle, New York was already wired to an extent that would surprise us today. So instead of adding to the unsightly confusion, Edison put his wires underground, making the distribution of electricity as convenient, unobtrusive, and safe as the distribution of coal gas. Indeed, his ultimate goal was to run the wires of his electric grid through the existing infrastructure of coal gas pipes, and directly into the lamps that already decorated homes and offices. Once Edison had his system in place, he provided free electricity for the first three months of operation, hoping to convince customers of the superior quality of incandescent light. After that trial period, he installed electricity meters—another Edison patent—and began the tradition of billing customers for the convenient average rate per month still employed today.

Even so, it took about 15 years before Edison's light bulb became a hit with consumers. There were a variety of reasons for the delay. For example, technological improvements to the coal gas lantern had brought it closer to the light bulb's level of light quality, so many consumers did not feel compelled to make the switch. But in 1906, when the carbon filament inside the light bulb was replaced with a metal filament—the tungsten we know today—the light bulb suddenly became three times more efficient, and thus much more compelling than coal gas lanterns. Around the same time, the Edison-style screw-in base (fashioned in imitation of the screw cap on kerosene containers) became industry standard. This meant that any light bulb made by any manufacturer could fit into any light bulb socket. Finally, starting in the 1920s, the production of light bulbs became automated. Until then, most light bulbs were actually made by hand, a slow, laborious, and expensive process. Factory production led to cheaper prices, and by 1940, the price of a light bulb in inflation-adjusted dollars was approximately the same as it is today. This lowered the barrier to entry for new customers and made the switch to electricity as compelling as possible.

People expected electricity to change their way of life immediately. As early as 1890, a popular song put forth this idea:

If Edison is still alive

In 1892,

Electric horses we shall drive

In 1892.

Electric dinners we shall eat.

Electric brooms will clean the street.

Police will have electric feet

In 1892.[1]

In fact, it wasn't until the 1970s that the United States achieved almost full adoption of the light bulb.

Of course, the light bulb, as a break point innovation, only whetted our appetite for electricity. As the popular song predicted, Edison's power grid made consumer demand for other electricity-consuming products and services possible. It was those secondary innovations and proliferations that really changed our world.

At first, the electrification of America occurred mostly in public spaces. Electric street, building, shop, and theater lights became common, and factories, trolleys, and elevators became powered by electricity, too. Then stores and offices adopted electricity and work hours were no longer limited by daylight or lamp fuel. At home, the housewife was the key early adopter as electricity-powered consumer goods made their way into stores, starting in the early 1920s. The electric iron, toaster, fan, mixer, vacuum cleaner, washing machine, refrigerator, and hair dryer reduced the housewife's burden. Advertising, traveling road shows, and appliance demonstrations fed the excitement. On November 19, 1910 *Scientific American* reported, "A novel method of demonstrating the advantages of electricity in the household has been adopted by the Edison Company of Boston. This house is portable, and will be set up in the various towns reached by the lines of the company. Demonstrations of electrical kitchen work, laundry work, house cleaning, etc., will be given each evening."

Electricity and the household devices it runs are considered nearly indispensable today. Edison might well have been able to imagine the sweep of such change (after all, his inventiveness seemed without limit). But I suspect even he didn't consider the scale of issues that would be raised by electrifying the world.

A Car in Every Driveway

Henry Ford idolized Edison and became successful for the same reasons. He turned a break point innovation—the internal combustion engine, invented in 1876 by Nikolaus Otto—into a consumer product of compelling appeal: the cheap, efficient, and highly functional automobile.

Like Edison, Ford was not the first to build an effective gasoline-powered car and there were many others like him striving to make the same advancements. At the turn of the twentieth century, the consumer need for an automobile was almost palpable. With a national train network, we had entered the age of travel, but technology had not yet made independent transportation available for individuals. Other than the bicycle—which was extremely popular at the time—the other alternatives available were still walking or the horse. It might sound idyllic, but in truth horse drawn carriages and trolleys crowded nineteenth century New York City, London, and Chicago, creating traffic jams that would stress out any commuter today. Disease was a problem, too, as dead horses were often left to rot on the street where they had fallen. Even worse, horse manure was a constant source of pollution. According to an 1899 issue of *Scientific American*, two-thirds of the dirt on city streets was due to horses and, it declared, if automobiles were to replace horses, cities would be two-thirds cleaner.[2] To describe the situation even more bluntly, in 1900 in New York City, the streets were polluted each day with 40 dead horses, 2.5 million pounds of manure, and 60,000 gallons of urine.[3] For the amount of food they ate and waste they produced in return for "useful work" they produced, horses were many times less efficient than even rudimentary automobiles. Ironically, in its early days, the automobile was heralded not only as a wonder of individual transportation but an environmental savior, too.

Even so, no one was sure what kind of automobile should rule the day. Once, when Henry Ford was twelve years old and driving a horse and carriage into the city with his father, he saw a strange contraption making its way slowly toward them, smoking and clanging along the road. It was a Nichols, Shepherd, & Company steam-powered tractor, the first motorized vehicle Ford had ever seen. He jumped down and ran over to the driver to ask questions before his father knew what was happening. According to Ford, the tractor was "simply a portable engine and boiler mounted on wheels with a water tank and coal car trailing behind."[4] One man could operate it, but he needed to steer, manage the throttle, and shovel coal at the same time, and the maximum speed was probably around 12 miles per hour. Still, Ford was hooked.

Within a few years, he built his own steam car, using kerosene rather than coal or wood to heat the boiler. But he ran into some discouraging problems. The car had a lot of power, but the boiler was unstable and could explode. The ride itself was unpleasant, and Ford found that even after two years of experimentation, he could not get the weight or cost down sufficiently to make the car economical.

In the end, Ford gave up on steam and turned his attention to a new device called the Otto engine, which he'd read about in England's *World of Science* magazine. By 1890, he was working on his own double-cylinder Otto-style engine and struggling to make it light enough to be functional on a moving vehicle. Wanting to be free from farm work, he moved to the city with his wife and took a job at the Detroit Edison Illuminating Company, in part because he believed that an understanding of electrical systems would help him build a better starter for his gasoline-powered engine. At nights, he worked on his engine and horseless carriage in the outdoor garage, his work space illuminated by one of Mr. Edison's light bulbs. When his "gasoline buggy" was ready for the road, Ford had to knock away part of the wall of his garage to make the doorway entrance big enough for the car. He put a thousand miles on the vehicle driving through the streets of Detroit over the next two years; scaring horses, stalling at corners, and always tinkering and improving its design.

Birth of an Industry

Ford's may have been one of the first gasoline-powered vehicles in Detroit but there were soon many others like it, as the city became the hub of experimentation and capital of the nascent automobile industry—a clustering of innovators and investors not unlike Silicon Valley today. Still, for several decades around the turn of the twentieth century, the gasoline-powered car had a much smaller market share than steam cars and electric cars.

The Stanley Steamer was the most famous of the early steam cars. Powered by an external combustion engine that heated a boiler and generated the steam needed to turn the wheels, the stylish Stanley Steamer motto was, "Power, correctly generated, correctly controlled, correctly applied to the rear axle." Unlike the steam tractor that Ford encountered as a boy, the new steam cars did not chug along at a pokey pace. In 1906, a streamlined steam racer designed by the Stanley Brothers set the world land speed record at 127 mph at a race in Daytona Beach, Florida. Indeed, the power, speed, and smooth-running engine of a steam car made them very appealing to many motorists, but they had their downsides. They could take anywhere from 12 minutes to 45 minutes to warm up when first started, and were complicated to maintain. Most significantly, steam cars consumed a tremendous amount of water, and without a system of water-filling stations in place, it was inconvenient to travel in them any great distance from home.

The electric car was another popular option. At the turn of the century, about one-third of all automobiles in the larger cities of America were battery-powered. Electric cars were fast enough (an early Belgian model set a speed record of 65.79 mph in 1899), nearly silent, and did not produce any of the exhaust fumes already being criticized as a major problem with gasoline-powered cars. For this reason, they were particularly desirable in urban settings; in fact, 90 percent of the taxis in New York were electric in 1899. The most compelling feature of an electric car, however, was its easy and quick start. All you had to do was push a button or flick a switch to power one up. In comparison, the steamer took a lot of time and the gasoline-powered car required cranking. While that might seem like a minor (and nostalgic) inconvenience, turning the crank of an internal combustion engine took brute strength, and sometimes the handle snapped back, breaking an unfortunate motorist's arm.

Not surprisingly then, electric cars were primarily marketed to women, and women loved them in turn. But the significant downside of an electric car was, as Edison had pointed out to Ford in 1896, the limited range of travel. At best, an electric car could travel around 20 miles before recharging was necessary, a distance that could never secure a lasting hold on the public imagination. Despite his advice to Ford, Thomas Edison was among those who put a lot of time and energy into developing a better, more reliable battery to give electric cars farther range. He never succeeded. Indeed, that's an innovation many are still striving for today.

During the first decade of the 1900s, Henry Ford kept working toward the perfect automobile. Most of his contemporaries saw the gasoline-powered automobile as a luxury item for the rich, and decked their models out accordingly, but Ford was of a very different view. Obsessed with efficiency and utility, Ford aimed to develop the best quality automobile possible at the lowest possible price. If he achieved this goal, he believed he would succeed in turning the automobile into the greatest mass-market product in history.

Ignoring his competitors and even the wishes of his investors, Ford worked relentlessly on making his product increasingly compelling. For example, the Model A competed with Oldsmobile's Curved Dash—the first mass-produced motor car ever developed. Ford's Model A was lighter than the Curved Dash, had more horsepower and many of the convenience features we associate with automobiles today, like room for two in the front seat. It was also the first automobile to drop below the $1,000 mark. A few short years later, Ford's Model N expanded on those differences and established a new benchmark for the industry. Though it offered a rough ride, the Model N was lightweight, with a better clutch and braking system than other cars, plus it had a six-cylinder engine that could crank out plenty of horsepower. Even more important, it cost a mere $500. The Ford Motor Company sold 8,500 of them in 1906, making it the American automobile market leader.

By this time, Ford had developed a keen understanding of the threshold an automobile must exceed to be a true mass market phenomenon. In early 1906, he wrote a letter to *The Automobile* magazine to describe what a "compelling" automobile would look like:

> *The greatest need today is a light, low-priced car with an up-to-date engine of ample horsepower, and built of the very best material. One that will go anywhere a car of double the horsepower will; that is in every way an automobile and not a toy; and most important of all, one that will not be a wrecker of tires and a spoiler of the owner's disposition. It must be powerful enough for American roads and capable of carrying its passengers anywhere that a horse-drawn vehicle will go without the driver being afraid of ruining his car.*[5]

Since his Model N didn't completely satisfy these requirements, Ford kept experimenting. Two years later, he refined his stated aim: "I will build a car for the great multitude. It will be large enough for the family car but small enough for the individual to run and care for. It will be constructed of the best materials by the best men to be hired, after the simplest designs that modern engineering can devise. But it will be so low in price that no man making a good salary will be unable to own one—and enjoy with his family the blessings of hours of pleasure in God's great open spaces."[6]

The Model T, unveiled in 1908, was that car. It was elegant, light in weight, and easy to drive. Women embraced it. Men loved it. A downside of automobiles in general was the expense, time, and effort required to keep such a complicated machine in working shape. But Ford's Model T, while still needing regular tinkering from its owner, was considerably cheaper and simpler to maintain. The Model T was not plagued by mechanical breakdowns, and its high carriage and wheel base allowed it to surmount bad conditions in a nation with few paved roads. Its flexibility of use was another point of pride for Ford. Seating five, it allowed families to go on Sunday drives, but it was also sturdy and powerful enough for a farmer to use as a makeshift tractor. Of course, the most important feature was the price. Once again, in a market that still produced cars as luxury items for the well-to-do, Ford's car was made affordable to the masses. As a consumer product, it was a tremendous hit from the beginning, able to go farther, faster, and with more comfort and convenience than automobiles twice its price. By 1913, with the timely development of the electric starter, another barrier to acceptance was passed and the gasoline-powered automobile began to eclipse electric and steam cars, too.

In 1914, Ford became world-famous when he announced that his workers would be paid, after a probationary period, a minimum of $5 per day for eight hours of work. This was at least twice the rate for workers in other companies and industries and a truly revolutionary shift. From a public relations and employee retention standpoint, the campaign was an enormous success. From a social standpoint, the implications were perhaps more far-reaching. Other business owners were pressured to follow suit, and as wages rose, American workers were able to consume more products and raise their standard of living. Of course, this meant they could buy Model T's as well. The mobilization of America now had unstoppable momentum.

Ford didn't take his fame or success for granted. He knew the lessons of mass adoption as well as Edison. On the sales side of the business, his company worked to improve the distribution system with dealers throughout the country. On the manufacturing side, Ford kept pounding away at the efficiency of production. Frederick Winslow Taylor became famous for his time and motion studies that brought the principles of scientific management into the factory, but Henry Ford was a hands-on practitioner independent of Taylor. He designed ever-bigger, ever-more efficient factories transitioning production from individual work crews to the modern assembly line. Every worker had a precise job, repeated over and over, and every automobile produced was exactly the same.

At the beginning of 1914, Ford's workers could produce a single automobile in 13 hours. Before the end of the year, they'd knocked that time down to 93 minutes. By 1920, Ford's factories were making one automobile every minute, and by 1925, one every ten seconds. The price of a Model T fell accordingly, from $850 in 1908 to $360 in 1916. The scarcity of materials during World War I forced prices slightly higher for a few years, but by 1921, the cost per unit was back down to $310. The consumer impact of such low prices was enormous. In the early 1920s, two-thirds of all cars in the United States were made by Ford.

The Insistence of Comfort, Luxury, and Plenty

In 1900, there were only a few thousand vehicles registered in America. By 1925, there were 17 million. By 1940 there were 50 million. Now, there are over 250 million. With the automobile, the country's system of roads and highways became more sophisticated, connecting towns, reducing travel time, and changing the very idea of geography. A system of fueling stations sprouted up along these roads so that cars could travel any distance without inconvenience. Families could drive wherever they needed to, so they moved away from crowded cities and isolated farms into what became suburbs. That picket fence and driveway became the American dream, and the automobile inserted itself into the national psyche as a symbol of status, freedom, style, and coming of age.

It has become nearly impossible to imagine life in America without the automobile or electricity. But that's what happens when something that offers compelling convenience, efficiency, or entertainment enters our lives. The Internet has not even been with us for 20 years, but now we conduct much of the business and pleasure of our lives online. The iPod was launched in 2001, and now there are 150 million of them in people's pockets and music has gone almost completely digital. A compelling product is not only easy to adopt, it's practically impossible to give up. Ask yourself to give up your cell phone, let alone your car or your television set. For most of us such sacrifices would be a painful exercise in self-discipline.

In the meantime, our problems are growing. Edison and Ford may have made their mark here a century ago, but their inventions are just gaining hold of markets in developing countries. In New Delhi, India, on January 10, 2008, Ratan Tata, chairman of the Tata Group, unveiled a new vehicle for the great multitude to the musical flourish of the theme song from the film, *2001: A Space Odyssey*. What he said next resonated with Henry Ford's remarks and notions from a hundred years prior:

> *I observed families riding on two-wheelers—the father driving the scooter, his young kid standing in front of him, his wife seated behind him holding a little baby. It led me to wonder whether one could conceive of a safe, affordable, all-weather form of transport for such a family. Tata Motors' engineers and designers gave their all for about four years to realise this goal. Today, we indeed have a People's Car, which is affordable and yet built to meet safety requirements and emission norms, to be fuel efficient and low on emissions. We are happy to present the People's Car to India and we hope it brings the joy, pride and utility of owning a car to many families who need personal mobility.*[7]

Closely resembling a Mercedes Smart Car in style, the Tata Nano (Nano means "small" in the Indian dialect Gujarati) is slightly larger and half the price of its nearest domestic competitor, the Maruti 800. This price-point is critical, because at approximately $2,500, the Nano will be affordable to India's vast middle class, a déjà vu strategy harkening back to Ford's thoughts on his Model T, ". . . it will be so low in price that no man making a good salary will be unable to own one." Tata was able to achieve an ultra-low $2,500 price tag by stripping all luxuries and using materials and engineering approaches that were as cheap as possible while still being safe. For example, the struts will wear down quickly (though safely) if the car is driven over 45 mph on a regular basis. Most encouragingly, the Nano gets 50 miles per gallon, an achievement that would give it super-elite gas mileage status in the United States.

But think of our adoption of the cheap light bulb and automobile over the last century. Now think of the huge populaces of China and

India, as they experience their own industrial revolution by adopting compelling pivotal devices that will change their lives. While cars are old news to us, the Tata Nano will materially increase the appetite for energy in India and throughout the two or three billion people ready to join the ranks of the middle class in the developing world. It's a waking nightmare: hundreds of millions of new consumers lining up to put even more pressure on the world's energy supplies and the environment. What's a gasoline-addicted nation like the United States to do? Tell these newly empowered buyers they can't own cars? Put them off with cautionary tales of pollution, traffic jams, and car jackings? Good luck—they have the right to aspire to higher standards of living and social status, too!

As we look for answers to our energy problems, it's important to understand just how difficult it is to halt such a trend. The already developed world North America and Europe may not want another 200 million car drivers in India, but how do you tell a couple of billion people in a striving middle class that they should refrain from chasing the lifestyle goals that we in the wealthy world take for granted? We've had a hundred years to make our cars more economical, safer, and environmentally friendly. Instead, North American roads today are congested with energy obese SUVs.

We need to remember the tremendous allure of the lifestyle of convenience, comfort, luxury, and plenty that has historically been made possible by the proliferation of energy consuming devices. Products that are compelling will always succeed with the great multitude. We must now seek a new class of break point innovations that help us consume less energy rather than more—without sacrificing everyone's desire for greater convenience and comfort.

Chapter 3

The First Principle of Energy Consumption

My First Principle states that our personal wealth and well-being is directly related to our energy consumption. Very simply, the wealthier we become the more energy we use and vice versa. So, with all those break point innovations, all those lifestyle improvements, all that prosperity and wealth, the way we consume energy must have grown. It's time to step on the scales and see just how energy laden we have become.

The Way We Eat

If you wanted to determine whether your daily diet is healthy or not, you'd probably first examine whether the food you eat contains more energy than your body requires. If your appetite is too large and too many calories are ingested, obesity may eventually follow.

That chocolate bar you crave contains about 200 food calories that your body will gladly "burn." A *calorie* is a unit of energy that nineteenth century physicists used to measure the amount of heat in their experiments, which should not be confused with a *food Calorie*, which is equal to 1,000 calories. But while most physicists migrated to using the *joule* to measure energy, nutritionists continue, to this day, to describe the amount of energy in food using food Calories or kilocalories. Qualitatively, a chocolate bar may contain enough energy to allow you to jog around the block before you're hungry again. For a technical benchmark, one food calorie is the amount of energy required to raise the temperature of one kilogram (2.2 lbs) of water by one degree Celsius (1.8°F).

In North America, our high-calorie food diets have led to an obesity epidemic. While an abundance of cheap, unhealthy cuisine is the main cause, other key contributors include genetic and family histories, as well as lifestyle and behavior choices. Whatever the causes, the results are yielding serious social problems such as high health care costs, loss in productivity, and reduced quality of life for millions of people.

Our energy diet works in the same way. We consume gasoline in our cars, and use sources like coal to generate electricity to power our homes and offices. We buy goods to improve our standard of living—thus indirectly consuming the raw materials that make up those objects, and the fuels used in their transportation to market. The good news is that we have tremendous variety and abundance of consumer goods. More concerning is that the long-term availability of cheap energy has enabled many to cultivate a lifestyle of excess fuel consumption. Because it was easily affordable, many in North America traded in their economical cars for gas-guzzling SUVs; moved into larger houses, further from work; and grew accustomed to ubiquitous central heat and air conditioning, year-round access to fresh fruits and vegetables, and cheap, foreign-made consumer items.

Let's compare food appetite against what we use to power our lifestyles and comforts—or what I term our *energy appetite*. The average person eats around 2,200 food calories a day, meaning that, on average, we each ingest 800,000 *food* Calories per year. By contrast, North Americans use 110 times that amount in fuel energy, or around 88 billion physics calories annually.

Keeping calories with the nutritionists for the moment, another way we can quantify a standard unit of energy consumption is by considering how everything compares to a barrel of oil. Our energy diet consists of five primary menu items: coal, oil, natural gas, uranium, and hydro-electric power. And for dessert we layer on solar, wind, and biomass.

If you burn a 42-gallon barrel of oil you will liberate 1.46 billion calories of potential energy, which is also what's contained in 433 pounds of coal, 5,800 cubic feet of natural gas, or around .003 ounces of uranium. So instead of standardizing everything to calories, I will express our energy consumption in terms of *barrels of oil equivalent*, or BOE. For example, a ton of good quality coal contains the same amount of energy as 4.62 BOE. It's like expressing the food energy in a cup of cornflakes as 0.4 bars of chocolate equivalent. (In which case we could use the abbreviation BCE!) Both contain 80 food calories of energy.

Altogether in 2007, the total appetite of 300 million Americans was 18 billion BOE of coal, oil, natural gas, uranium, and renewable energy. Dividing it down to a personal level, the average American citizen has an energy appetite of around 60 BOE per year.

So what? Does this mean Americans are energy obese and others are not? Compared to what standard? To answer these questions I need to show you energy appetite from different world perspectives, how those appetites relate to wealth creation, and how to understand the means by which our insatiable energy hunger is fulfilled.

WealthyWorld and WantingWorld

Let me start at the highest level. Our planet is divided into two economic worlds. One world, representing 56 percent of a $65 trillion global economy (2007), and containing 800 million people, includes 28 "rich" countries, principally the United States, Canada, the nations of Western and Central Europe, Australia, New Zealand, South Korea, and Japan. This group is sometimes referred to as the OECD, as the countries it contains belong to a rich nations' club called the Organisation for Economic Co-operation and Development. Dispensing with that dry label, I will simply call this group "WealthyWorld." Historically, countries in WealthyWorld have grown their economies at a modest and mature rate of 2.5 percent per year.

The 150 or so countries that are not in WealthyWorld host our planet's remaining 5.9 billion inhabitants—seven times the population of WealthyWorld! I call that world "WantingWorld." Within Wanting-World are 30 rapidly "emerging" countries like China, India, some nations in Southeast Asia, South America, and Eastern Europe—a non-trivial 4.1 billion people eagerly chasing the well-heeled lifestyles we in the rich half of the planet enjoy. Notwithstanding the deleterious effects of the 2008 financial crisis, an important event that I will discuss later, countries that are in their wealth-creation phase typically grow their economies two to five times faster than rich, mature countries. As a result, the two worlds on our planet, each as different as a Sumo wrestler and a lean sprinter, have distinctly different energy appetites and diets.

Aggressively developing countries within WantingWorld, principally led by China, are now going through a twenty-first century version of the original Industrial Revolution—building bridges, roads, dams, and power plants; generating wealth; and buying consumer goods similar to what all the WealthyWorld countries went through since the unveiling of the Iron Bridge in 1779. And while I can point to the Iron Bridge and say, "Here, this is where mankind moved away from basic farm life and started industrializing," it's not so easy to identify a specific location or object marking the start of economic momentum in places like China or India. What I can do is point out an energy chart that clearly shows when the industrial revolution in today's WantingWorld countries started.

Figure 3.1 shows the growth in total energy appetite over the last 40 or so years for the 150 WantingWorld countries. I also show what composes the WantingWorld energy diet as layers of primary fuels—all standardized to BOE per year.

I will be talking about how diet grows over time in Chapter 5, but for now notice how total energy appetite in WantingWorld started rising dramatically after 2001; this is the marker for the beginning of the New Industrial Revolution—the aggressive pursuit of western economic standards by a world of 4.1 billion people, hence the prefix "Wanting." After rising steadily and sometimes slowly for 35 years, energy appetite in that world rapidly grew by 40 percent between 2001 and 2007. Skyscrapers began claiming the sky, humble farmers put down their hoes and started migrating to the cities, and shoppers took to shiny new malls and auto dealerships. Note how burning coal, which is the fuel of choice to make lots of cheap electricity, has satisfied most of the recent

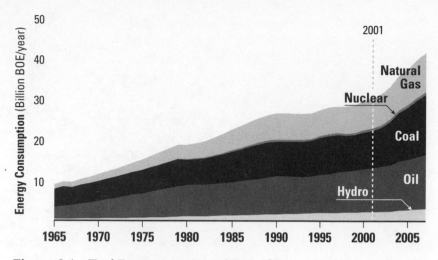

Figure 3.1 Total Energy Appetite and Diet of *WantingWorld* Countries: All Primary Energy Sources Converted to BOE
SOURCE: BP Statistical Review 2008, ARC Financial Research.

growth in WantingWorld's appetite. Hunger for oil has been intense too, as middle class citizens from China to the Middle East buy their first car, and go on their first airplane flight with newfound wealth.

Now look at Figure 3.2, representing the energy consumption profile for WealthyWorld countries. High growth between 1965 and 1973 is a continuation of the post–World War II era in which WealthyWorld became even richer by adopting the legacies of Edison and Ford on a grand scale. Successive dips in appetite during the energy crises of the 1970s are evident in the middle of Figure 3.2—issues to be addressed in Chapters 5 and 9. Fast-forward to the beginning of the twenty-first century and we see a somewhat surprising trend, or lack thereof: the energy appetite of WealthyWorld looks as if it's leveled off at the same time as WantingWorld's took off.

To those who follow global economic news, my tale of two energy appetites since 2000 should not be surprising. Emerging, industrializing countries like China (that are building infrastructure and manufacturing everything from shirts to ships at a frenzied pace) exhibit much stronger energy growth than those that are mature and rich.

An important observation from Figures 3.1 and 3.2 is that each of the two worlds, WealthyWorld and WantingWorld, has almost the same total

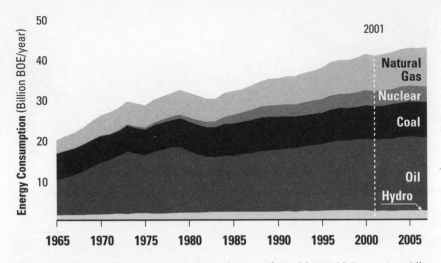

Figure 3.2   Total Energy Appetite and Diet of *WealthyWorld* Countries: All Primary Energy Sources Converted to BOE
SOURCE: BP Statistical Review 2008, ARC Financial Research.

energy appetite—a staggering feast of 45 billion barrels of oil equivalent per year! I will emphasize this point repeatedly throughout this book: the scale of our planet's collective energy appetite is staggering and its sheer magnitude represents the biggest impediment to finding quick and easy solutions.

On the surface, comparing my two energy appetite charts during the past 10 years would seem to suggest that rich nations have finally got their consumption growth under control. Metaphorically, their plates are always full, but at least the portion size doesn't seem to be growing. On the other hand, WantingWorld nations are just beginning to achieve the lifestyle gains WealthyWorld residents already enjoy, and their energy appetite is becoming increasingly voracious.

A comfortable conclusion appears to present itself: that the problem of energy consumption is most acute throughout WantingWorld, while those in WealthyWorld have learned how to sustain and even grow their standard of living while keeping energy appetite almost constant. But before rushing to such a sweeping judgment, let's look at energy appetite at an individual level. After all, population growth leads to new inhabitants burdening the earth with all sorts of needs, including energy.

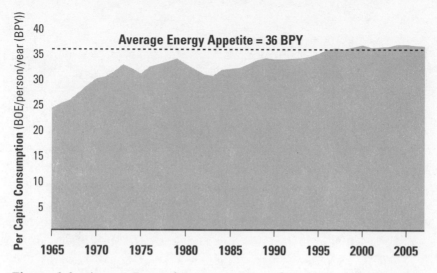

Figure 3.3 Average Personal Energy Appetite of *WealthyWorld* Residents: All Primary Energy Sources Converted to BOE
SOURCE: BP Statistical Review 2008, IMF, ARC Financial Research.

For each year in WealthyWorld's chart (Figure 3.2), I'm going to divide total energy appetite by the number of people. The result is Figure 3.3, which shows the long-term trend of *personal energy appetite*. Looking at the flat part of this chart, between the mid-1990s and 2007, leaves WealthyWorld residents feeling very good about themselves. For at an individual level, it really does look like residents of this privileged land have learned how to keep their energy appetite steady at around 36 BOE per person, per year (or simply 36 BPY). To be clear about what this says: the average person in WealthyWorld—principally the citizens of Canada, the United States, nations of the European Union, and Japan—consume the equivalent energy contained in 36 barrels of oil every year, and this level of appetite has not changed since 1995.

However, there's a major problem with this flat-appetite interpretation, and it's created by the way goods are consumed in WealthyWorld. Let's say you want a new shirt, so you go to your local Wal-Mart and buy one that's reasonably priced. Hidden from view is the fact that the shirt was made in China and has traveled halfway around the world to get to you. Who is really responsible for the energy consumed in manufacturing that shirt—you, or the person operating the sewing machine in China? After all, Chinese energy and materials wouldn't have been consumed to produce it if there weren't people in WealthyWorld wanting to buy such items.

Here is another example. If you were in the United Kingdom and you wanted to buy a shirt, there's a good chance you'd go to a Marks & Spencer store to do so. The chain is the country's largest clothing retailer, and has long been part of the British identity; almost every High Street in the United Kingdom has a Marks & Spencer shop on it somewhere.

As recently as 20 years ago, 90 percent of Marks & Spencer's clothes were made in the United Kingdom. But textiles and clothing are labor-intensive industries, and cheaper imports from low-wage countries began replacing the company's expensive domestically-manufactured products. By 1999, only 55 percent of Marks & Spencer's clothes were British-made. At that point, the company said it would shift 70 percent of its textiles sourcing to overseas suppliers as it sought to cut costs. The British textile industry shrank as Marks & Spencer and other retailers began offshoring. A similar transition occurred in other traditionally British industries, such as shipbuilding and steel production, as well as more broadly across other WealthyWorld countries.

We have a tendency, whether we're talking about energy consumption or carbon emissions, to think in terms of national boundaries. But our lifestyles are integrated within the global economy. If we raise our standard of living by consuming goods that are manufactured in other countries, we are, in effect, consuming energy that has been used in those nations. It's like ordering take-out food from a restaurant every now and then. Just because the stove is outside your house doesn't mean you can shirk responsibility for the energy that was used to cook your meal.

Since the mid-1980s WealthyWorld inhabitants have been buying vast, and increasing, amounts of manufactured goods from WantingWorld to sustain and improve lifestyles. Because it is cheaper to produce these goods abroad, WealthyWorlders are increasingly relying on a long list of WantingWorld countries like China to make them, and have restructured their own economies to become more service, rather than manufacturing, oriented. Providing retirement advice in New York requires a lot less energy than making a dishwasher for export in China.

As our economy gets lighter and more service-based, we become further alienated from the physical manufacturing of things. In a way, it's reminiscent of the shift in how we eat. Once, we slaughtered our own animals for meat and grew our own vegetables. Now, the production of food is done out of sight, in giant farms and meat processing plants. We buy our groceries—bags of lettuce, avocados from South America, packaged meat—in convenient, well-lit supermarkets while giving little thought to where that food was produced or how it arrived, so long as it is cheap, appealing, and healthy.

Likewise with energy, we are increasingly unaware of where it was "spent," how we are consuming it, and how much of it our lifestyle requires. If we are going to learn to modulate, let alone reduce our energy appetite, we need to understand exactly how much we consume without fooling ourselves.

This worldwide dynamic is vital to understand. In WealthyWorld, offshored energy must be repatriated if an honest assessment of personal appetite is to be made. Of course, our calculations can't overlook the fact that WantingWorld also buys from WealthyWorld.

If we take WealthyWorld's personal energy appetite in Figure 3.3, and adjust it to take into account the offshoring phenomenon, we find that WealthyWorld's energy appetite is not flat past 1995 after all. Instead, personal energy appetite is still growing at a pronounced rate, the difference of which is shown in Figure 3.4.

I call the gap between a region's basic energy appetite and the appetite that accounts for the net energy that has been sent out of the region the "Offshored Energy Wedge." Nearly all countries in WealthyWorld have an offshored energy wedge, including the United States. Note how the wedge starts to take shape in the mid-1980s when the trend of offshoring really began to take root. But it was in the late 1990s when the wedge becomes most pronounced, a time when there was a stampede by WealthyWorld countries to manufacture their goods in WantingWorld—a progression intimately linked with the phenomenon of globalization.

So in reality, our energy appetite in WealthyWorld isn't really slowing as an initial glance at Figure 3.2 would suggest; we've just convinced other countries to take on some of our energy burden.

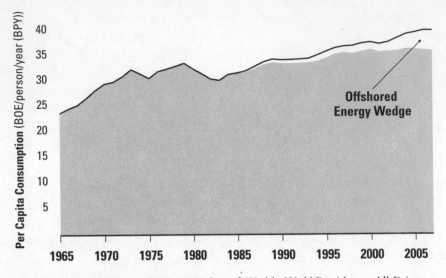

Figure 3.4   Offshored Energy Wedge of *WealthyWorld* Residents: All Primary
Energy Sources Converted to BOE
Source: ARC Financial Research, BP Statistical Review 2008, IMF.

The First Principle and the American Dream

Let's relate these findings to the United States, the biggest economy
in WealthyWorld, where compelling, energy-intensive devices such as
Watt's steam engine and Henry Ford's Model T have long spurred higher
standards of living. History shows us that as factories, cities, homes,
offices, and transportation systems consumed more energy, and the infrastructure of energy distribution became increasingly seamless and in-
visible, Americans consumed more refrigerators, automobiles, television
sets, pharmaceuticals, packaged foods, vacations, houses, and light bulbs.
The two trends went hand in hand, and the standard of living, as measured by real wealth per person, rose as a result. There are many qualitative and quantitative ways to measure a nation's standard of living from
happiness indices to personal income levels; however, overall wealth per
person—as measured by gross domestic product (GDP) divided by total
population—is acknowledged to be a good numerical indicator that can
be compared "apples-to-apples" around the world.

In Figure 3.5 the First Principle of Energy Consumption is illustrated
using U.S. economic and energy data going back to 1800. The two

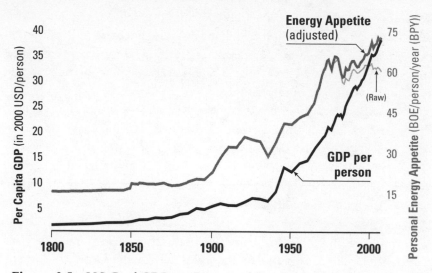

Figure 3.5   U.S. Real GDP per Person and Personal Energy Appetite (1800 to 2007)

SOURCE: ARC Financial Research, BP Statistical Review 2008, IMF, OECD, UN.

side-by-side time series are U.S. wealth per person and personal energy appetite (which I have adjusted for offshoring).

First, let's take a look at the broad trend in wealth creation. Note that the climb is steady but unremarkable through the period of the American Industrial Revolution, from about 1800 to 1900, but it begins to steepen after 1900 with the introduction of two break point innovations: electricity and the automobile. It rises even more sharply following World War II, when industrialization, suburbanization, and the modern consumer lifestyle accelerated with seemingly unbounded momentum.

Validating my First Principle of Energy Consumption, Figure 3.5 also shows that personal energy appetite followed the broad rise in American wealth creation. This relationship is not exclusive to the United States and can be demonstrated for almost any country in the world, wealthy or wanting. If you look closely at Figure 3.5, you will see that there has been one historical episode (so far) during which my First Principle can be traced in reverse; showing that energy appetite actually decreases in times of wealth destruction. This occurred during the early 1930s, at the pinnacle of the Great Depression. Back then, domestic energy consumption fell by approximately 20 percent, as industrial production in the United States was cut almost in half. Although numerically not quite as remarkable as the fall-off in energy appetite, an average American's real wealth was cut by 8 percent during that calamitous period of impoverishment.

You will also notice that there are two periods when the relationship between energy appetite and standard of living breaks down, or "decouples." The first decoupling of energy appetite and standard of living can be seen in the period from 1973 to 1980 that is known as the "Oil Shocks" or the "Energy Crisis." During this time, a combination of political and economic forces inspired by turbulence in the Middle East led to a sharp spike in the price of crude oil worldwide, first in 1973 and then in 1979. With America being the world's largest oil consumer, the spiking prices caused a sharp jolt to the country's lifestyle and economy, as Americans experienced long lines at the pump. Americans and American businesses alike were told to lower their thermostat, turn off the air conditioning, dim unneeded lights, and conserve energy. Speeds were reduced on highways and new regulatory standards were imposed on the automobile industry. Consumers who'd once bought heavy, gas-guzzling automobiles began to seek out lighter, smaller cars with better fuel economy. Nevertheless, despite the difficulties that the country experienced—the stagflation, the high unemployment, the general malaise—the economy as a whole grew. Does that disprove the First Principle of Energy Consumption?

The answer is important, but we'll save it for Part II of the book. Before then, let's continue to examine the broad trend lines of economic growth and energy appetite. In the 1990s, appetite picked up again, but at a slightly slower pace even after repatriating offshored energy. This period marks improvement in domestic energy efficiencies and processes, but not enough to convincingly break the stronghold of the First Principle.

As a footnote to American energy appetite I also show in Figure 3.5 *raw* energy appetite, unadjusted for offshoring (grey line). If you were just looking at this rendering of basic appetite, your first guess might be that the decade in question was one of very slow economic growth. But life was good in the late 1990s, a heady period of economic well-being and global stability. Unemployment was low. Incomes were rising. Certain people in the right industries at the right times were becoming very rich, as is evident by the steeply rising wealth-per-person line.

In the absence of repatriating the large component of offshored energy, it would be easy to come to the conclusion that Americans have learned to tame their energy appetite while still growing their personal wealth and well-being. However, this would represent a false sense of accomplishment, because offshoring your energy is a disingenuous way of claiming that you've truly broken the First Principle of Energy Consumption. Neither America, nor most of the broader set of countries in WealthyWorld, can truly claim to have broken the domestic efficacy of the First Principle that has remained intact since the days of the Orata's hypocaust.

Getting Everyone on the Scales

So the trend of energy appetite is broadly increasing, but what I want to measure now are the average, personal energy appetites of people living in individual countries and comparing them against each other. Does an individual consume more energy living in Korea or Italy? Russia or Austria? The United States or Australia?

In Figure 3.6 you can see how the appetites of 30 sample countries from around the world compare to each other. These personal appetites have *not* been adjusted for offshoring, because the detailed trade data to do the calculations for several of the countries in the list are not available.

In this exercise, compensating for offshoring of energy is not important, because what I want to illustrate are the big relative differences in basic energy appetite between nations. Whether the average Australian's repatriated appetite is actually 45 BPY instead of 40 BPY doesn't really make a difference when they are contrasted against an average Colombian, who uses less than 10 BPY. Either way you cut it Australians, who live in WealthyWorld, consume at least four times as much energy per person as Colombians.

It's clear from the far left of Figure 3.6 that WealthyWorld countries like Canada and the United States are consuming energy at voracious rates. It may surprise you that Canadians consume so much energy—in excess of 75 BPY in basic terms (and above 90 BPY after adjusting for offshoring). In terms of lifestyle and behavior, Canada shares much in

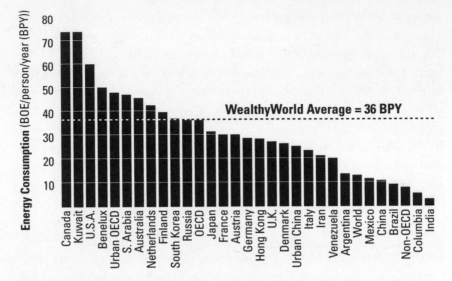

Figure 3.6   Comparison of Personal Energy Appetites for Various Countries:
Raw Energy Appetites *Unadjusted* for Offshoring
SOURCE: BP Statistical Review 2008, IMF, ARC Financial Research.

common with the United States: a reliance on large gas-guzzling vehicles, the comforts of spacious temperature-controlled homes and offices,
and long-distance commutes. In fact, geographically Canada is even
larger, and its population more dispersed, than the United States. Canada
is more of a resource oriented economy and much, much colder—all of
which exacerbate its energy obesity problem. In comparison, European
nations, like France, Germany, the United Kingdom, and Denmark, as
well as Japan, have energy appetites very much in line with the Wealthy-
World average of 36 BPY.

Living the "American Dream" means consuming at least 60 BPY or
more (without energy repatriation), a level double Denmark's—another
WealthyWorld country. In fact, being at the far left of the spectrum,
the energy appetite of Canadians and Americans is about twice the
WealthyWorld average of 36 BPY, which makes it hard *not* to conclude
that North Americans are energy obese.

It's too early to rush to a hasty judgment, as there are still many
factors to consider —geographic, demographic, and economic to name
but a few—when considering the right level of energy appetite for

countries given their unique set of circumstances. I am not one to jump to conclusions, point fingers, and criticize people who contribute to our economy by consuming more goods and services. On the other hand, there are no gains to be made vindicating unsatisfactory practices and hiding the fact that poor choices about energy consumption come at the expense of everyone's security and prosperity as well as overall environmental sustainability.

In the end my objective is to understand the roots of how and why energy appetite grows, propose pragmatic and innovative solutions to curbing such growth, and in the exciting world of tomorrow suggest that reducing energy appetite is not only virtuous, but also very possible and appealing. Ending energy obesity is about learning how to restrain and reduce personal energy appetite in both Worlds, Wealthy and Wanting.

Finally, think of Figure 3.6 as a steep energy staircase rising up from right to left. The First Principle of Energy Consumption takes countries up the staircase as they grow their economies, industrialize, mobilize, and improve their standards of living. At the bottom of the staircase, 1.1 billion citizens live a mostly agrarian existence in India, consuming only 4 BPY. At the top, 30 million Canadians enjoy a comfortable and sanitized (and cold) 75 BPY lifestyle. It's easy to see that in this sampling of 30 countries, WealthyWorld citizens are well up the staircase, while WantingWorld countries are just starting to climb. The average for the world is 14 BPY, which is about one-third of the WealthyWorld average of 36 BPY.

Putting different countries on the scales gives us a sense of the wide variation in personal energy appetites at a point in time—in this case 2007. What the scales don't give is a sense of the staggering population issue that I mentioned earlier. What happens when the weight of a few billion WantingWorld residents with hungry energy appetites start marching up the staircase?

Chapter 4

The World's Factory

I t's no mystery that China grew to be the world's factory in the first half of the twenty-first century. The energy we in WealthyWorld avoided using by sending out a portion of our manufacturing was being consumed instead by nations in WantingWorld, of which China is a leader. This globalization of manufacturing was motivated largely by the enticement of cheaper labor and production. But there are also instances when manufacturers sent their production to nations within WantingWorld with less strict environmental policies in order to reduce their nominal carbon footprint at home. The irony is that by consuming less energy domestically we're consuming more energy globally, and producing more pollution, too.

In the early stages of industrialization, WantingWorld factories and power plants can be up to four times less efficient than those in Wealthy-World, and are far more polluting. Also, trucks delivering fuel, raw materials, and manufactured goods produce more carbon emissions than tightly regulated trucks in WealthyWorld's distribution infrastructure. Exporting goods back to the countries that offshored their production yields still more energy consumed and more carbon emitted. And yet, despite the complaints about tainted products reaching the West, worries about the amount of energy China consumes, and charges that China is polluting too much, the offshoring of manufacturing goes on. The reason, of course, is simple: In part, our lifestyles and standard of living in WealthyWorld are being supported and enhanced by cheaper labor and the processes of others outside our borders.

When we think about the challenges of energy obesity in the West and the global problems of environmental sustainability, it's vital to understand that while WantingWorld and WealthyWorld nations constitute two very different industrial circumstances, we remain one planet. That is an aspect of globalization few in WealthyWorld appreciate fully.

The political leadership of China is aware of our cultural blind spot in this regard. Discussing the pressure on China to reduce its carbon emissions and other greenhouse gases, the Chinese foreign ministry spokesman, Qin Gang, spoke frankly about the consequences of globalization in 2007 when he said: "Some people call today's China as the World Factory, where we see a shift of manufacturing from the West. Much of what the developed world wears, uses and eats is made in China. It is not fair for mature countries that have already industrialized to increase their production in China whilst at the same time attacking them over greenhouse gas emissions."[1] Qin Gang understood that WealthyWorld is partly responsible for the economic growth occurring in China. He called upon us to recognize that our outsourced manufacturing needs are contributing to China's consumption of energy.

But while China's energy appetite may have been stimulated or perked by the demands of Western affluence, China has since been developing the conditions and capacity to become less dependent on trade with WealthyWorld. In other words, the energy consumption growth trend in China over the last 20 years may be interrupted by recession, but will not be reversed in the long-term even if WealthyWorld ceased all offshoring altogether. China, with its vast land, labor, and now capital, has established many of the conditions that Adam Smith wrote about at the dawn of the world's first Industrial Revolution. Notwithstanding the near term consequences of the 2008 financial crisis, what we are seeing now is the historic occurrence of the world's latest Industrial Revolution. Increasing the stakes, China's version of industrial development is occurring at an astoundingly accelerated pace, taking mere decades instead of centuries. Its energy appetite—along with that of other hungry WantingWorld nations—was one of the major reasons why the world as a whole was on the verge of an energy break point in the summer of 2008 when the price of oil nearly breached $150 a barrel. The scale of WantingWorld's future energy appetite will assuredly make us face the pressures of high energy prices again.

WealthyWorld's development makes it imperative for us to deal with our looming energy issues. At the same time, a country like China is also showing us, as in a sped-up laboratory experiment, why energy appetite grows so persistently. Looking at China, we can understand clearly that breaking the First Principle of Energy Consumption is incredibly difficult.

The Second Banquet

In my first book, *A Thousand Barrels a Second*, I explained our addiction to energy, how the pressure forces of scarcity, politics, and environment were building, and foretold that oil prices would soon enter a volatile phase with rising prices. As an energy economist, I had known for years that our global energy needs were growing larger than our ability to keep up with demand, a fact that was proven out when a barrel of oil sold for a painful $147 in July 2008, a record high and over five times the price only a decade prior.

However, the rapidity and magnitude of the oil price rise took me off guard because I was initially dubious about some of the fantastic growth figures that were coming out of WantingWorld, particularly out of China. Frankly, I hadn't seen anomalous numbers like that before in my career, and I was cautious if not skeptical about drawing alarmist conclusions.

Inspired to experience and validate what was happening firsthand, in the guise of a vacation, I took my family to visit Asia in 2007. After traveling to Japan and observing the way that highly industrialized nation carefully manages its energy appetite, we moved on to urban and rural China, snapping about 3,000 pictures to photo-document what was witnessed. I'm no expert in Chinese culture, history, or politics, but the everyday reality of such a rapidly developing lifestyle provided the direct evidence I needed to more deeply understand the economic data I had already seen. To me, a picture was worth a thousand spreadsheets.

As a newcomer to China, I was awestruck by the physical reality of its enormous population, as well as by the intensity of the urban development going on, and by the determination and pride that the Chinese people show over that progress. The sleeping giant had indeed awoken, as Napoleon had once foretold, and the energy of that return to economic ascendance, along with the vast land and labor supply already in place, led me to wonder why the industrialization of China—a culture with 4,000 years of uninterrupted existence—hadn't occurred centuries before. Chinese civilization was old when Rome became an empire; you need only walk a short length of the Great Wall, and contemplate the litany of technological innovations and the sophistication of Chinese society and thought, to appreciate the grandeur and scope of China's ancient past.

Sophisticated explanations abound as to why China, historically a technological powerhouse, didn't have its own industrial revolution to match the one that began in Europe in 1776. The question is not new and is otherwise known as the "Needham question," named after the famous British sinologist Joseph Needham, who wrote the seminal, multivolume tome, *Science and Civilization in China*. One explanatory theory, a Malthusian argument, is that medieval Europe's population was kept in check (by such calamities as the plague) just enough to allow for net growth in food and livestock (in other words, capital). This catalyzed the wealth generation that suddenly exploded when the first Industrial Revolution ignited at Coalbrookdale. Because China's dense population historically lent itself to a more subsistence-based existence, some experts speculate there may have been less opportunity to focus on wealth-producing activities beyond the necessities of daily life. On another front, trade and an interest in exploiting distant parts of the world also created a significant difference between the paths taken by China and Europe. Europe, lacking some of the land resources that China had in plenty, was inspired to go further afield to colonize and tap the resources of the Americas, Africa, and Asia. This eased demand on its own land, freeing it up for other uses, allowing some people to save and build up more capital instead of instantly consuming all the fruits of their labor. In contrast,

China was largely content to stay within its boundaries and utilize its land intensely. Finally, some experts contrast the interesting history of technology in Europe and China. With such pivotal innovations as paper, printing, gunpowder, and textiles, to name only a few, China was more technologically advanced earlier in its history than the nations of Europe. However, by the early 1700s, certain key technological advances in Europe, like mining and the steam engine, gave it the potential for greater economic growth, even as China retained a significant edge in other areas such as social infrastructure, public health, and textile making.

An alternative theory with an energy overtone suggests it was probably the availability and usage of fossil fuels, particularly coal, that allowed Europe to gain the productivity and efficiency advantages that led to the Industrial Revolution. China was never lacking in coal, but its plentiful reserves were located in the north and northwest. There is evidence of iron smelting and the use of coke in that region as early as 1000 C.E., long before it was happening in Coalbrookdale. But a series of tumultuous events, such as the Mongol invasions and severe floods and disease, caused a cultural and economic shift to the south, where coal was not plentiful. Iron was still made in this new center of civilization, but lacking an abundant supply of ready coal, China used wood and charcoal as adequate energy alternatives.[2]

England might have been content to subsist on wood and charcoal, too, if not for the problem of massive deforestation throughout northern Europe in the early 1700s. The high premium on wood led to the use of more coal and therefore deeper coal mines in England, leading in turn to the development of the steam engine. The abundance of coal around Coalbrookdale (along with financial capital, local entrepreneurial culture, and easy access to the sea) was ready to be tapped by a foundry industry on the rise. In China, on the other hand, the problem with coal mines was not water seepage, but dryness. Sparks led easily to explosions—so there was no need for a steam engine to pump out water. Perhaps the explanation for the Industrial Revolution was as simple as these basic coincidences and conditions. Without coal and the steam engine, Europe would never have produced iron in large quantities or have been able to generate the power necessary for its factories to produce goods more cheaply and plentifully. From that ever-expanding energy appetite, as the First Principle states, came wealth and improved standard of living.

It was said that emissaries from China were among the many visitors to the Iron Bridge in Coalbrookedale at the beginnings of the Industrial Revolution. But for the next three centuries, for many political and economic reasons, China was unable to follow the path taken by Europe. When I traveled through the country in 2007, it was blindingly obvious that things were different. Despite the upheaval of a rapidly changing society, there was enormous pride in the progress of development, in the accomplishments that had been made, and in that nation's entry onto the world stage, epitomized by the 2008 Beijing Olympics. The message I kept hearing and observing over and over was one that I could best articulate as: "We can do it too, and we can do it better."

For instance, I was struck by the iconic presence of the Oriental Pearl television tower in Shanghai. Only weeks before, I had seen the Tokyo Tower in Tokyo, a replica of the Eiffel Tower in Paris. The Eiffel Tower was built in 1887 as a declaration of industrial arrival. The Tokyo Tower, erected in 1958, was a similar expression, marking the resumption of Japan's progress of industrialization after defeat in World War II, and foreshadowing the global economic preeminence to come. At 468 meters high, the Oriental Pearl Tower, built in 1994 and taller than both the Tokyo Tower (333 meters) and the Eiffel Tower (324 meters), seems to announce the same satisfaction of arrival and determination of future greatness. Like a coming-out party, building a tower—or an iron bridge—is a statement declaring entry into a new age of modernization and industrialization.

New skyscrapers are everywhere in Shanghai, many over 80 stories high. So many construction cranes straddled the horizon in 2007 that tour guides joke, "That's our national bird." Forty thousand new kilometers of concrete highways are added each year, twisting into tangled arteries, overlapping each other like competing power lines, connecting the cities, while the cars shuffle along and the trucks are loaded to the brim. Airports bustle with activity, with one plane leaving every ten minutes to connect Beijing with Shanghai, a continuous conveyor belt of domestic travelers. Electronic billboards illuminate the cities and encourage the consumption of more and more goods. There is a sense that comfort, convenience, and ease have become prized commodities within the reach of many, as the air conditioners, flatscreen monitors, computers, cell phones, refrigerators, and family cars attest. Urbanization is rapidly leading to suburbanization. Cheap coal-fired stoves are being replaced by gas stoves. The cost and energy-efficient system of "just-in-time" food available in neighborhood markets is being replaced by energy-intensive household refrigerators and an infrastructure of grocery stores.

The industriousness of China's society was obvious not just in the building, transportation, and moneymaking, but also in the way people were behaving. Everyone was working and buying. Of course, despite the growing affluence and the number of new millionaires and billionaires, the *average* standard of living in general is still well below that of WealthyWorld. The rural migrant laborers with their simple pickaxes and shovels lead very hard lives on less than $200 a month, but they are constantly working and rarely take breaks, even in the fetid heat of a tropical city. Outside the cities, the farms are mechanizing too, their productivity increases coming courtesy of inefficient tractors and dump trucks expelling black smoke into the air.

What was powering all this industriousness and wealth? Where was the electricity coming from? You can follow many massive power lines stretched along the highway to the Three Gorges Dam, soon to be the largest hydroelectric power generator in the world. China already has more than half the world's dams, three times as many as the United States, and many future hydroelectric projects will go online in the coming decades.[3] We visited the headwaters of the mighty Yangtze River in rural Yunnan Province; at about 10,000 feet elevation we saw the churning untapped power of that water tumbling down. Hydroelectric water power is directly proportional to the depth of water you can achieve in front of a dam, so over the next ten years much of the picturesque valley below will also be flooded with more displacement. Such, apparently, is the cost of industrialization and modernization.

Even at such a scale, the Three Gorges Dam power plant provides only a small 0.3 percent of China's total, ever-escalating energy appetite. To fuel the hungry nation's energy diet, coal is the main menu item. Until 1994 a self-sufficient oil producer, China is now one of the world's largest oil importers, with double the consumption of 15 years ago.[4] The huge run-up in oil prices up to August 2008 was not so much a function of the marginal increases in North American demand or the steady pace of the relatively flat consumption rates in Europe and Japan, but because of the entry of this latest participant and all its peers from WantingWorld to the splendid banquet. Indeed, the price of all primary commodities—steel, nickel, and copper—skyrocketed to record heights in large part due to the growth in China.

The Power of Wealth

China's story is astonishing because of its scale and pace, but its economic growth is not an isolated event in WantingWorld. For much of human history, life has proceeded at barely subsistence level for most people on this planet, with an average annual energy appetite that's less than is contained in one barrel of oil (1 BPY). However, in the past 15 years, the world has experienced more widespread economic growth than ever before in its history. While the European and American Industrial Revolution generated amazing affluence, only a select few countries and a small overall portion of the global population truly benefited. Today, economic development is becoming more widespread and China, with one-fifth of the world's total population, is still the country with the greatest potential.

From an energy perspective, perhaps even more worrisome than the economic growth of China and other WantingWorld countries is the global population trend. More people, of course, means more energy consumption—but not all population growth is created equal. Urban and suburban lifestyles consume much more energy than rural lifestyles. I estimate that the minute someone puts down their hoe, sells their ox, and adopts an urban lifestyle their energy appetite jumps by at least 20 BPY. As of 2008, the world's urban population has finally come to equal its rural population. This massive shift, a trend that is continuing, will dramatically increase global energy appetite.

Consider Hong Kong, one of my favorite cities. Spectacular topography, great restaurants, and shiny buildings form the hub of what is not only one of the world's great financial markets, but a city that buzzes with life. A densely-packed economic powerhouse, Hong Kong has continued to thrive since it reverted to Chinese control in 1997, and operated as a Special Administrative Region (SAR). By virtue of geographic constraints, Hong Kong's seven million inhabitants live in very small dwellings that rise vertically, not horizontally. Navigating the busy metropolis, there are multiple choices for getting around Hong Kong: ferries, trolleys, buses, subways, and plenty of inexpensive taxis. Elevated walkways between buildings make it easy to walk, notwithstanding summer heat and humidity. As a result, Hong Kong has a very lean energy appetite, with inhabitants using only an average 25 BPY, after making the necessary adjustment for the large amount of embedded energy they export to WealthyWorld.[5]

Few cities in the world are as compact and efficient as Hong Kong, which is why I believe it represents a lower bound for modern city energy appetite. In other words, there aren't any templates for big city living today that can offer a lifestyle lower than 25 BPY (notwithstanding futuristic eco-city designs). Even so, this level of appetite is far greater than living a 5 BPY or less agrarian lifestyle on a rural farm, which accounts for the minimum 20 BPY rural-to-urban energy premium that I'm talking about. In fact, many of the migratory destinations in China—Shanghai, Beijing, Chengdu, and ChongQing, for example—have templates that are well in excess of 25 BPY.

The urban-rural split in China produces a barbell energy appetite that leads to a deceiving national average of 9 BPY. Some 750 million people in rural areas actually sustain on less than a meager 1 BPY, while 550 million in cities are already at an average 25 BPY and rising. "Upward mobility" takes on a new meaning in China when it comes to energy—at a 25 times multiple in consumption. Again, the point I want to make is that urban migration, which is tied to wealth accumulation, drives a quantum jump in energy appetite. This is true of any country in WantingWorld, not just China.

Urban and suburban lifestyles are dominant in WealthyWorld. In Canada and the United States, about 90 percent of the population lives in the cities or suburbs. In the developed nations of Europe, the number is a little lower at 80 percent. In China, it is a mere 45 percent, but of course, with a total population of 1.3 billion, 550 million city dwellers amounts to almost double the entire population of the United States.

While all this notionally makes sense, it doesn't become clear until we distinguish between population growth and aggressive wealth creation.

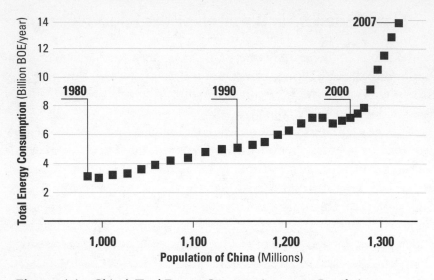

Figure 4.1 China's Total Energy Consumption versus Population (1980–2007)
SOURCE: IMF, BP Statistical Review 2008, ARC Financial Research.

Figure 4.1 shows a plot that relates China's total energy consumption for any given year since 1980 with its associated population. For example, for the data point marked 1980, China's population was 980 million people, as read on the horizontal axis, and its national energy appetite was 3 billion BOE per year as read on the vertical. Each point thereafter represents a subsequent year marking a population–energy appetite pair.

Prior to major economic reforms taking hold in the late 1990s, China's energy appetite grew steadily upward with population growth of about 15 million people per year under a steady, agrarian-dominated economy. China's energy hunger really started burgeoning in 2001 when appetite soared, despite population holding around 1.3 billion people. In fact, if you look at the vertical scale of Figure 4.1 you can see that China's national energy appetite doubled between 2001 and 2007! This is the wealth effect taking over from mere population growth.

To be fair, some of the escalating energy use in Figure 4.1 belongs to WealthyWorld because of offshoring. Nevertheless, the vertical trend in China's energy appetite is much more a statement about what happens when a society makes a rapid and conscious move to industrialize, mobilize, and bring their people's standard of living up to WealthyWorld norms.

The Hidden Consumption of the Middle Class

As standard of living grows, people not only buy more energy-consuming "luxury" goods like computers, stereos, and televisions; they also increase their consumption of goods that have an indirect energy cost we don't normally count.

Every good and service in the economy has an embedded energy cost at some level, if only we calculated it. Consider a cup of coffee. It takes energy to operate a coffee shop and a coffeepot. It also takes energy to produce the coffee cup, the plastic lid as well as to roast, transport, and grow the beans. That's why, when oil prices rise we see a corresponding rise in the cost of everything else, even goods that we normally don't think of as oil-related.

With affluent urban living come more lattés, more clothing, more bottles of wine, more energy-intensive food. The old maxim, "the more you make, the more you spend," must be extended into the realm of energy and the context of the First Principle to read, "the more you make, the more you spend—and the more energy you use." Just consider the energy appetite among U.S. citizens as a function of their personal income.

The energy appetite data in Figure 4.2 are raw and not adjusted for offshoring. Such nuances don't matter here, because my point is to show that the more money you make, the more energy you use. The First Principle applies not just on a national scale but right down to the personal income level.

At the low end of the income scale, $15,000 a year, the average American consumes 37 BPY. As they enter the middle-income grouping their appetite rises to the national average of 60 BPY. When they enter the flush income brackets, above $100,000 per year, they will probably have a bigger home that may be located at a more distant location from the city, and two or more larger vehicles to support that lifestyle. They'll travel by airplane more, possibly have a second home in the country, and perhaps enjoy an expensive energy-consuming hobby like motor boating. This is not meant to infer blame or guilt for such a lifestyle, otherwise known as the "American Dream," but to validate the truism that people with disposable wealth consume more energy than people who live closer to the paycheck regardless of what country they live in.

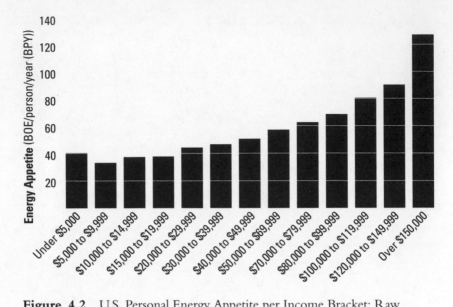

Figure 4.2   U.S. Personal Energy Appetite per Income Bracket: Raw
Appetite *Unadjusted* for Energy Offshoring 2005
SOURCE: ARC Financial Research, U.S. Department of Labor, IMF, BP Statistical Review 2008.

Notice that once the middle-class threshold has been breached, energy appetite begins to move up faster. The escalating relationship I'm showing in Figure 4.2 does not permit middle-class readers to shrug off their concerns about personal energy consumption with the excuse that, "The rich are different than you and me, they use more energy." Rather, because a majority of people in WealthyWorld nations are middle or upper-middle class, they actually comprise the group which, in aggregate, consumes the most energy in total, despite the "super-consumption" of the rich (see Figure 4.3).

The central idea I want to make clear is that energy appetite does not increase with rising standard of living on some kind of one-for-one basis demonstrating a linear relationship. Instead, a rising standard of living leads to an *exponential* growth in energy appetite. This spells trouble. Globally, WantingWorld is getting wealthier in the long run. As their middle class grows, more people are going to be buying more goods and gadgets and consuming more energy at an exponentially greater rate.

In 1990, average income in China was US$1,150. Ten years later it was US$ 2,440. By 2007 the average "middle class" Chinese person

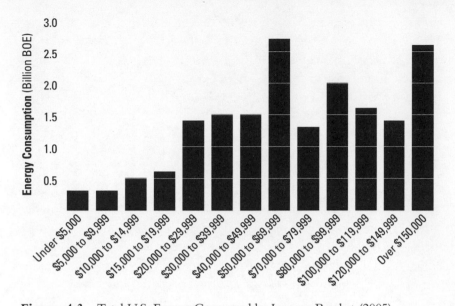

Figure 4.3   Total U.S. Energy Consumed by Income Bracket (2005)
SOURCE: ARC Financial Research, U.S. Department of Labor, IMF, BP Statistical Review 2008.

earned $4,180 per year. Though this is still not much by WealthyWorld standards, there are two points to be made: First, notwithstanding economic fluctuations, the long-term trend in China's income is growing by about 10 percent per year; and second, being middle class in China is not the same as being middle class in the United States or Germany. In straight, currency-converted dollar terms a relatively well-off citizen in China appears to earn considerably less income than someone of similar social stature in a WealthyWorld nation. But a dollar goes a lot further in China than in the United States, between two and three times further, in fact. After adjusting for comparative purchasing power, an average Chinese person is already at the equivalent of US $14,700 per year and rising.

The implications are clear. As China's income distribution approaches WealthyWorld levels, consumption and energy appetite all increase at an accelerating pace. Again, it doesn't really matter what country you live in—"the more money you make, the more energy you consume." And that relationship is exponential, not linear.

Throughout the first decade of this century and at the same time as the stresses on our supplies were building, WantingWorld countries like China have been getting wealthier and demanding more energy. That was one of the big reasons why, halfway through 2008, oil prices reached such lofty heights. But the First Principle also holds true in reverse. When wealth shrinks, energy consumption goes down, as we saw in the second half of that most interesting year.

A Two-Sided Principle

In late September 2008, I was in Hong Kong only a couple of days after the storied, 160-year-old investment bank Lehman Brothers imploded, an event that marked the moment when the global financial downturn turned into a full-blown crisis. While visiting financial institutions, I could sense the tension among Asian money managers as stock markets lost between 3 and 5 percent of their value day after day.

Over the next couple of weeks, stock markets would continue their tailspin as the most severe financial crisis since the Great Depression worsened and bank after bank toppled. Politicians and financial mandarins from WealthyWorld scrambled to pull all the levers at their disposal to right the economy, promising bailouts to banks in order to keep the wheels turning. But those efforts failed, and economies around the world faltered—or teetered on bankruptcy, as in the case of Iceland.

The biggest fear was that WealthyWorld countries would fall into recession, which by the commonly applied rule of thumb is when a country's economy, visible in real gross domestic product, actually shrinks for six months or more. In fact, instead of growing, the collective $35 trillion worth of annual commerce incumbent in the WealthyWorld nations was about to get smaller by a few hundred billion dollars. On an individual level, a recession translates into the hard reality of pay cuts, an end to easy spending, and losses in savings. At the more difficult end of the recessionary spectrum, millions of people lose their jobs and homes and pension plans are threatened. As President Truman pointedly said, "It's a recession when your neighbor loses his job; it's a depression when you lose yours."

Much will be written about the financial crisis of 2008. Though wholly unsettling, the most remarkable aspect about the crisis was that the mature WealthyWorld economies went into a *rapid* recession, followed by rapid contraction. Any time major economic events occur without forewarning it serves as a laboratory for observation and validation of theory. Extreme events provide a tremendous amount of data. Large earthquakes and hurricanes, unwelcome as they are, have the positive benefit of giving scientists a wealth of information from which to learn. Likewise, we will inevitably learn volumes from the seismic events shaking the global economy in the fall of 2008.

Back then, we saw that as wealth generation turned into wealth destruction, the need for energy diminished just as fast. Individuals and corporations stopped buying goods and services and the impact on energy was almost immediate. In the United States and Europe, oil demand slipped more than 3 percent in a matter of weeks. Under these extreme and sharp financial conditions, the First Principle of Energy Consumption was vividly validated in reverse: less wealth meant less spending, that in turn meant less energy use.

Clearly, this is not the prescription we're looking for to end energy obesity. Like going on a starvation diet that adversely affects your health, shrinking the economy quickly is not an acceptable way to tackle our energy predicament. And that shows just how difficult it can be to reduce energy consumption. According to the First Principle, doing so implies a reduced quality of life.

If the financial crisis confirmed the First Principle in reverse, the first half of 2008 demonstrated the First Principle in overdrive. Easy access to capital for most of the prior five years lubricated wealth creation and consumption. Economic growth was synchronous around the world, like a well-oiled V12 firing on all cylinders and revving close to the red line. Most of those cylinders were attributable to WantingWorld economies. Led by China, these countries were growing at an average of 6.7 percent, equivalent to about $2.5 trillion of new wealth being created each year. Even the United States and mature countries of Europe were generating new economic activity of $1 trillion per year. As a result of this wealth generation, the pull on all energy commodities—coal, uranium, oil, and natural gas—were showing increasingly excessive stresses and strains.

By July 2008, we were on the verge of a break point. A demand response was starting to happen at $4.25 per gallon of gasoline. Americans were taking "staycations" and opting to relax in backyards and front porches instead of the ritual packing up of the SUV, roof rack and all, and heading out with kids and dogs. Automakers found themselves responding to a sudden demand for smaller, more fuel efficient vehicles.

There was an awakening in the summer of 2008, but the prices of energy commodities weren't high enough for long enough to catalyze a meaningful change in the tight relationship between energy consumption and wealth. Our energy demand was not cut by a conscious, widespread desire to reduce energy appetite; it was cut due to a reduction in wealth, which is not a long-term solution. When wealth creation returns, as it always has following recessionary periods, the character of energy appetite growth will return unchanged.

During an economic slowdown, most of us cut back. We consume less. But no one likes to tighten a belt when they don't have to. It requires discipline, attention, and sacrifice—an ability to resist the impulse to buy, use, or consume what we've become accustomed to having in our lives. Recent essays about the "science of happiness" point out what most of us understand firsthand. It doesn't matter how much money or material belongings you have, you're never fully satisfied and always want more. That's the essence of economic growth. The strict corollary of that idea of dissatisfaction should be that the less we have the less we want or need, but unfortunately such a sentiment doesn't often hold true in reality. Instead, it would seem that the only thing that upsets us more than not getting what we want is losing what we already have. It's almost counter to human nature, or the capitalist culture most of us are born into, to give up what we've come to enjoy.

In his 1927 essay titled *Comfort*, the English writer Aldous Huxley wrote, "The more comfort is brought into the world, the more it is valued. To those who have known comfort, discomfort is a real torture." Those of us who are fortunate enough to live in one of the Wealthy World economies are loath to willingly give up on the lifestyle advantages we've come to enjoy, and indeed, deem essential to our very quality of life. We're programmed to strive for a growing economy, and drive for more personal wealth. This means that most of us will find it difficult to significantly reduce our personal energy appetite. Of course, there are times when an energy diet gets forced upon us, as happened during the 1970's energy crises and as was imminent in the summer of 2008. When oil reaches record prices and the cost of filling up a tank of gas or heating our homes becomes "uncomfortable," many of us are increasingly willing to put up with a little discomfort temporarily.

But while high energy prices help change behavior and somewhat reduce energy demand, the impact is disproportional and not as helpful to our overall energy obesity problem as one might hope. Naturally, those who have the least amount of disposable income—the lower-middle class and the poor—are the ones who are hit the hardest. While the middle class grumbles about the cost of filling up the tank, the people with less disposable income are leaving the car parked on the street and riding the bus, or heating their homes through nontraditional and sometimes unsafe means involving open flames. But if we recall Figure 4.3, my chart on energy appetite as a function of income bracket, we can see how little impact this might have on a nation's overall energy appetite. The middle class may drive a bit less, too, and adjust the thermostat, but transportation and household energy use is only a small part of the energy appetite of the affluent. The more significant portion goes toward the creature comforts of life; the new suit, the skim-milk latté, the Chilean-grown tomatoes available in the local grocery store in the middle of the winter. Those pleasures might seem trivial compared to the looming energy issues we are facing, but try giving them up. Once lodged in our psyche as fixtures of the quality of life we've come to enjoy, it can seem like torture to forego them. It is for this reason that I believe we will need to find some other way to end our energy obesity that doesn't involve sacrificing our standard of living.

And if it is so difficult for us to give up on the creature comforts we're accustomed to, imagine the citizen of a rapidly developing WantingWorld nation willingly resisting the achievement pleasures in the first place? The American Dream—the suburban house with two cars, the upwardly mobile and comfortable lifestyle of plenty—is not limited to Americans. It is becoming a tantalizing reality for hundreds of millions of newly affluent citizens of China, India, South-East Asia, South America, and Eastern Europe. Now, we must brace ourselves as their standard of living rises and their energy appetite surges over the next two decades.

China, in particular, shows a trend akin to a troubling movie we've seen before. The faint hope exists that a rapidly developing nation might choose to learn from hard-earned WealthyWorld experiences and avoid the mistakes made that have led to societal templates of energy obesity. But the likelihood that China will choose the path of an energy-fit neighbor like Japan and avoid the excesses of North America appears slim. In this, it would seem that geography is destiny. The smaller confined energy-poor nations like Japan, Western Europe, and, more recently, South Korea, have shown a strong tendency toward careful management of their energy appetite, unlike sprawling, energy-affluent nations like Canada, the United States, and, it would seem, China. Indeed, if we do a projection of where China's energy appetite is headed, we see that it is chasing the American Dream of 60 BPY, not the Japanese reality of 35 BPY. And the strength of China's growth means that while the current financial crisis will temporarily slow its economy, in years to come the turmoil of 2008 and 2009 will likely be seen as no more than a pause.

When they get there, what will be the result? Can our planetary energy distribution system sustain the entrant of such a behemoth? Can our environment? Those types of questions are studied in a discipline of applied mathematics called "game theory," which provides a framework of characterizing and solving problems in which one person's gain is another's loss. Insights developed from game theory can be applied to the world of energy, where there is always a complex interplay of participants sharing a finite resource, like oil, or a common problem, like the environment.

A Common Tragedy

Garrett Hardin, the late American ecologist, investigated the sharing of finite resources in a seminal 1968 article entitled *Tragedy of the Commons*.

> *Picture a pasture open to all. It is to be expected that each herdsman will try to keep as many cattle as possible on the commons. Such an arrangement may work reasonably satisfactorily for centuries because tribal wars, poaching, and disease keep the numbers of both man and beast well below the carrying capacity of the land. Finally, however, comes the day of reckoning, that is, the day when the long-desired goal of social stability becomes a reality. At this point, the inherent logic of the commons remorselessly generates tragedy.[6]*

To wit, the game here is that it is in the short-term best interest of each herdsmen to introduce one or more additional cows into the commons, and so every herdsmen does. But the cumulative impact of overgrazing ruins the commons for all. The metaphor is easy to follow. China and the other WantingWorld nations, as the new herdsmen, are introducing not one cow, but as many new cows as are already comfortably grazing. Undeterred by this development, WealthyWorld is still bringing more cows of its own onto the commons, too. Hardin's anecdote would hold that we are all, therefore, headed rapidly for tragedy.

The optimists will argue that there are solutions. Game theory would suggest one solution to be "Mutual coercion, mutually agreed upon," which means that we must strike deals and cooperate. In the case of global energy consumption, this would imply some sort of diplomatic solution. But as we saw with the Kyoto Protocol, even a pressing issue like global warming can have its detractors, and when all players in the game—especially a significant player like the United States—do not agree to be mutually coerced, no player is likely to live up to what has been agreed upon. To me, regardless of the pros and cons of the Kyoto treaty, this resistance by the United States only reaffirms the inexorable calculus of the First Principle. Curbing status quo energy appetite means reducing standard of living, and countries are not likely to submit to such measures willingly. Speaking in June 1992 at the Earth Summit in Rio de Janeiro, Brazil, the first President Bush, George Herbert, expressed his concern about the negative economic impact of imposing climate change policies on U.S. society. "The American way of life is not negotiable," he said. Whether in word or deed, many would agree with that sentiment privately. After all, what politician in any country is eager to bargain for a lesser standard of living for their people once a certain level of wealth and comfort has been achieved?

But if contrived international diplomacy doesn't work—or isn't completely sufficient—there are other solutions, the optimists insist. Perhaps we can expand the yield of the commons by making it more efficient, or we can find a new commons that better serves our demand, or discover some miracle alternative, or curb our use of the commons without backtracking on our standard of living.

Yet others suggest that you can best change energy consumption by changing the values that direct people's behavior. Those who see things this way usually consider the human spirit to be the driver behind history and downplay the importance of technology and economic development. And what has been a more central shaper of the human spirit and values than religion? Curiously, religion often tends to see appetite as negative and restraint as a virtuous path to happiness. Just think of religious or fringe groups who demonstrate their disregard for worldly possessions by taking vows of poverty. From their perspective, it's almost natural to regard any crisis that stems from energy gluttony as a kind of deserved retribution!

There is no straightforward relationship between human happiness and economic well-being. Just as wealth doesn't guarantee happiness, neither does poverty. Nevertheless, cultural values are constantly changing, so it cannot be ruled out that society might one day even voluntarily revert to a more primitive, less energy-intense lifestyle—as some religious, environmental, or other groups advocate. Having said that, such a reversion on any meaningful scale strikes me as very unlikely, because relative concepts like spirituality, happiness, and human values invariably lead to sharp disagreements and even fights over an even more rigid type of commons: the commons of the mind.

Mental games, whether mathematical, philosophical, or both, are always insightful and interesting to consider and debate. However, in this book I have chosen to minimize philosophical arguments, preferring to stay with ideas that have been developed upon the solid ground of historical guidance, empirical data, and quantitative analysis. Those effects show that when we have faced seemingly intractable energy crises in the past, we have always found broad-based solutions when we needed them most—though now, nothing is easy when the world already has a total energy appetite the equivalent to 240 million barrels of oil per day.

Part II

ELUSIVE SOLUTIONS

Chapter 5

Breaking Our Energy Diet

The problem with energy is not that it is bad for us, but that it has been too good. As the First Principle makes clear, increased energy consumption leads to a higher quality of life. Wood, coal, whale oil, or waterpower—to name just a few forms of fuels we've enjoyed over the last 300 years—promote the development of more goods and services and, in turn, generate wealth. As wealth in the economy is generated—as people become richer, assume higher standards of living, and desire more goods and services—our reliance on that form of energy gets progressively stronger.

Looking beyond the valley of the severe global recession that took root in 2008, we're looking at new territory with respect to this formula of wealth creation. The world's population has become much larger *and* much wealthier even since the energy crises of the 1970s. As a result, the scale of the global energy problem has grown to a point almost beyond comprehension. In 2008, the world's population was estimated at 6.7 billion and growing by 75 million every year. That's like adding a new France *plus* a new Czech Republic to our planet every year; a lot of people to feed, clothe, shelter, and provide with the comforts of modern life. While it's true that today's *rate* of population growth is 1 percent and declining, big regional trends in places like Asia, the Middle East, and Africa suggest the planet will host a peak of nine billion people by 2050.

If that's beyond your retirement plans, consider that the world will need to find the means to host another one billion people by 2020. By that time I forecast that the current population trend, combined with everyone's desire to increase their standard of living, will push the world's energy needs up 37 percent, or another 32 billion BOE per year. The world's historical energy appetite and composition of its diet back to 1965 as well as a projection of all dietary components through to 2020 are illustrated in Figure 5.1 (note that individual fuel source forecasts are *unrestricted*; in other words, the forecasts in Figure 5.1 assume that the supply of each fuel is readily available without constraint).

Perhaps you think that the steep upward slope in my forecast to 2020 is alarmist or out of context with the prior 35 years of energy evolution. It's not—and you don't need a spreadsheet to understand this.

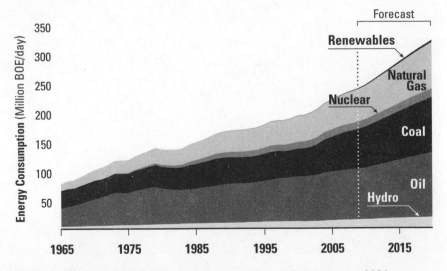

Figure 5.1 World Total Energy Consumption with Forecast to 2020 (Unrestricted): All Primary Energy Sources Converted to BOE
Source: ARC Financial Research, BP Statistical Review, IMF.

The post–World War II period up to 2000 was predominantly due to 800 million people growing wealthy and increasingly comfortable. Looking ahead, the story is about keeping those 800 million WealthyWorld residents happy, while also making room for another two or three billion WantingWorld citizens on our planetary commons.

The irony of the financial crisis that started in 2008 is the high probability that WantingWorld, in particular China, is positioning itself for even faster growth of its energy appetite. In November of 2008, in response to fears that the global economic slowdown would temper China's extraordinary growth and cause politically unacceptable unemployment, the Chinese government announced a U.S. $586–billion fiscal stimulus plan to spur the expansion of the country's economy over two years. Specifically, the funds were to be spent on upgrading infrastructure, roads, railways, airports, affordable housing, and the national power grid.[1] Besides costing China about one-sixth of its expected 2009 GDP, this plan will require an enormous amount of energy. Even more staggering perhaps is the fact that when all of the infrastructure projects are completed, China will be ready to use more energy and grow even faster in the future (though the severity of the global economic downturn precludes knowing exactly when).

In fact, we don't have to go back far in history to find a parallel story with a similar conclusion. The "New Deal" was the name that U.S. President Franklin D. Roosevelt gave to a series of economic programs he introduced between 1933 and 1936 to jump-start the American economy following the Great Depression. Its central mandate was to allocate a then-incredible $3.3 billion (equivalent to $55 billion in 2007 U.S. dollars) to public works projects. Schools, hospitals, post offices, roads, and dams were built at record speed. Not surprisingly, total U.S. energy demand soared—growing at an average rate of 4.5 percent between 1936 and 1939. More importantly, when the U.S. economy finally recovered after World War II, America had a modern infrastructure and a network of new highways to grow into. Thanks in part to the availability of this infrastructure, the United States became one of the greatest powers of all times, boasting an equally "super" and continuously growing energy appetite.

The scale of WantingWorld's growing energy appetite projected over the next 20 years will make the rise of WealthyWorld in the twentieth century seem like an appetizer enjoyed before a decadent feast. That doesn't mean China or India or any other country in WantingWorld is in trouble; rather, it is our energy appetite in WealthyWorld that will be stressed the most. A citizen in a developing nation may be frustrated when their improving standard of living gets stalled by high-priced energy. But that frustration pales in comparison to the anxiety that will befall us if our current standard of living actually declines. WealthyWorld lifestyles may not be open for negotiation, but that doesn't mean they won't be compromised as others fight for their fair share.

Dietary Evolution

Let's take a step back from current problems and consider the natural evolution of energy appetite in general. Man, as the father of humanistic psychology Abraham Maslow noted when formulating his hierarchy of human needs, is a "perpetually wanting animal."[2] Over time, different energy sources and systems have supported our perpetual desire for more security, shelter, comfort, luxury, and freedom. But there comes a period in the life cycle of every energy source when our demands for it are so great that the supply itself or the infrastructure of its delivery are taxed beyond capacity. When that happens, we reach what I call an "energy break point"—the moment when a society's energy sources, or the way those sources are supplied, is no longer sustainable. At that point, either our energy consuming habits, the proportional mix of the fuels we consume in our overall diet, or some of the fuels themselves, must change.

In *A Thousand Barrels a Second*, I used historical examples to describe the evolution and dynamics of energy break points. In the premodern era, wood was the predominant fuel source in agrarian Europe but a break point occurred in the 1700s. At this juncture the need for fuel and shipbuilding materials—as well as a burgeoning population's demands for more land for crops and grazing animals—outstripped supply and decimated Europe's forests.

A similar story unfolded in the 1800s with whale oil—then one of the world's premier sources of illumination. Tallow candles may have been more common, but they were a poor substitute for the clean, sweet-smelling, and brighter light of spermaceti candles. In its day, the industry for slaughtering sperm whales as well as processing, distributing, and selling the oil was as developed as the industry for drilling, refining, and distributing crude oil is now. But our demand for whale oil began to exceed the supply from sperm whales living in the oceans—it even exceeded the capacity of the industry, as several untimely maritime disasters crippled the whale fishery fleet. And so, the combination of those two calamitous events ended our easy access to whale oil and precipitated a break point.

Energy break points bring about changes, often drastic, in our economic behavior and in our lifestyles. Reacting to public complaints about high prices and a slowing economy, governments typically intervene to modify the energy diet in order to find immediate relief for their constituents' pain. A bit later, they look for actual legislative or regulatory solutions, sometimes in denial of the seriousness of the problem, sometimes desperate enough to tackle matters head-on. In any case, the ultimate solution to a break point—a rebalancing of our energy diet—usually originates not from the grassroots or the political process but from an energy-related innovation on the supply side that allows us to expand our appetite once again.

Through the help of some timely innovations—a pivotal device like the steam engine, the combustion engine, the kerosene lamp, or nuclear power plant—and some timely social and economic trends, a new and different energy source can be exploited that rebalances our diet and eases the pressure on our addiction. In this way, the forests of Europe were saved by coal, and the majestic sperm whale was saved by the discovery of the illuminating properties of crude oil, distilled as kerosene. The irony of this should be noted. No solution is black and white in the intersecting worlds of energy and the environment.

When a new energy source, paired with one or more sufficiently compelling conversion devices, is introduced into our economy, our overall energy diet changes. Our hunger for wood, coal, or waterpower doesn't immediately disappear, but our energy diet is altered as part of a more diverse mix of sources on the menu. For example, when oil was introduced as a viable energy source to propel automobiles and ships and churn generators, it began to aggressively supplant coal, even as coal remained an important, though diminished, part of our overall diet.

Another way to understand our energy evolution is to think of fuels as products competitively jockeying for shares of our appetite. Occasionally, break point innovations in energy systems allow fuel sources to opportunistically take market share away from incumbent fuels—especially when the new entrant has a compelling advantage. Sometimes market share is reshuffled with existing menu offerings, or new entrants come in and steal another fuel's share. The evolution of primary energy market share in the United States since 1635, shown in Figure 5.2, vividly illustrates how market share of energy sources changes over time, sometimes smoothly, sometimes abruptly.

Until the 1800s, wood was the dominant fuel in the United States. Other fuels like whale oil and tallow for candles were significant too; possibly 10 percent or more of the mix, but unfortunately there's insufficient data available to accurately reconstruct the numbers. Coal's aggressive market share grab from wood started in the mid-1800s when steam engine technology crossed the Atlantic—the greatest energy break point period in history. But technology was not the only facilitator of coal's market share grab; environmental sustainability was a major pressure point in both Europe and the United States. The unsustainability of

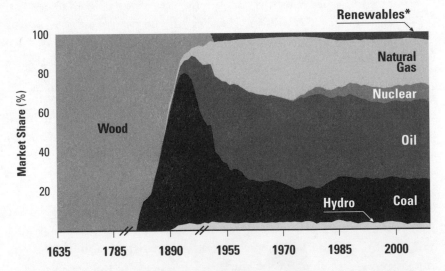

Figure 5.2   U.S. Market Share of Primary Energy Sources (1635 to 2007)
SOURCE: U.S. Energy Information Administration, ARC Financial Research.
*Renewables are primarily biomass, wind and solar.

heavy logging was a major environmental issue requiring quick resolution in order for early American society to keep advancing its standard of living.

I've talked much about Henry Ford and the introduction of the automobile as a stimulus for expanding energy appetite. Not only did the appetite for oil products take off at the start of the twentieth century, but the compelling qualities of oil relative to coal reduced our dependence on that solid fuel. Natural gas also muscled in on the menu, especially after the 1920s, an important dynamic to be discussed further in Chapter 14.

Renewables appear to have started emerging in the United States around 1940. This doesn't stem from any fantastic innovations or pivotal circumstances, but from the mundane fact that statisticians began to pay attention to them. In actuality, the use of renewable energy like wind power dates back to the 1600s in the United States. Both whale oil (in a macabre sense) and wood can be considered renewables, too. Water power goes back thousands of years, but it wasn't until the late 1800s that it was used to generate electricity and took on the moniker hydropower.

The pattern of energy diet that evolved in the United States is very similar to what happened in Europe, with variations in timing and proportion. In fact, we can generalize quite easily that the rebalancing and diversification of a nation's energy diet seems to be a hallmark of an economy's state of development. An easy parallel can be drawn with the way our nutritional diet changes as we grow older. When we're infants, we feed on milk and simple cereals. As toddlers we begin diversifying into solid foods like meat, vegetables, and grains, while still consuming plenty of milk. By the time we're teenagers, the demands of our growing bodies have us devouring everything in the fridge and pantry—milk, bread, fruit, chocolate cake, leftover pasta, potato chips—and we seem impervious to the negative effects of cheap calories in junk food. But as we reach adulthood and transition into middle age, we typically find that a diet skewed toward the wrong foods can lead to health problems. In response, we often try to exert personal discipline, with varying degrees of success, to curb the urges of a lifetime. This usually means eating less, but quality food, sometimes at the dismaying sacrifice of taste, enjoyment, comfort, and easy access.

Similarly, as economies develop from agrarian subsistence through industrialization and into the maturity of widespread wealth, we see energy diets diversify. The agrarian society burns wood because it's cheap and abundant. The early industrial society relies on rivers and a modicum of coal. Large-scale industrialization, like the teenager entering puberty, requires a tremendous expansion of energy appetite to satisfy. Coal certainly provides cheap energy calories, but oil—because of its ease of distribution and its robust power generation—is a GDP booster rocket that rapidly propels societies from developing to advanced levels of economic activity. In a maturing economy, natural gas and nuclear power arrive as dietary supplements. Eventually, we reach for renewables and other alternative sources that can allow us to maintain a lifestyle of plenty while postponing the inevitable consequences of unhealthy addiction to dirty fuels in the same way people reach for dietary alternatives to combat the deleterious effects of aging. Of course, each country's overall diet has its own unique proportions of coal, oil, natural gas, nuclear power, and renewables, just as each country has its own appetite. It all depends on its natural resources, its geographical location, its political friends, and the money it's willing to spend or invest.

So far, so good. As our society grows, we adapt to new circumstances by diversifying our energy diet and rebalancing the fuels on our menu. However, the cycle of energy evolution is neither simple nor clean. Unlike changes in nutritional diet from childhood through adolescence and into adulthood, transitions in energy diets are not a natural result of aging. Rather, each significant change is typically punctuated by a reaction to some crisis of sustainability or access to supply. In other words, it takes a break point to make us change the dietary habits of several generations. Unfortunately, as the scale of our addiction grows it becomes progressively more difficult to respond to that break point and rebalance our diets.

Two Heart Attacks and a Menu Change

The breakpoint of the 1970s remains the modern touchstone for understanding what an energy crisis felt like and how it impacted our lives. The headlines are easy to recall. Turmoil in the Middle East sent prices skyrocketing. Long lines formed at the gas stations. The era of classic gas-guzzling automobiles came to an end, while reduced speed limits were introduced. President Jimmy Carter in his cardigan sweater told America that a national economic malaise had set in, and the nation would need to conserve energy if it was to have a secure and stable future.

We'll examine that turbulent era in more detail later, but for now it's worth remembering some of the numbers and facts behind the headlines. Unrest had been rife in the Middle East for several decades without unduly affecting oil prices in the West. But in the 1970s, the political will of the Organization of Petroleum Exporting Countries (OPEC) coalesced, creating a new global power capable of influencing crude oil prices. The timing of OPEC's emergence was particularly unfortunate for the United States. After more than half a century of seemingly inexhaustible production that had started with the gushing Spindletop oilfield in 1905, American reserves peaked in 1970. Domestic production began to decrease for the first time, although demand remained unchecked.

We create an unbalanced understanding of the turbulent 1970s if we restrict our focus to Middle East politics. That's easy to do since the drama of sudden war, oil boycotts, and the conflict between civilizations paints the era in striking colors. But the 1973 energy crisis arrived after several decades of turbo-charged post-World War II wealth creation. The oil appetites of America, Europe, and Japan were growing by an aggressive 9 percent per year because of rapid "adolescent" industrialization and mobilization.

In any event, the world's developed economies were therefore vulnerable when the first heart attack hit. The crisis started in late 1973 after talks between the major western oil companies and OPEC broke down over negotiations for setting the price of oil. In response, and to also show outrage over their support for Israel in the so-called Yom Kippur War, OPEC began to embargo supplies of oil from the Middle East to America and the Netherlands. Per barrel prices surged from $4.30/B to $10.00/B in short order and, as mentioned, actual gasoline shortages occurred at service station pumps.

If you have a heart attack in early middle age, it's a wake-up call that may be ignored if life returns to normal. It's all too common that people resist making real behavioral change until the subsequent health crisis strikes. The oil embargo lasted just five months. The price of oil stayed higher but WealthyWorld did its best to ignore the domestic reasons for its vulnerability, and grew accustomed to higher prices. In short, the United States was unwilling or unable to make the kinds of serious structural changes to its energy diet that would be necessary to mitigate future problems.

It must be acknowledged that President Carter tried. He promised a national energy policy soon after taking office. Carter seemed to understand the nature of the simmering crisis, but was unable to sufficiently rally the public or the United States Congress. In 1978, in the midst of the crisis of the Iranian revolution, the National Energy Act was passed. That legislation included the Fuel Use Act, severely restricting the burning of oil and natural gas for the purpose of electric power generation.

This signaled the first wholesale shift in many decades in the U.S. energy diet. When Edison's generators first made their appearance in America's cities, they were typically fed by coal, which was cheap, plentiful, and perfectly suited to the task. But after Spindletop and the arrival of the Model T, the infrastructure for distributing oil and natural gas became increasingly sophisticated, turning those fuels into attractive, inexpensive, and accessible alternatives for power generation. With regard to power generation, Carter's Fuel Use Act simultaneously turned the clock back, encouraging more coal and forward by putting nuclear power onto the main menu.

And yet, as people fall back into complacency following the first heart attack, the shift did not come quickly enough. While stress had been building with the Iranian Revolution and the sense that all the rules in the Middle East were changing, the big heart attack arrived in earnest in 1979 when the Iran-Iraq War broke out. The world's oil distribution infrastructure, that functioned like life-giving arteries to the world economy, became clogged with geopolitics. Taking advantage of oil's new competitive disadvantage, both coal and nuclear power began opportunistically taking market share, a dynamic that can clearly be seen in Figure 5.2.

It was the 1979 meteoric rise in oil prices that finally triggered the break point, forcing the developed countries of the world to significantly change their energy diets while also reducing their actual appetites. For example, new rules were introduced in the transportation sector. American industry had long argued against fuel economy standards, while the American people were resistant to mass transit. As Henry

Ford II noted, "We are just not attuned to getting anywhere any other way than by automobile. Some people ride buses. Now trains are coming back—but it's a fad. This country developed in a particular way because of the automobile, and you can't just push a button and change it."[3] Even so, Washington mandated new fuel economy standards for passenger vehicles. Detroit automakers grudgingly responded by making technical improvements, lightening their vehicles, and making them smaller, even as they complained about the added production costs. To an industry and a public weaned on the marketability of the large fancy automobile, this was a difficult adjustment. Perhaps equally hard was the mandating of new speed limits. No one liked that curtailing of freedom, especially given the limited success of the policy; cutting highway speed to 55 miles per hour, fuel economy was improved by anywhere from a mere 0.5 to 1.0 percent.[4]

Japan and the other developed nations in Europe reacted differently according to their circumstances and domestic politics: changing energy diets, developing their mass transportation infrastructure, or imposing conservation methods in ways that were neither feasible, nor particularly popular in the United States. For example, at the time of the 1973 oil crisis, most of France's electricity came from foreign oil. Following the oil price shocks, the French government invested heavily in building nuclear reactors. Today, over 38 percent of France's total energy demand is met by nuclear power. Likewise in Japan, following the price spikes of the 1970s, new government policy resulted in the increased use of natural gas, nuclear power, and coal to generate electricity, thus reducing the nation's dependence on oil. In Denmark, a 1970 report from the Danish Ministry of Trade concluded that it may be possible to introduce up to 10 percent wind power into the grid. By 2007, wind power provided 19.7 percent of Denmark's electricity, a significantly higher proportion than in any other country.

Those paths, of course, were significantly influenced by the unique circumstances that each nation faced. Features of Japan's culture enabled energy-related choices in a modern lifestyle that a North American would find strange. Although air conditioning devours electricity in the hot and humid summer months, Japanese houses and offices are unheated and uncomfortable during sharply cold winters. The compromises the Japanese have made seem somewhat primitive in comparison to North

American indulgent lifestyles: portable kerosene stoves, chemical heating packs for underclothes, electrically-heated tables and toilet seats, hot baths, and warm drinks. But Japan's houses and apartments are far less energy intensive than suburban, convenience-loaded castles in North America. Japanese business workers in suits and women in dresses find nothing objectionable about cycling to destinations. Neighborhoods are built around convenient mixed-use facilities—offices, restaurants, coffee shops, stores, schools, playgrounds, and train stations are all within easy reach while parking spaces are scarce. Mass public transport, high gasoline taxes, and strict emissions controls further encourage people to avoid using their personal vehicles whenever possible.

In countries like France, England, Germany, and Denmark, similar kinds of lifestyle choices and limits exist. But before we criticize the United States and Canada for being energy gluttons, we need to appreciate certain substantial differences between nations. In many respects the United States can hardly be compared to Japan, Britain, or Germany. I'll expand on this discussion in Chapter 15, but in terms of geography and the potential for expansion the United States probably bears a closer resemblance to China. This does not mean, however, that Americans or any other energy-consuming citizens on the planet can't make better, more sustainable lifestyle choices.

A Restrictive Menu

When I talk to audiences now, I find I no longer need to conjure up historical anecdotes to explain what the lead up to an energy break point feels like—after all, we were experiencing the early stages of one in 2008, in real time. As many of us can now appreciate, when a break point seems imminent, the pressure on our supply or distribution infrastructure reveals itself most obviously in terms of sharply increasing prices.

Although Maslow may characterize us as a perpetually wanting animal, we're also an adaptive one. In our reaction to a looming break point, we begin to change our behavior to consume less energy. By the first half of 2008, as the elevated price of oil drove up the prices of gasoline, jet fuel, electricity, home heating fuel, and even food, we thought twice about taking unnecessary automobile trips. We hesitated to turn on the air conditioner or the furnace, avoided the gourmet grocery store, and visited the value supermarket more often. We skipped the second latté in the afternoon. Our lifestyle felt restricted, as we became anxious about how the dollars in our wallets flow out the pump nozzle.

Yet the oil price spike of 2008 was not the first energy crisis we've faced, so why can't we resolve imminent energy problems like we have in the past? The core issue is that our ability to manipulate the respective share of different energy items on our fuel diet has been curtailed.

First of all, I come back to the scale issue. What was happening immediately before the 2008 global financial crisis was far more expansive in scope and more challenging in complexity than the energy heart attacks of the 1970s. Back then price shocks mostly affected a handful of WealthyWorld countries, such as the United States, Canada, Great Britain, France, Germany, and Japan, and there was plenty of scope on the supply side to rebalance the world's energy needs back to health. Indeed, 30 years ago we could alter our energy diet relatively easily by diversifying into other large-scale alternatives. Pushing oil out of the power generating market to ease our problems was relatively easy; we simply unplugged the oil power stations that provided 20 percent of our power generation and turned to coal and nuclear power to make up the difference. Today, WealthyWorld countries like the United States use almost no oil for the purposes of electrical power generation—it's already been cut from the side-dish menu so there's nothing left to replace.

In the past, we have always been able to "supply" ourselves out of our oil problems. Metaphorically, whenever the hungry cries for food sounded in the dining hall the cooks always managed to bring more food out to the tables. Large oil fields in the Western hemisphere, under the stewardship of independent companies, were discovered in the mid-1960s in places like Prudhoe Bay in Alaska and the North Sea in Europe. After over a decade of development, those barrels had a major impact on alleviating the pressure we felt in the 1980s. But today, large "elephant" oil fields are increasingly hard to find, costly to tap, and too often encumbered under an opaque web of political machination or civil unrest.

And if the politics of oil isn't curtailing our ability to exert control over our fuel menu, the environment will. In the 1970s, we were beginning to grow concerned about the environmental impact of our oil-consuming lifestyle, but global warming hadn't yet moved from a fringe issue to a mainstream one. As a result, there was less political pressure on governments, corporations, and even individuals to be discriminating about where oil was being produced and what kinds of energy were being consumed. We're becoming more selective about the kind of energy we want on our plates, which is a problem when you realize that not all crude oil is created equal. Some of it is so high quality it needs little refining, like the light sweet crude that comes from Saudi Arabia. Other crudes, like those derived from the oil sands of Alberta, involve costly extraction and upgrading processes, release a lot of CO_2 in the refining process, and entail a host of other environmental challenges. As an industry description from 1980 described it: "The oil is the most expensive in the world, because it is so hard to obtain. Instead of huge underground reservoirs of black gold, the tar sands resemble nothing so much as their name implies—clumps of dirt and black tar pressed together."[5]

Given such qualities, oil from the oil sands wouldn't be anyone's first dietary choice for energy consumption. Yet the reality is that the world now relies on them for nearly 2.0 percent of its oil supplies. That fact by itself should tell anyone that our menu of *conventional oils* (meaning oil produced or extracted using traditional drilling and completion methods as opposed to mining or assisted recovery techniques) has become restricted. After all, why would any oil company spend billions of dollars bringing a high-cost marginal energy source like the oil sands to the table if lighter and sweeter oil alternatives were plentiful? If you're looking for proof to validate peak oil theories, there you have it.

Although I've been talking primarily about oil, it should be understood that the near break point of 2008 was also distinct from previous ones, such as that of 1979, in that oil was not the only fuel in the diet to be challenged. The striking thing about the first half of 2008 was that every energy commodity was under pressure. Like a restaurant that abruptly jacks up the price of everything on the menu because there's a constant line up of patrons at the door, the market for oil, coal, natural gas, uranium, and even corn (for making biofuels) was inflated by multiples alongside oil (see Figure 5.3). In contrast, back in the 1970s, though the price of oil spiked, all other energy commodities were relatively stable. This made the economic advantage of switching away from oil

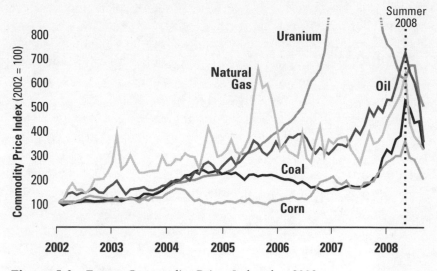

Figure 5.3   Energy Commodity Prices Indexed to 2002
SOURCE: Bloomberg Data, ARC Financial Research.

to other sources like uranium, coal, and liquefied natural gas compelling and manageable in the 1980s.

The 2008 financial crisis obscured a lesson that the energy markets were trying to teach us that summer: When the next heart attack comes, we are unlikely to find refuge from expensive energy in alternatives that are cheaper and easier to adopt. This markedly distinguishes our present day circumstances from previous break points.

In Need of a Break Point Innovation

Despite a common plight of tight supplies, we remain, for the foreseeable future, two worlds occupying one planet. In the event of a global squeeze on an energy commodity like oil, what options are available? To countries like China, the choices are sober but contain a measure of hope. WantingWorld economies are able to diversify their diets by supplanting a voracious appetite for oil, coal, and hydro with alternatives like nuclear power and natural gas. Indeed, China is already trying to rebalance its diet by putting more liquefied natural gas on the table and building 19 nuclear power plants by 2020.[6] Nuclear and natural gas are highly scalable and that is what a rapidly growing economy needs. Notably, China is diversifying its diet into renewables, too. Solar and wind are very much on the menu; in fact, by 2009 China will become the world's leading manufacturer of wind turbines. All this is fine, if not necessary, when we remind ourselves that China's population today is almost double that of all WealthyWorld.

In comparison, WealthyWorld options for expanding energy diet are limited. We've already adopted the easy choices, and we're quickly learning that other alternatives like biofuels, in which we put so much hope, have both much less nutritional value and scalability than anticipated. Like a gourmand who has indulged in every staple and course available, we're finally reaching the limits of what we have thus far regarded as an exquisite menu. Satisfying an increasingly picky palette with fewer ingredients at our disposal is getting very difficult.

Even if WantingWorld nations migrate to more nuclear power and natural gas, that doesn't mean we will all enjoy a return to a new phase of cheap energy. That's not the way dietary transitions work. Instead, WantingWorld will consume as much oil as possible, and supplement what's lacking with the easiest and most scalable of alternatives. In Wealthy-World, we'll still feel the pressure as our own appetite grows. Further, even if we engage all-out on a successful drive to pare back our oil appetite to healthier levels, that won't solve our problems in an absolute sense. WantingWorld economies will simply take up the spare capacity that is created.

Think of it this way: If WantingWorld reduces its appetite it will eat less. But over time WantingWorld will readily eat whatever portion of food is leftover on WealthyWorld's plates. Reducing our appetite may be a good thing for the health of our own society, but don't expect the benefits of that new healthy lifestyle to translate into lower prices. The growing and very hungry nations of WantingWorld, sitting at the same table, though in different stages of appetite, will devour everything that we virtuously pass on.

If that sounds daunting, it should. We cannot easily "supply" ourselves out of the problems we are in this time. The scale of the challenge is massive. Also, juggling market share is much more difficult due to the pull on all energy sources. Look back at Figure 5.2. The portion of fuels in the U.S. market has been steady since the early 1990s: hydro

3 percent, coal 22.5 percent, oil 40 percent, nuclear 8 percent, natural gas 23.5 percent, and renewables 3 percent. How realistic is it that any one of these sources can take market share away from the others? Our big rivers are dammed up; coal and oil are about as palatable as tobacco; nobody wants a nuclear kitchen anywhere near them; natural gas is stigmatized as being too price volatile; and then there are the renewables like solar, wind, and biomass. Flip back to Figure 5.1 to be reminded of the world's stupendous appetite. You may be wondering, if you can see it, what the very thin strip of primary energy is on top of natural gas in the stack. It's the fraction of the energy diet, 0.3 percent of today's energy appetite that represents renewables like biomass, solar, wind, and geothermal, even after accounting for their aggressive growth prospect of attaining 1 percent of total market share by 2020. There's been little variation since the data started being tracked. Is there anything on or off the menu that is compelling enough to challenge the status quo diet? Surely we're in need of another break point innovation.

In the chapters that follow I will show you why the options that get frequently talked about—alternative energy sources, dramatically improved efficiency levels, a focus on reducing carbon emissions, and a renewed dedication to conservation—will be insufficient, if taken as stand-alone measures. To the extent that any one of such options gets described as a miracle solution by lobby or political groups, it constitutes distracting fallacy. And yet, if we roll them all together into a customized package that best fits our specific needs and situation and combine them with another consumer-driven miracle or two, I'll show you what just might see us through.

Chapter 6

Price and Value

In the past, as I've said, we've often swung heavily toward new fuels or gone back to old ones as a way of rebalancing our energy menu following a break point. Sometimes new alternatives have come from places completely off the map. What sailor on a whaling ship, carving up raw blubber and heaving the greasy lumps into a cauldron-like-pot to render it into oil, could have imagined that in a few short decades the illuminating fluid used in lamps would come from a viscous black tar bubbling up through the ground in the backwaters of Pennsylvania? What housewife lighting her kitchen with one of those kerosene lamps could have imagined that soon she'd be driving a Model T propelled by a differently distilled variation of that same crude oil? Similarly today, we may be skeptical as to whether oil executives can see the future in such unlikely fuel sources as algae, animal waste, or even solar power.

We're searching for the next answer. We have a trio of urgencies to motivate us: energy security, environmental sustainability, and volatile prices. Notwithstanding the crimp of the 2008 financial crisis, the investment capital will continue to reach the innovators. There's nothing that isn't possible within the bounds of the laws of physics, and it would be foolish of me, or any industry expert, to discount the idea that some unexpected new source will one day comprise a significant portion of our energy diet.

Yet there are reasons why a stalwart energy source like crude oil has been king for a century. Compared to it, there are still serious shortcomings with all of the other menu items being proposed as its replacement. I'm not a pessimist by nature. I fully believe technology and innovation will yield new break point innovations and help move us forward. But I have spent too many years grappling with such issues as the dynamics of adopting new energy systems, the hidden shortcomings of erstwhile alternatives, and the scale of our energy needs not to be skeptical when well-meaning people, politicians, and entrepreneurs become excited about the latest "magic bullet."

Renewables and other alternative energy solutions will have an important role to play in augmenting tomorrow's diet. But in terms of transitioning through our next, inevitable break point and creating a cleaner future for the next 10 to 30 years, an honest discussion is warranted and some inconvenient truths need to be confronted. That in hand, it will be critical for us to understand what type of attributes a healthier menu must have before it can make a meaningful contribution to our overall energy appetite and the betterment of our world.

More Inconvenient Truths

Today, only 6.3 percent of the world's 240 million barrels of oil equivalent a day (BOE/d) appetite is supplied by renewables. Indeed, that's a deceiving number, because almost the entire fraction, 6.0 percent out of the 6.3 percent, is dominated by hydroelectric power, a result of the big rivers we dammed up in the mid-twentieth century. Only the remaining 0.3 percent is sourced from other renewable offerings—mostly solar, wind, and biomass. To get a sense of the proportions, just look at Figure 6.1 for the market share of each of the world's primary energy sources.

When I talk publicly with groups about energy issues, the potential of renewables and alternatives always come up. Of course, we are all concerned about finding new energy sources that can satisfy demand

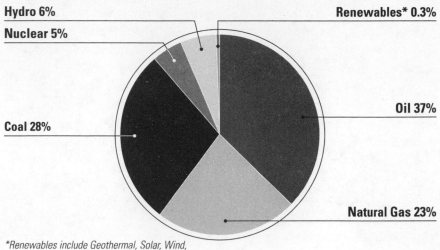

Figure 6.1   Market Share of World Primary Energy Sources (2007)
SOURCE: BP Statistical Review 2008, ARC Financial Research.

while also reducing the harmful impact of energy use on our environment. Yet the immense scale of our energy consumption needs is rarely grasped, most do not fully appreciate the catalysts required to encourage adoption of healthier energy choices.

We've sunk multi-trillions of dollars into the carbon-based energy distribution complex over the past 200 years. Countless peripheral devices feed off that standardized and entrenched infrastructure. That system is so successful because coal, oil, and natural gas have a high degree of utility and new entrants find this incredibly difficult to match, let alone beat. The "other" inconvenient truth is that we won't eagerly dump what's working now for something different unless we are *compelled* to, either by law, by crisis, or—most optimistically—by the quality of life improvements that can be gained as a result.

I'll come back to that last notion, but first let's get some perspective. Global interest in developing renewable energy has accelerated over the last two decades. Many innovations and technological improvements have already been made, and many more are to come. Government incentives and policies in numerous WealthyWorld countries are forcing a menu change. The trend in generating electrical power illustrated in

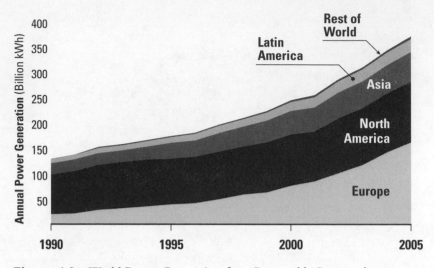

Figure 6.2   World Power Generation from Renewable Sources, by
Region (1990–2005)
SOURCE: U.S. Energy Information Administration, ARC Financial Research.

Figure 6.2 clearly shows that worldwide use of renewables, excluding
hydro, has tripled over 20 years and is still accelerating. The question is,
will these innovations and measures be able to change the world's energy
diet in a meaningful way?

The easiest menu to change at our energy banquet is the one for
electrical power. Those needs are more flexible than in transportation,
where we're stubbornly attached to a diet of oil products.

Electrical power can be generated in a multitude of different ways,
oblivious to the end user, and channeled into a grid of wires for distribution. Notionally, it can make sense to remove a 500-megawatt coal-fired
plant from the menu and insert a few 200 unit arrays of two-megawatt
wind turbines, a 50-megawatt solar farm, and a smattering of biomass
plants that cleanly burn wood. Never mind, for the moment, that the
sun doesn't shine all day and the wind is intermittent—our feeding time
may have to be shuffled to accommodate the new schedule. But the idea
that a lighter fare of environmentally sustainable renewables can replace
a single-course, heavy meal of coal is appealing.

Many WealthyWorld countries, especially those in Europe, have
adopted "renewable portfolio standards" that mandate a certain fraction

of renewables in power generation by a target date: 20 percent by 2020 is typical. Figure 6.2 shows that such mandates are working, because it's notably the European appetite for renewables that has been growing significantly, pushing up the global total.

Looking more specifically to Germany, where they've had a major policy push to put renewables into their electrical power diet since 1997, the results are starting to become convincing as the market share trend diagram shows (see Figure 6.3). About 14 percent of Germany's electrical power needs are now generated from renewable menu items—mostly wind, solar, and wood.

However, Germany's laudable trend loses some sense of major accomplishment when taken in the greater context of the country's total energy appetite. Like most WealthyWorld countries only about 30 percent of the main diet goes to generating electricity. So 14 percent of 30 percent means that Germany, one of the most determined countries trying to put renewables into their diet, has only really been able to displace 4 percent of their total appetite. The inconvenient truth is that renewables merely represent a nice side dish to the overall diet, not a main course.

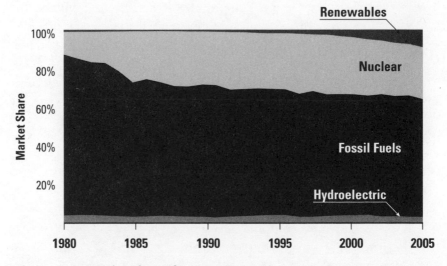

Figure 6.3 Market Share of Primary Energy Sources in Germany: For Electrical Power Generation Only (1980–2005)
Source: U.S. Energy Information Administration, ARC Financial Research.

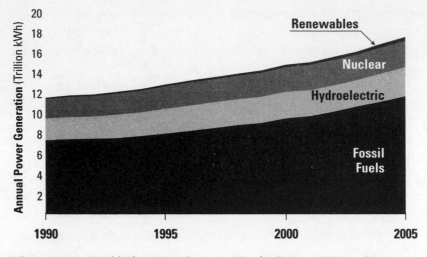

Figure 6.4 World Electricity Consumption by Primary Energy Source (1990–2005)
SOURCE: ARC Financial Research, U.S. Energy Information Administration.

From a world perspective the challenge appears even more daunting. Figure 6.4 breaks out the trend of the world's energy appetite for electricity. Coal largely dominates the fossil fuel category labeled "Fossil Fuels." The slice at the top are the nonhydro renewables, which have a long way to go to make a meaningful dent in the electrical power market, let alone the total energy diet that I showed earlier in Chapter 5 (Figure 5.1).

Returning to my question: Will innovations and policies for energy sources be able to meaningfully alter the world's energy diet in the coming decades? As with prior break point innovations in history, it depends on the compelling attributes of the available options.

Nine Energy Attributes

Think of the last time you bought a new high-tech gadget. You may have been reasonably happy for years with your old TV set until your eye caught a glimpse of a flat screen high definition plasma model. The price probably struck you as prohibitively expensive, but now that the sticker shock has lessened, you're thinking of taking the plunge. With dozens of high definition channels now being broadcast, and many more promised in the near future, the fancy new TV set has finally become *compelling* enough to warrant the switch. Millions of people are feeling the same way.

Similarly, for an entire society—or even a significant portion—to undertake the mass-market adoption of a new energy system, it has to be convinced that what's new is truly *compelling*. When Edison distributed electric power to people's houses, he knew he needed to displace the convenience of coal gas pipelines so he designed his system to run its power lines through the outlets of coal gas lamps. When he designed the common screw-base of the incandescent light bulb he used the same cap threading that people were familiar with from kerosene containers. Similarly, Ford's Model T used the same roads as horses and buggies while Watts' steam engine replaced the water turbines in textile mills to power the same machinery inside the factory. "Plug and play" is not just a catchy slogan; in the energy industry it's long been the standard mode of transition.

Let's take a moment to define what exactly it means for an energy system to be *compelling*. The following framework of nine energy attributes will serve as a useful reference point for assessing how energy sources—renewable and nonrenewable—jockey for market share, and for predicting how successfully we can incorporate them into our energy diet. As you read through these attributes, think of oil-based processes, because they are as I will shortly explain, the current "gold standard" of utility as far as compelling energy systems are concerned.

1. Versatility

Crude oil is remarkably flexible and versatile. Its chain of hydrocarbon molecules can be "cracked" into gasoline, diesel, jet fuel, kerosene, and naphtha, to name a few. Those byproducts can be used in a wide variety of devices: from leaf blowers to 747 aircrafts; from cruise ships to power plants; from motor scooters to farm tractors; from portable heaters to helicopters and trains. All of our needs—heating, transportation, lighting, and more—could be easily served with fuels made from crude oil. Indeed, if oil were secure and clean we would probably need look no further for powering our lifestyles.

On the other end of the versatility spectrum is uranium. You can't put fuel rods in your car or your home furnace. Nuclear fuels can serve only one function and that's making electricity in a fortified reactor. That's pretty much the same for wind turbines.

Indirectly, converting primary energy sources like solar, wind, and nuclear into electricity does create the versatility we're looking for, because so many devices can be "plugged in." In the future, cars may be plugged into wall sockets the same way we recharge cell phones. Until then, oil remains the overall king of versatility.

2. Scalability

Any new market entrant wanting to take away meaningful market share from the big incumbents, especially oil and coal, has to be scalable. I can't stress enough the importance of being able to deliver large amounts of energy, given the scale of our global issues. Consider nuclear power, which can deliver incredible amounts of energy. Even so, nuclear power has only been able to garner 10 percent of the world's primary energy market since its commercial introduction a half century ago.

One major reason why renewables find it difficult to take away market share from incumbents is that their ability to scale up is limited. It takes 1,500 two-megawatt wind turbines to put out the same power as a single 1,000-megawatt nuclear power plant running 24/7. The reason we switched away from windmills and water wheels to coal, oil, natural gas, hydroelectricity, and nuclear power was because the latter are much more scalable energy sources.

Scalability also encompasses the ability to go small. And that's another reason why oil is tough to beat. The devices that oil works with span the entire scale spectrum. The fuel can be used in a tiny model airplane and the largest cruise ship—and everything else in between.

3. Storability and Transportability

To qualify as compelling, an energy source must be easily storable and transportable. Oil and its many products can be put in anything from small hand-held jerry cans to pipelines, trains, trucks, and supertankers. Jets and fighter planes can even be refueled in flight by flying tankers.

What's more, petroleum products are not corrosive so they do not need exotic materials to contain them.

No energy alternative is as robust as oil products when it comes to storage and transportation. Gases are more difficult to contain and handle while solids like coal are heavy and cannot be sent down a pipeline. Indirectly, the energy in wind, solar, coal, and nuclear can be converted into electricity—a "carrier"—and be transported to customers via wires, but the energy sources *themselves* are much more difficult to contain. Moreover, both the conversion to electricity and its transmission take a heavy toll on the original energy quantum. In other words, the process is inefficient in that much of the energy is lost along the way. I will discuss this further in Chapter 10.

Batteries have long conquered small-scale storage of electricity, but large-scale storage has historically been more difficult and costly. Progress is being made, but it's still meager relative to the best of what is already available. At the moment, the ease and scalability of storing electrical energy in big batteries or other physical devices is not compellingly better than keeping an equal amount of energy as liquid hydrocarbons in a big tank.

4. Deliverability

We like our energy to be there when we want it, in a small or large quantity, either individually or collectively. For example, we want the option to accelerate our cars quickly, or hold our gas pedal steady on a freeway. We like to turn on our lights, TVs, stoves, and coffeemakers when we wake up, and then turn them off when we go to work—then do the same when we return home from work.

Energy sources that allow us to "throttle" up and down to satisfy our needs quickly, safely, and with precision have high utility that we have grown to take for granted. Devices that feed off of oil and natural gas—like cars, furnaces, and power plants—have a wide range of deliverability. Coal and nuclear power plants can't throttle up and down easily and are much happier providing power at a constant rate. Wind and solar power are highly dependent on the weather. As such, their deliverability is highly uncertain in the absence of electrical storage devices.

5. Energy Density

Can you imagine the energy you would expend putting your shoulder to your car and pushing it 20 miles? That's what a gallon of gasoline can do. The amount of energy stored in a one-gallon jerry can is truly remarkable.

Setting aside nuclear fuels, no other safe energy source comes close to the energy density of oil by weight and volume. That was one of the biggest motivations for Henry Ford to choose the internal combustion engine over the battery-powered car. How far we can drive on a single fill-up is a selling feature on which we place a great deal of emphasis, and it is directly related to the energy density of the fuels we use. Again, it is one of the primary reasons why king oil has managed to reign supreme for so long.

6. Power Density

Not to be confused with energy density, power density refers to the amount of power (energy per unit of time) that can be delivered by a device relative to its size or weight. A nuclear power plant can deliver a lot of energy, but it has to be housed in a big concrete bunker. Solar farms can deliver clean electricity, but the real extent of row upon row of these flat, shiny panels can devour acres; in other words, the power density is very low. On the other hand, the next time you fly take a look out the window and check out the size of the jet engines relative to the girth of the airplane. Then consider that an average sized Boeing 747 jet engine puts out the same amount of power as 125 acres of solar panels.

Jet fuel combined with the combustive capacity of a jet engine delivers a tremendous amount of power from a highly compact volume. That is what high power density is about and it's a compelling and desirable characteristic for many applications we demand.

7. Constancy

I use this term to characterize energy sources and devices that can be used in any place, at any time, and during any season or weather condition. Generally speaking, oil products can power everything from tanker engines to camp stoves, winter or summer, day or night, rain or shine, wind or calm. Natural gas is almost as robust, as is coal. Nuclear can operate 24/7, but is not flexible on location. Similarly, without storage devices and intricate mechanisms of dissemination, solar and wind have little constancy, as their performance is hostage to time of day, season, geography, and weather conditions.

8. Environmental Sensitivity

Depending on the energy source, the issues of environmental sensitivity may include, but are by no means limited to, greenhouse gas emissions, excessive water use, deforestation, habitat destruction, toxic effluent and so on. Energy sources like solar, wind, geothermal, and wave power, to name a few, have clear advantages over fossil fuels on many environmental dimensions, but there are several nontrivial caveats.

Consider the case of biofuels where scientific and popular opinion have fallen just as dramatically as they had risen. Recent reputable studies have declared that biofuels may actually emit more greenhouse gases than gasoline because forest and grassland absorb far more carbon dioxide once converted to growing biofuel-related plants Moreover, the plants in question require tremendous amounts of water. And rapid deforestation in countries like Brazil and Indonesia, where biofuels are a growth industry striving to meet global demand, are leading to a loss of biodiversity.

What's more, devoting such a growing percentage of American farmland to biofuels exacerbated rising corn and wheat prices in 2008. I've been using food consumption—including appetite, diet, and calories—as a metaphor for energy consumption throughout this book. Now the metaphor is literally coming back to haunt us. We've reached a stage in our societal evolution when the fuel energy we require and the food energy we require are pitted against each other in stiff competition. It's neither a sustainable proposition nor a morally prudent trade-off.

9. Energy Security

This is an attribute that can potentially trump the preceding eight. We have grown to regard certain features of our lives as indispensable, and they include the unambiguous feeling you have when your lights go on when needed, the heat is there in winter, and the gas pump is always ready to flow. Once we have this entrenched comfort we're highly intolerant of disruptions, such as when foreign political agendas or turmoil hold our energy supplies hostage. In the United States the top-of-mind issue is foreign oil, which is a genteel term for any oil coming from the Middle East. In Western Europe, it's the winters that are greeted with nervousness, because 25 percent of the natural gas to heat their homes and businesses comes from Russia, a country that has not been shy to use energy supply as a political or economic weapon.

There are only a handful of countries rich in primary energy resources—such as Russia, Saudi Arabia, and Norway—that can claim complete energy security in the sense of being self-sufficient. Big energy importers like the United States, the EU, Japan, China, and Korea all have reason to be nervous about relying on others for large quantities of oil, coal, or natural gas to run their economies and provide comfort for their citizens. Having homegrown, sustainable energy is becoming increasingly priceless in an increasingly turbulent and uncertain world. You can expect the premium on energy security to grow even higher as WantingWorld puts greater and greater pressure on the energy commons. Clearly, renewable sources excel in this attribute, subject as they are to the vagaries of their local geography, climate, and vegetation.

■ ■ ■

These nine attributes collectively embody the usefulness, or in economic parlance the "utility," of an energy source. It is important to recognize that though we may have a common understanding of what makes a fuel "useful" by definition, the individual utility or *value* we derive from using it varies from person to person and from time to time. For example, as people wake up to the reality of environmental pressures or increasing tensions in the Middle East, the "utility" of using gasoline may decrease.

Although utility is neither a static nor uniform concept the following generalization can be made: Incumbent processes—like gasoline-powered cars, jet-powered airplanes, and even coal-fired power plants—have given us such a high standard of overall utility that we are reluctant to compromise their use by considering other options. This holds true especially, and most importantly, at the prices we have historically paid.

Price, Value, and Relative Utility

It's really easy to be cynical about energy prices, especially when it comes to the popular suspicions about Big Oil and price manipulation. But let's put things in perspective by taking a page from Oscar Wilde. In the 1892 play, *Lady Windermere's Fan*, Wilde pens his famous definition of a cynic as, "A man who knows the price of everything, and the value of nothing."[1] I don't intend to broad-brush all of us as cynics, but standard theory and everyday experience tell us that it is ultimately *price* that will dictate whether we choose to purchase the next gallon of gasoline. "Value," as I touched on, is a subjective concept that we develop by assessing an energy source based on the preceding nine attributes. Price, on the other hand, is taken as a given by the end-user. From here, the relation is simple: If the "value" you attach to a product exceeds the price of the product, you'll buy it; if it does not, you won't.

Try the following mental exercise: How much do you value not having to walk to work on a cold winter day? If you can't immediately attach a number to such a question, consider your alternative: buying a gallon of gasoline to do the job. If you're anything like me, to avoid the work and the discomfort you may incur by walking, you would take the gallon and gladly pay $2.00 for the "luxury" of driving (excluding ownership, insurance, and maintenance costs). Given North American commuting statistics, it's easy to see that few commuters believe that the value of work a gallon of gasoline can accomplish is expensive at a price of $2.00/gallon. At $20.00/gallon on the other hand, we would undoubtedly be able to find a few additional cynics. My point here is that gasoline has historically been incredibly cheap relative to its perceived utility. In basic terms, the fuel has given us good "value" for our buck. On one hand, that's good news, and definitely helps explain why gasoline gained market share so quickly and kept it for so long over the last 150 years. On the other hand, this constitutes a challenge for energy sources vying to displace petroleum products.

Pushing oil off the table is incredibly difficult. Not only does oil prove robust across nearly every criterion I've discussed, it is startlingly cheap for the work that it does to power our prosperity and way of life. Even in the United States, the record national average high price in the summer of 2008 ($4.17/gallon), gasoline originating from oil deep in the earth's crust, distributed halfway around the world, and refined with state-of-the-art technology—remains cheaper than milk or bottled water. That's incredible to contemplate. Indeed, this is one very, very tough product to beat.

Any new system of energy hoping to take market share away from the incumbents must have a superior value proposition. Break point innovations in the history of energy have occurred when the utility of what's been offered by the new has surpassed that of established energy systems in a compelling way. To a consumer, a Model T running on gasoline offered compellingly better utility than a horse running on food, or an electric car hosting a weak battery charged by a coal-fired power plant. Very quickly, Ford's vehicles demonstrated superior range, productivity, reliability, power, scalability, all-weather capability, and, most importantly, cost. No wonder its market debut marked a break point innovation.

Do any of the new menu choices being proposed for the future, such as wind, solar, or biomass, offer compellingly better utility than the staid incumbents? This is of course subject to varying degrees of importance ascribed to the series of energy attributes. From a societal point of view, however, the thin slivers of market share taken by new energy sources suggest that the overall utility is not yet able to surpass the threshold required for these alternatives to be truly compelling.

Again, I'm not saying that new innovations won't bring us energy systems that can definitively outperform the incumbents, especially given that the two big incumbents are losing collective utility. Coal's main weakness stems from its CO_2 emissions and link to climate change. In the case of oil, it too has emissions issues, but is suffering perhaps more from loss of confidence with respect to the energy security attribute than anything else.

Improvement in the utility of new energy systems, in conjunction with deterioration of utility among incumbents, can narrow or flip the utility gap such that adoption can accelerate. As for price, governments can and often do intervene. Introducing policies that disadvantage incumbents, for example, through carbon taxes, or giving incentives to new entrants through subsidies is intended to shift our preference toward the alternatives. In effect, that's what some of the climate change policies in the European Union and other regions (including many jurisdictions in the United States) have been seeking to do.

But again, I stress that we need to be honest with ourselves if we are going to make meaningful and timely changes to the problems that ultimately stem from acute energy obesity. Developing alternatives that materially surpass the utility of fuels like oil and coal will take a great deal of time and money. What's more, at the end of the expensive process, we would still be caught in the paradigm of supplying, as opposed to substituting, our way out of our problems. We need to take a close look at an attribute that is little talked about to understand why.

The Tenth, Overlooked Attribute

In the world of energy supply there is one more attribute that is not well recognized, but has substantial societal repercussions when thinking about putting together the best, healthiest energy menu for the future. That attribute is what I will call "sustainability."

Imagine that you have a plot of land that produces 1,000 units of grain. To plant, grow, and harvest the grain you need to feed work animals—say, a couple of horses and maybe an ox—and those animals will consume 100 units by the time you have reaped your crop. The net gain is 900 units, or we can say the output is 10 times the input. That's not bad as long as the land keeps yielding the same and your animals don't need more food. Clearly, if your animals suddenly require more than a 1,000 units of feed, while your output is still 1,000 units, your net yield is negative and you would starve.

The tenth challenge an energy system faces is highly analogous to this farm metaphor. On the one hand we have the dream of limitless, environmentally-beneficial power, reminiscent of the historical quest to develop a perpetual motion machine. Humans have long observed that nature seems to operate in a perpetual state. The wind moves the trees. The water rushes downstream. Plants grow on their own accord. Why can't a machine be invented that creates or supplies its own energy such that its fuel never needs to be replenished? The earliest recorded attempt was in India in 1150 A.D. when the revered mathematician and astronomer, Bhaskara Acharya, described a wheel that would turn indefinitely. Other theories of perpetual motion were hypothesized in the early Middle Ages but it was Leonardo da Vinci who legitimized the search for such a device around 1495, offering engineering designs for machines that would create "free" energy.

Four hundred years later we learned why such attempts had failed. Hermann von Helmholtz's First Principle of Thermodynamics, commonly known as the law of conservation of energy, which states that energy can neither be created nor destroyed. In practical terms, a device cannot create its own energy but must draw on energy from some external source to perpetuate its motion. Even devices that receive an initial boost eventually lose that energy due to the friction of moving parts. While there are no doubt scientists and garage engineers secretly working on gadgets that can stay in motion forever, such devices would need to overcome one of the fundamental laws of the universe.

It always takes energy to liberate energy and the coefficient that relates energy input to energy output is a critically important consideration. Although we don't often think about it, every source—including oil, coal, uranium, solar power, wind power, biomass, cellulosic ethanol, and whatever else you can name—requires a certain amount of energy to produce. It takes energy to drill an oil well, refine the crude into gasoline, and deliver it to the pump. It takes energy to mine uranium, process it as nuclear power, and generate electricity. It takes energy to grow switchgrass, construct a windmill, or build a battery. We call this the "energy to make energy" or, more technically, the "energy return on energy invested" (EROEI, pronounced E-Roy).

In order to assess the overall value of a particular fuel, it's essential that we determine its EROEI, which is not a trivial exercise. For that assessment, let's consider some parameters. The closest WealthyWorld came to having free energy was on January 10, 1901, when an oil derrick sent a gusher of black crude 150 feet into the sky at an oilfield in Beaumont, Texas. "Spindletop" produced 100,000 barrels of oil a day, tripling total U.S. production at the time, and signaling to Americans that there was a seemingly limitless supply of domestic oil available for their growing appetite.

Tapping Spindletop was so easy it only cost the equivalent of about one barrel of oil to produce 100 barrels from the ground. While that 100:1 ratio was not rare in the early days of the American oil industry, the ratio has been dropping ever since. The reason is simple: as our easy barrels of oil have run out, we've needed to travel farther, drill deeper, and accommodate ever-harsher conditions to find what we so desperately need. The costs incurred, and the energy requirements, of meeting such needs have risen exponentially.

By the 1970s, the EROEI for oil had dropped from 100:1 to 30:1. Obviously, there's great variability depending on the source, but America's average oil EROEI today is estimated to be about 16:1. In Texas, for example, where Spindletop was once the epitome of limitless production, the remaining mature oil fields are laden with water. Typically, for every 5 barrels of crude brought to the surface, 95 barrels of water come with it. As anyone who has carried a bucket of water any distance knows, water is not light. For an oilman, water is not only heavy, it's useless from an energy perspective, and it means that we are using far more energy to produce energy than we did when light sweet crude gushed from the ground.

Even worse than water-laden oil is bitumen, a gooey, heavy oil that is bound with sand, gravel, and water. There's nothing new about bitumen, its potential value as an energy source has been known for centuries, but there has been little need to exploit it until recently because better quality, cheaper oil was available in abundance. The Alberta oil sands, where much of the world's bitumen is developed today, has been widely rebuked for many environmental reasons, including the amount of greenhouse gases produced over the course of the entire extraction and refinement process. It also takes a tremendous amount of effort—in other words, input energy—to separate the oil from the sand, gravel, and water and eventually upgrade it to the light quality that our refineries are capable of processing into the various petroleum products. Given that difficulty, it shouldn't be surprising then that the EROEI of oil sands amounts to a mere 7:1 just for extraction, and the number drops to 3:1 by the time the oil is upgraded and refined into jet fuel, naphtha, or gasoline. In other words, it takes one barrel of energy for every three barrels of product produced.

In the previous section, we saw how ethanol has been much maligned for its unintended environmental consequences and its poor utility track record. But ethanol doesn't gain any points back with its EROEI score. The debate as to whether the EROEI of corn ethanol is greater or less than 1:1 rages on, with a seemingly equal number of pundits supporting both sides of the inequality. An EROEI of 1:1 is an important benchmark because it is the break-even EROEI. Unless EROEI is at least greater than 1:1, meaning that you get more energy out of a system than you put in, the process is ultimately unsustainable.

Solar energy has surpassed ethanol and other wonder fuels as a lauded source of renewable energy. This makes plenty of sense. All fossil fuels ultimately come from the sun, so why not cut out the middleman? Our sun has enough energy to burn for another 13 billion years. It should follow, then, that solar power is an energy investment with wonderful returns—as close to a perpetual motion machine as we've ever discovered.

But solar panels are not the panacea many proclaim them to be. The problem is that they take a great deal of energy to manufacture and maintain. There have been several studies done to measure this inherent energy cost. The average of those studies works out to an EROEI of 7:1.[2] In other words, solar panels are currently not much better than oil sands at giving us energy for the energy we put into them.

The EROEI of solar panels will improve over time, as technology improves and as the economies of scale kick in. Nevertheless, it's important to do the analysis before we commit our rhetoric and our dollars to an energy source that we currently lack the technology to exploit as economically as we would hope (see Figure 6.5).

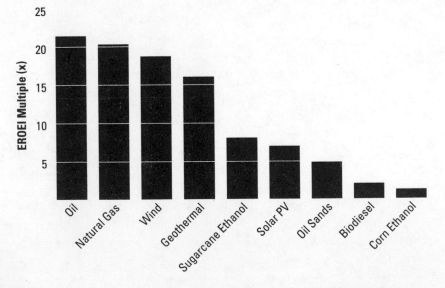

Figure 6.5 Average Energy Return on Energy Invested (EROEI) for Various Energy Systems
Source: ARC Financial Research, IMF, USDA.

From the list of all the energy sources in Figure 6.5 it's easy to see the standouts. Among the hydrocarbons, natural gas is clearly the second-best option after crude oil. For good reasons, it is being talked about now in terms of a substitute for gasoline in our transportation industry. Indeed, as I will discuss in Chapter 14, I believe we will see a renaissance for natural gas in the near future. Among the renewables, wind power is clearly the best option, and just as good as natural gas in terms of EROEI. Remember from my previous discussion, however, that the overall utility of wind power is not nearly as broad as that of natural gas or petroleum.

The Perfect Garden

If we are to displace more hydrocarbons from our diet, what is the best approach? You have seen that the answer is far more complex than expected. We must ask how the alternatives measure up on the spectrum of compelling utility and how much "energy" they cost. We cannot get discouraged by this complexity because asking these questions will allow us to address the principal issue: "Does it make sense to displace these hydrocarbons at all?" Coming up with a concise answer will require digging deeper into the problem and assessing *why* we started wanting and needing to displace the hydrocarbons in the first place. But that is a discussion for further chapters. For now, consider the following analogy.

Imagine planting a simple vegetable garden. For years, you've relied on five basic vegetables to satisfy your nutritional needs. In the biosphere of that garden, everything is in balance. The weeds are under control, only a modest amount of water is required, and the soil has stayed fertile. Then, one spring, you find that one of the five vegetables has to be replaced because the seeds are getting too expensive, not to mention its overgrowth is beginning to degrade the soil quality. So you choose a new vegetable that seems like it will provide the nutritional value your diet requires.

Within a year, however, you realize the new vegetable is doing more harm than good. It's detrimental to the other vegetables, it needs a tremendous amount of fertilizer, and it's even consuming far too much water. The impact is so dramatic that the sustainability of this "alternative" vegetable is called into question. What made sense when you planned the switchover turned out to be a poor choice in the long-term.

Are we going to make the right choices as we change our energy diet going forward? If a shift is imminent, which shift is the right one? Only by taking *all* the attributes and data into account can we begin to make reasoned choices. In the world of energy—and in our world where energy is the basis for every item or service we consume—economic factors end up balancing the equation. One thing is for sure: if we ignore the data before we make those choices, that data will surely come back to haunt us when we have to face the unintended consequences of our inadequate planning.

Chapter 7

Eating Our Efficiencies

The song goes, "O Christmas Tree! O Christmas Tree! Thy candles shine so brightly!" In North America, most of us associate Christmas trees not with candles but with strings of multicolored bulbs adorning spruce branches. Certainly, for three-quarters of a century in New York City, the 80 foot tall Norway Spruce that is erected each year at the Rockefeller Center has been brilliantly and colorfully lit. Then, for Christmas of 2007, the tradition was tweaked. The dazzling incandescent light bulbs strung on five miles of wire were replaced by 30,000 multicolored LEDs.

"O Christmas Tree! O Christmas Tree! Thy *light-emitting diodes* shine so brightly!" may not have the same ring, but LEDs and CFLs (compact fluorescent lights) are more energy efficient than the modern version of Thomas Edison's incandescent bulb. A standard light bulb only delivers between 8 and 21 lumens per watt of electricity. To put its inefficiency into perspective, if all the electricity flowing out of the socket was actually used to make light, the maximum illumination from the little filament inside the bulb would be 240 lumens per watt. So, 130 years after Edison struggled to beat the competition in coal gas, kerosene, and spermaceti candles, incandescent bulbs are still only between 3 percent and 9 percent efficient at doing the work we want them to do (dividing 8 and 21 lumens into a maximum 240). Compact fluorescent lights, on the other hand, are between 30 and 40 percent efficient, while LEDs can be over 50 percent efficient. By replacing the light bulbs on the Rockefeller Christmas tree with LEDs, electricity consumption is reduced from about 4,800 kilowatt hours per day to 1,300.[1]

That amount is enough to power a middle-class family home for about a month. It's inconsequential, perhaps, in a city of nine million, but New York Mayor Michael Bloomberg was using the switchover as an opportunity to encourage energy efficiency. As the price of fuels rise and environmental concerns mount, almost every level of government is doing something to encourage, provide incentives for, and even force energy efficiency on manufacturers and consumers. Just in time for Christmas in 2007, for instance, the U.S. Congress passed legislation mandating energy efficiency levels for light bulbs by 2012. These standards are so high that the conventional incandescent bulb cannot possibly meet them, effectively banning the bulb. Meanwhile Wal-Mart, the influential North American retailer, is among those that have made a major push to market CFLs. Perhaps seeing the light, General Electric, the long-term maker of Edison's iconic product, decided to shut down many of its light bulb manufacturing plants in 2008 and has contemplated selling off the division altogether.

Poets are already waxing nostalgic about the soft glow and gentle warmth of the incandescent light bulb—something that would surely make Mr. Edison's heart glow (in innovators' heaven?). But viewed in the cold, harsh light of a compact fluorescent, it's easy to understand why we are focusing on efficiency. If we cannot "supply" our way out of our current predicament by producing more oil or even perhaps displacing oil with an alternative fuel, then perhaps we can get more work out of the energy sources we have by increasing the efficiency of the devices we use. A single light bulb may mean very little, but when we consider the scale of billions of light bulbs in use around the world, saving an extra 60 percent or so of that end-use electricity is pretty meaningful.

And if we take the thinking a step further, the savings aggregate. Neither an SUV nor a pickup truck is much better than an incandescent light bulb in terms of the work they do for the energy that's put into them (often just transporting one person around), and they are responsible in absolute terms for a lot more fuel consumption. Logically then, to avoid a double standard, why stop with the banning of the bulb? Why not ban obese energy-devouring SUVs, too? As a policy move, banning big vehicles would avoid the hypocrisy of outlawing one inefficient device and not another. Why stop there? To be consistent with the policy logic, shouldn't big plasma televisions be banned too?

Of course it's not that easy. A personal vehicle is a lot more important and sentimental for people than a mere light bulb, which is why elected officials are unlikely to go near the idea of limiting choice. Nobody wants to be told what they can and can't drive or watch. And for that reason it is very hard for society's leaders to make energy decisions that inhibit the free market, create discomfort or otherwise impede our lifestyle desires. Indeed, it's all too easy for any well-meaning policy to be twisted through hypocrisy, special interests, and plain old misunderstanding to become misdirected and toothless.

But there's a bigger and more serious problem with the idea of banning the bulb and taking other steps at efficiency improvements. History shows us that saving energy through efficiency doesn't always improve our overall energy situation.

The Rebound Effect

It's common sense that introducing devices that do a better job of putting the full potential of energy to work will lead to a reduction in fuel consumption. Metaphorically, the idea is similar to squeezing oranges to make orange juice. Let's say the human hand is an efficient squeezer, leaving 25 percent of the juice remaining in the pulp. We can say then that the human hand is 75 percent efficient at making orange juice. But if we use some kind of mechanical squeezer, we may able to recover over 95 percent of the juice in the orange. According to basic logic, this leads us to use fewer oranges per glass of juice, because we are now getting more juice per orange. Furthermore, the mechanical squeezer reduces the *cost* of producing the next glass of orange juice.

Putting economics aside for a moment, this approach to maximizing our resources fits with a kind of moral imperative that most people share. Just as there's virtue in a hunter or a farmer using all the parts of a slaughtered animal, or a child in finishing all the food on his or her plate, so it is sensible and even moral to make optimal use of the energy our planet provides. The moral imperative is enhanced by the twin urgencies of global overconsumption and secure, sustainable supply.

But the first thing we usually consider when dealing with energy efficiency is not morality but potential savings. When we account for all the energy released during the passage of oil from ground to gas tank, only 15 percent of the barrel's original energy content remains to turn the wheels of the car. The other 85 percent is dissipated in heat lost in the gear boxes and exhaust pipes, as well as in the refinery stacks that processed the product. If driving a car were to be likened to eating an eight-ounce steak, for every ounce eaten, seven would be thrown into the garbage. This would be a rather pointless end to a carefully raised animal.

But if we do get better at squeezing oranges, does that mean we use fewer oranges because we now get more juice per orange? Or do we just drink more orange juice?

Known as Jevons' paradox, the question of an efficiency "rebound" was first discussed by the famous nineteenth century British economist William S. Jevons. In his 1865 book, *The Coal Question: An Inquiry Concerning the Progress of the Nation, and the Probable Exhaustion of Our Coal Mines*, Jevons posited the alarming idea that efficiency gains actually increase rather than stem the use of energy. Taking note of the vast increase in coal consumption that came with Watt's improvements over Newcomen's steam engine, Jevons wrote, "It is wholly a confusion of ideas to suppose that the economical use of fuel is equivalent to a diminished consumption. The very contrary is the truth."

Coal was king in Jevons' economy, aggressively fueling Britain's industrial revolution and widely improving the standard of living. Expressing the First Principle of Energy Consumption in his own terms, Jevons described coal as above all other commodities and serving as "... the material energy of the country—the universal aid—the factor in everything we do. With coal almost any feat is possible or easy; without it we are thrown back into the laborious poverty of early time."

The "question" in Jevons' treatise was whether or not Britain should be exporting this precious commodity to countries like Belgium, when it was so essential to the growth and prosperity of the British Empire. It was not lost on Jevons that miners in the United Kingdom were going deeper and deeper into the earth in search of coal, and that the incessant growth of coal consumption as the industrial revolution picked up steam was making the resource increasingly expensive. He postulated that those industrializing countries with access to the cheapest coal would be the empires of tomorrow. So why export this wealth-generating commodity?

Expanding on his theory of utility, Jevons pointed out that inefficient coal consumption was already a major problem in the United Kingdom. The work done by coal, he wrote, was only about one-sixth the work that the fuel had the potential to do. Even the best steam engines of the day provided only about one unit of work for every six units of energy, or about 16 percent efficiency. In terms of domestic heating and industrial steel making, most of the heat generated by coal was wasted in open grates and up the chimney.

And yet, despite the pressing reasons to consume coal with more care, Jevons showed that progressively improving energy efficiency did not translate into less coal consumption. Actually, the opposite was true as the freed up coal promoted the adoption of even more steam engines, factories, and heated homes, and greater coal appetite.

Jevons diarized the work of Charles Williams, who noted in his book, *The Combustion of Coal and the Prevention of Smoke*, "Whatever, therefore, conduces to increase the efficiency of coal, and to diminish the cost of its use directly tends to augment the value of the steam-engine, and to enlarge the field of operations." The data was so convincing that it led Jevons to formulate a rule, which stated that "new modes of [fuel] economy will lead to an increase of consumption." Economists today call this stimulus of greater energy demand through efficiency gains the "backfire" effect.

So what was so convincing about Jevons' data? Jevons observed that there are three sets of dynamics that come into play when more fuel efficient devices are employed. First, there is the "direct rebound effect." When consumers are offered a device like a more efficient steam engine, they actually buy more steam engines and run them longer. Second, there is the "indirect rebound effect." This happens when coal saved from using a more efficient steam engine is used elsewhere, such as in a fireplace. As Jevons put it, "no-one must suppose that coal thus saved is spared—it is only saved from one use to be employed in others."

Finally, there is the "indirect economy effect." This is when the money saved from energy efficiencies are spent on goods and services that don't use energy directly, but require substantial energy in their manufacture or supply. In other words, because you save so much money with your new fuel-efficient furnace, you spend more money on furniture (which takes energy to manufacture and deliver) or on a trip to the Mediterranean (which takes energy for travel). The net impact of the "indirect economy effect" is to free up more wealth. And as we understand by now, that means more energy consumption.

In other words, energy efficiency encourages energy consumption, which drives an improvement in standard of living. History has shown us that energy efficiency, therefore, doesn't break the First Principle, it propagates it.

The Rebound Effect Today

Since Jevons' day, more academic research has been conducted to understand the rebound effect. Consensus is difficult to find, but the validity of the rebound effect is universally affirmed. The only debate is the nature of the conditions under which it occurs and the extent of its impact.

Regardless, the validity of the rebound effect has serious implications for energy and climate change policy. Most critically, simplistic calculations in relation to energy savings—and, by extension, emissions reductions—are incomplete. Policymaker and special interest groups need to understand that the full savings of greater energy efficiency improvements never materialize, because human and economic behavior ensures that we will eat there a portion of what we saved from eating here. In worst-case scenarios, the expected benefit of new energy-efficient devices actually backfires and leads us to eat more than we save, accelerating our energy use.

To think about what the rebound effect means in terms of today's lifestyle, let's expand on the idea of saving energy by banning the bulb. Imagine a couple named Frank and Helen, who live in a 2,700 square foot home in suburban North America with their two children, Ben and Jane. Inspired by skyrocketing oil prices, Frank and Helen are on an energy conservation kick. Unfortunately, it's easier said than done.

As any parent will understand, Frank and Helen have had a hard time getting their children to turn off the lights and the television when they leave a room. Frank started cracking down in the summer of 2008 when the household electricity bill jumped by 50 percent, reducing the little ones' monthly allowance by a dollar every time he caught them red-handed. Now, Helen thinks the kids are finally catching on and the conservation measures seem to be helping, even though it's difficult to assess how much of the net savings is due to turning off the lights. Other measures have certainly contributed; they decided to put up a clothesline in the backyard that eased the need for using the dryer once a day. The thermostat was turned up a degree to cut down on the need for air conditioning. Altogether, these small sacrifices put a few more dollars into the family wallet instead of the coffers of the local utility.

Frank is aware that in a couple of years, the government intends to ban incandescent light bulbs in favor of the more efficient compact fluorescent lights. Neither he nor Helen really liked the twisty lights that take a minute to warm up and don't actually fit their lighting fixtures, nor did they like the quality of the light that CFLs radiate. But the dual concept of saving electricity and saving the planet made the sacrifice seem like a good idea. Frank thought they might as well start now.

A scan of their house suggested that Frank and Helen could re-place ten 100-watt and seven 60-watt light bulbs right away. The price tag of doing so ($150 for all 17 CFLs) was fairly hefty, but the pay-back calculation over the light bulbs' life span made sense—at least on paper.

After buying and installing the bulbs, Helen did the rough calcula-tion, dredging up her high school math and physics. A 23-watt CFL gives off the same light as a 100-watt incandescent using the same amount of electricity, or a four-times gain in efficiency. A 14-watt CFL substitutes for a 60-watt of Edison's best. Therefore, Frank and Helen's total savings, in terms of wattage across 17 light bulbs, is 1,092 watts.

On the one hand, that amount is about the same as used by Helen's powerful blow-dryer. On the other hand, Helen only blow-dries her hair for five minutes a day. Frank estimates that, on average, their 17 lights are on for three hours a day, taking into consideration that not all the lights are on all the time, and that there are seasonal differences, too.

Making the effort means that Frank and Helen's household will theoretically save 3,276 watt-hours, or about 3.3 kilowatt-hours (kWh) per day. Frank checked his last electricity bill and found that the utility is now charging him 11 cents for every kilowatt-hour. Great, he thought sarcastically, noting that the family's saving will be about 36 cents a day, or $11.00 per month; "With that kind of extra pocket change, I'll be able to buy my family ice cream on a hot afternoon."

Frank's and Helen's light bulb savings doesn't sound like a personal retirement plan. But imagine how that kind of energy reduction can add up when we scale to the level of a neighborhood, community, or city. In a region where a utility may serve a million households, the cumulative savings are significant. Assuming Frank and Helen live in a region with a million households, 3.3 kWh per day per family multiplies into 3.3 million kWh per day. Putting this into perspective, if each of the million households acted like Frank, the local utility could notionally take a small coal-fired power plant offline.

It is such logic that utilities and policymakers are using to justify banning light bulbs or giving incentives to people who buy higher efficiency appliances. It's almost heretical to argue against that reasoning—and I wholly support the notion of ensuring that the work derived from a fuel, especially a nonrenewable one, is maximized. But do the theoretical savings actually match the results?

The evidence suggests not, because the rebound effect needs to be factored in. The clearest case of a direct rebound effect is observable in the world of transportation. Academic research shows that when people are given a more fuel-efficient vehicle, their inclination is to rebound by anywhere between 10 and 30 percent[2] off the assumed gains. For example, say a customer is thinking about a new car that is just as useful and appealing as the customer's old vehicle, but the gas mileage is so good that the new car will use 100 gallons less a year with the same driving habits. So the customer goes ahead and buys the car, but saves less than anticipated. Why? Research shows that for every 100 gallons saved thanks to the improvements in efficiency, the driver will drive 20 gallons worth further. As such, the *net* savings of this improvement in fuel-efficiency is only 80 gallons.

With household utilities the research conclusions are more variable. The direct rebound effect appears to be around 20 percent in advanced economies like the United States. You can imagine how this happens. Knowing the CFLs are in place, for example, Frank and Helen might be inclined to be less diligent about chastising their kids for leaving the lights on. After all, they're saving enough money without that kind of constant struggle.

The indirect rebound effect is more difficult to measure, but again the economic research is unequivocal in acknowledging that it exists and is probably higher than 50 percent. This is where Frank and Helen, after feeling good about their light bulb savings, decide to go buy a 1,000-watt home entertainment system, and turn it on for an average of four hours per day. The energy saved from the efficiency gains in one device is merely "eaten up" by use in another, *especially when the other device is less efficient than the first.*

From a community perspective, I observed a classic example of the indirect rebound effect on a business trip to London in late 2007. Back then, the British government was making noise about banning the bulb by as early as 2012. Yet I felt the emptiness of such policy talk as I descended an endless escalator to the bottom of London's landmark subway system, the Tube. All the paper billboard holders advertising products and West-End plays had been replaced by flat panel video screens (see Figure 7.1).

The irony was stunning. Paper billboards use zero energy to get their message across, whereas a typical flat panel screen consumes 250 watts or so. I could only imagine that Frank's British cousin would be upset to realize that each flat panel installed in the escalator offset the five 60-watt incandescent light bulbs he switched out, assuming the screens are only on for three hours a day. In reality, of course, most of the flat panel billboards are probably on for 20 hours a day, which means the real offset is more like 35 60-watt light bulbs. In such indirect and surprising ways, the psychology behind economic behavior leads us to consume more, even when we commit to doing the opposite.

It's also important to realize that the rebound effects add up. For instance, if 100 units of energy are freed up as a consequence of obtaining higher energy efficiency in a new device, 10 to 30 units are eaten up by direct effect and over 50 units are consumed indirectly. The good news is that the research generally shows that direct and indirect rebound effects amount to less than 100 percent "backfire," at least in advanced

Figure 7.1   Flat Panel Screens Used for Advertising in the London Underground.

economies. Only from this perspective does the enhancement of energy efficiency result in absolute energy savings.

What's more difficult to establish is the magnitude of the indirect economy effect. If Frank and Helen spend their light bulb savings on ice cream, they are buying a product that has taken energy to cool down and freeze. Even the cone took energy to make. From an economic perspective, was the share of energy used in the freezer for their ice cream greater than the 3.3 kWh Frank's light bulbs saved in a day? Quantifying this type of backfire is very difficult, but such considerations are not inconsequential when thinking about energy and environmental policy. Where will people spend the money they save from efficiency improvements? What has been gained if, in an extreme case, someone leverages their savings from efficiency improvements in lighting in order to afford the purchase of a large SUV?

If policy should be geared toward the reduction of energy consumption, and hence emissions, surely people should be thoughtful about not using efficiency savings on goods and services that are even more energy inefficient. In other words, they must be convinced to *conserve* energy. But President George W. Bush dismissed the idea of mandating conservation when he noted in the summer of 2008 that, "people can figure out whether they need to drive more or less. They can balance their own checkbooks. It's a little presumptuous on my part to dictate how consumers live their own lives. I've got faith in the American people."[3]

I support the idea that the free market will help us with solutions. But the energy efficiency rebound effect shows that balancing a checkbook is not a simplistic calculation. No one wants their lives to be dictated to (I certainly don't), but we all need to be aware that how we live dictates how much energy we consume.

Like the Energizer Bunny

Energy efficiency improvements are a kind of perpetual motion machine when you consider what they do for an economy. Just think about the world of Jevons' day. The Industrial Revolution was in full swing by the mid-nineteenth century. In Britain, the domestic economy was growing by an average annual real rate of about 2.7 percent, and the British Empire was at its glorious apex. In today's context, Britain was the leading, emerging economy of its era, with an energy appetite on steroids. It would be another century before the British economy would be considered "mature" or in an "advanced" state.

What Jevons understood was that because emerging, industrializing economies in their adolescent years need tremendous amounts of fuel to feed their growth, any efficiency gains are immediately devoured, leading to "backfire." In an emerging economy, there is a substantial amount of backfire because the objective is not to reduce energy consumption but to increase it significantly. I would argue this type of backfire is desirable and needed to improve the living standard of impoverished people. That's how countries like twenty-first century China or nineteenth century Britain facilitate industrialization, mobilization, urbanization, and of course, a higher standard of living for all. In effect, growing nations need energy efficiency to supply more work because that's how they increase their standard of living and perpetuate the First Principle of Energy Consumption.

Western policymakers fail to recognize that there is a significant rebound effect in their own advanced economies and have little understanding that the introduction of energy efficiencies in industrializing economies like China does not mitigate energy consumption, but actually stokes it further. When the steam engine was made more efficient, British industry devoured more steam engines and coal. In the same way, any improvements in China's power plants will result in the demand for even more generation facilities. Indeed, one of the few studies about energy efficiency in China shows that the rebound effect is greater than 100 percent, in other words "backfire".[4] Jevons would not be surprised.

Don't get me wrong. The pursuit of energy efficiency is a worthy endeavor. In fact, it's essential. But we need to understand what problems energy efficiency solves in order to better understand how to use it as a tool for achieving our goals. Most of us, including policy makers, think of energy efficiency as a "demand-side" moderator of our energy and environmental problems. They think that if we squeeze juice more efficiently, we'll waste fewer oranges. In fact, energy efficiency is not about the demand side, but the supply side. Greater efficiency just frees up more barrels of oil and more watts of electricity, as if we'd produced or generated more. Then, as Maslow's "perpetually wanting animals," we promptly take that extra energy and use it to do even more inefficient work. The only way to mitigate against rebound is if all energy-consuming devices in society, from toasters to pickup trucks, are mandated to become progressively more efficient. As you'll see in Chapter 15, this holistic approach is something that the Japanese have recognized.

If we really want to cut demand we need to think about *conservation*. Energy efficiency is often confused with conservation, but the two are not the same thing. As you'll learn in Chapter 10, there's a huge difference between screwing in a more efficient light bulb and turning the light off when not needed.

I support energy efficiency because under our current global circumstances, wasting energy is wrong, especially when that energy comes from a nonrenewable source. But better efficiency will not on its own solve our energy obesity. Think of it this way: eating everything on your plate is being efficient. Eating everything on your plate *and* figuring out how to live with a smaller helping is even better.

Chapter 8

Complex Carbons

Here is the stark reality: Over 88 percent of the world's energy needs are supplied by burning fossil fuels—coal, oil, and natural gas. Any discussion of climate change and greenhouse gases needs to acknowledge this fact first. The word carbon is a fixture in conversations about energy and the environment these days. While some are focused on efficiency, or more supply, or better alternatives as solutions to our energy problems, parallel discussions are taking place about carbon emissions, footprints, caps, trades, offsets, and taxes. But those who look more at the carbon problem than the supply side issues tend to overlook one important point. The reason why carbon dioxide poses such a complex and intransigent worry is because we are so thoroughly addicted to the amazing utility that carbon-based fuels provide. We use the cheap and plentiful energy to improve our lives, and we suffer pollution as a result—often willingly.

When we burn fossil fuels we release carbon dioxide and other greenhouse gases into the atmosphere. As simplistic as that sounds, I want you to keep that fundamental fact in mind throughout this chapter, because

I believe it impacts how we should think about carbon emissions and what we should do to alleviate them. Whatever your beliefs about the level or causes of global climate change, there is no debating that our overwhelming reliance on fossil fuels is inextricably linked to emissions of staggering volumes. That's unnerving enough regardless of how you evaluate the various scientific theories, political views, and policy proposals that are being debated.

Putting aside even the most rudimentary arguments about consequences and solutions, it's important to understand that energy use has always had an environmental impact, and that periodically the effect is so harsh it forces changes in our energy diet. In various regions and times in history, our reliance on wood stripped us of forests and destroyed habitats. Coal, a cheap and noxious fossil fuel, turned urban air into unbreathable smog in London in the eighteenth century and still does so today in many Asian cities. Our use of whale oil as a fuel for lamps nearly led to the extinction of the Sperm whale.

Even our reliance on hydroelectric power has overtaxed our environment at times, reducing water flows to an unusable trickle while destroying fish habitats in the process. Environmental degradation is one force, among others like geopolitical tension, excess demand, and tightening of supply, that can lead to an energy break point—a periodic shift, alteration, or wholesale change in our energy diet. Unfortunately, pressure on our environment, driven by our addiction to an energy source, is probably the easiest of such forces to ignore or overlook—that is, until crisis hits. We often react more slowly than we probably should because the costs show up on the social, rather than the financial, side of the ledger and because the effects are often so insidious. We may lose forests or biodiversity, have trouble breathing, or witness a rise in cancer rates. But curiously, none of those impacts hit us with the same immediacy and urgency as a sudden steep jump in the price of gasoline or heating oil. If our energy appetites do not markedly impact corporate bottom lines, national economies, or our pocketbooks, then the most powerful incentive to react is lacking.

Why is it so difficult to be aware of—let alone account for—the costs of environmental degradation? In his 1960 paper, *The Problem of Social Cost,* the Nobel Prize-winning American economist, Ronald Coase, discussed how to evaluate the harmful social impact that businesses or industry can have as a way of balancing any assessment of overall value. Coase's sensible and understated conclusion is worth thinking about in any energy discussion. As Coase wrote, "It would clearly be desirable if the only actions performed were those in which what was gained was worth more than what was lost."

Society has always used energy sources—renewable and non-renewable—under the tacit assumption that what is gained is worth more than what is being lost. Gains can be tangibly measured in terms of utility, productivity, and wealth creation. Costs, however, are more difficult to translate into measures that financial markets, corporate and government decision makers, and consumers can evaluate. Inevitably, we end up using our subjective social values as an imperfect compass to guide us in reacting to environmental problems. We resist the refinery being built in our backyard, but overlook the highway nearby. We ban the bulb, but allow the gas-guzzling pickup truck.

Ironically, there is evidence that as energy use drives up a society's standard of living, its members tend to become more concerned about the environmental consequences of their reliance on fuels. History has shown us that it is only after we attain a comparatively high standard of living from industrial production and when environmental pollution is at its greatest, that the focus changes from self-interest to social interest. In the economic lexicon, economists Gene Grossman and Alan Krueger refer to this relationship as the Environmental Kuznets Curve—a proposition first formulated in 1991.[1]

Consequently, the integrity of the ecosystem is not as high a priority in WantingWorld societies like China or India, which are eager for the WealthyWorld's standard of living. Conversely, in WealthyWorld, our concerns grow as our interest in comfort, quality of life, and other luxuries becomes more discerning. Of course, therein lies the irony of the relationship: the damage of pollution can be far harsher in an industrializing economy than in a developed economy. But if you want to view the barrel as half full rather than half empty, it's encouraging that we eventually become conscientious about reducing the negative side-effects of energy use, even if the solutions become harder to apply.

There have been times in history when we've abandoned a more environmentally harmful fuel for a more sustainable one. When we stopped chopping down forests and started mining for coal, that seemed like a good thing, though our overuse of coal soon revealed its own problems. Similarly, kerosene derived from crude oil was the miracle fuel that saved the whales, but spurred the creation of an infrastructure that now delivers our biggest addiction. Once upon a time, we relied on gas distilled from coal to light our cities, even though the effluent at the production facility was brutally toxic. The dirty and laborious process of distilling coal into methane was only abandoned after natural gas from the depths of the earth was able to offer compellingly better utility. Today, natural gas is one of the cleanest of fossil fuels and as I will discuss in Chapter 14, will figure larger in our future energy diet.

Even in our own lifetimes we've seen major shifts in appetite or behaviors that improved our environment. Although it can be argued whether environmental concerns were a main catalyst for the most recent switchover, the fact is that nuclear power replaced oil as a source of power generation following the break point catalyzed by the 1970s energy crisis. Other obvious cases are legion. For example, when heavy traffic on freeways generated a noxious soup of brown smog in the 1970s, automakers were forced to install catalytic converters to clean up tailpipe emissions. Similarly, when coal-fired smokestacks belched out the ingredients for acid rain in the 1980s, regulatory and incentive mechanisms were put in place to curb the practice.

So, we know it can be done. Depending on the problem, either geopolitics, fuel scarcity, market forces, or regulatory remedies have encouraged us to shift or alter our appetite, clean up our waste, and live in a cleaner world. But we're stuck with one conundrum that simply won't go away: carbon emissions are a problem because burning carbon-based fuels are so ideal almost right across the board of desirable energy attributes. But that still begs the question, what should we do this time?

Subordinating Policies, the Right Way up

Moral imperatives aside, environmental policy must be factored into our understanding of how our globally interlacing energy systems will evolve in the future. Setting aside the overwhelming issues related to the 2009 global recession, citizens and decision makers are talking more about carbon footprints and offsets than about our energy diet itself.

But we cannot lose track of the cause of the issue, namely that energy consumption results in carbon emissions. As such, I want to talk about the environmental consequences *of* our current energy diet.

Our appetite for carbon-based fuels, conventional vehicles, and conventional energy production shows no signs of flagging. In the 1960s, the world's reliance on coal, oil, and natural gas measured as a proportion of total fuel use was over 94 percent. That means virtually all of our energy consumption resulted in carbon emissions. By 1985 we dropped down to 89 percent because nuclear power was introduced into the energy diet as a means of reducing our addiction to crude oil. Along the way we became more efficient in our energy use, too. Today, despite all the efforts of green nations like Germany and Denmark to decrease their reliance on oil and coal, trends in the world's total carbon-dependency is reversing again, an uncomfortable phenomenon charted in Figure 8.1.

I come at the climate-change problem from the pragmatism of analyzing our energy needs, for that's where my expertise is grounded. Although some may discount my perspective as inherently biased, I'm strongly convinced that all should share this bias. We all need energy to live and work. The more energy we consume, the better our quality of

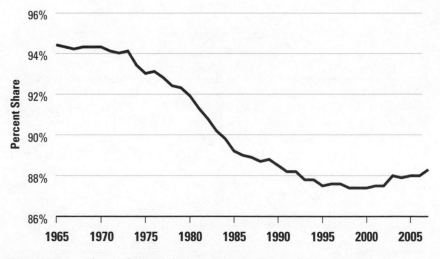

Figure 8.1   Share of World Energy Appetite Derived from Fossil Fuels (1965–2007)
SOURCE: BP Statistical Review 2008, ARC Financial Research.

life—that's the First Principle. And when we talk about regulatory curbs on energy use with respect to climate change we need to keep that in mind—unless of course we can learn how to break away from the First Principle, which is the focal point of this book.

While the First Principle doesn't often enter the standard environmental debate, climate change policy (specifically the mitigation of Greenhouse Gas [GHG] emissions) is, in contrast, becoming the de facto energy policy of WealthyWorld governments like those in the United States, Canada, and the European Union. Put another way, energy policy is becoming subservient to climate change policy. This is of major concern: though the two policies are inextricably linked, we are being conditioned to believe that the proverbial tail is wagging the dog, and not the reverse.

I have highlighted several times in this book that there are a trio of big issues that emerge from energy obesity: vulnerable security, limits to prosperity, and challenges to environment. My illustration in Figure 8.2 shows a simple causality diagram, top to bottom, between energy obesity and our vexing issues, and also points out that there are a multitude of subissues under the big three, too many to name, one of which is the emission of greenhouse gases.

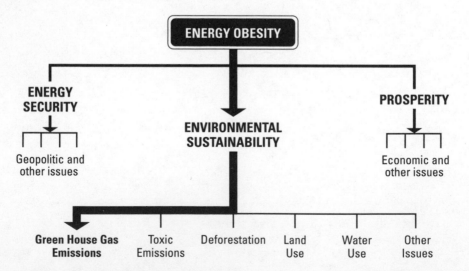

Figure 8.2   Direction of Causality and Consequences of Energy Obesity

Viewed in this simplistic way, the causality suggests that climate change policy should be subservient to energy policy and not the reverse. That is to say, if our energy obesity can be solved top-down, we will go a long way to mitigating *all* the issues under my causality tree. Seeking to solve the problem by going bottom-up from emissions— by instituting a myriad of complex mechanisms like caps, trades, offsets, and taxes—doesn't necessarily mitigate the urgency of our prosperity and security issues; in fact, in some cases, it can actually antagonize against them. The figure reminds us that in solving causally complex problems it's more effective to pull than push a rope.

Consider the large initiative to capture carbon emissions at the source. Carbon sequestration, otherwise known as Carbon Capture and Storage (CCS), sounds like science fiction. The technology is being developed to capture the CO_2 that a coal-fired power plant emits, compress it, pipe it, and bury it far into the crust of the earth in a secure reservoir such as a self-contained, sealed geological formation. We can also sequester carbon through "aforestation," using natural sinkholes filled with vegetation. And there are theoretical plans to seed the ocean with iron in order to grow plankton that can soak up carbon dioxide, then collect and burn that plankton as a renewable energy source. I've even read about the possibility of hurling carbon dioxide into outer space.

The Sleipner oil and gas field, operated by Norway's Statoil, is one functioning example of such a process. Since 1996, carbon dioxide has been captured in the process of drilling for natural gas, then compressed and pumped into a natural shale formation reservoir 3,000 feet below the seabed. This is all encouraged and subsidized by Norwegian tax breaks. Such technological practices are also advancing in Japan.[2] Meanwhile in Alberta, Canada, the provincial government is allocating US\$1.6 billion to help pilot carbon capture projects, especially for emissions emanating from the production and processing of environmentally contentious oil sands.

Yet capturing and burying CO_2 is not as easy as recycling pop cans. Isolating the CO_2 from exhaust gases takes energy. Afterward, you then have to compress it under high pressure and ship it long distances to the final burial ground—all of which takes energy. At this point you now have to compress the CO_2 even more to force it down a well partly encased in stainless steel that goes at least a mile underground.

This too takes energy. Lastly, it still takes energy to monitor the reservoir and ensure the CO_2 doesn't escape. The picture is clear: it takes a substantial amount of energy to capture, compress, ship, and store CO_2. If that increment of energy for all that work also emits CO_2, are we not engaging in a counterproductive activity? Philosophically, why are we promoting an inefficient, energy intense process to sweep under the carpet the emissions mess made by other, already inefficient processes? In fact, the numbers are not pretty, and have the effect of cannibalizing some of the EROEIs I discussed in Chapter 6. For example, the already poor 3:1 EROIE of oil sands production falls to a marginal 1:3:1 if emissions sequestration is applied. There is of course also the question of paying for the cleanup, which implementing a straightforward CCS policy ignores. Of the 6,096 million tons of carbon dioxide emitted in the United States in 2007, more than half (53 percent) were emitted by the transportation and residential sectors, while only 47 percent were emitted by the industrial and commercial sectors;[3] those which produce the goods and services that directly grow our economy. Mandating CCS policies puts the financial cleanup of our CO_2 emissions on the commercial and industrial sectors, leaving the end user scot-free. Such policies fly in the face of what the First Principle teaches, for they penalize an economy's wealth-generating mechanism without providing disincentives for the end user to trim down their energy appetite.

For conversion processes like coal-fired power generation, the energy drain of CCS also cannibalizes efficiency. Chapter 10 will demonstrate that electricity made from burning coal runs at a pathetic efficiency of 27 percent—that means 73 percent of the energy in a pound of coal is lost in the conversion process. In my discussions with utility experts, strapping on CCS equipment to coal-fired power stations will further reduce that efficiency to between 15 and 20 percent. Accounting for the burdensome cost of CCS, and thinking about this outcome in the context of Ronald Coase's thoughts, it's not clear that what is being gained is worth more than what is being lost. Through implementing CCS, we may end up sequestering our unwanted emissions, but our energy appetite will rise as an unintended consequence. In fact, many climate change policy implementations are perfectly synchronous with reducing energy obesity, especially those that encourage efficiency and conservation. As you'll read in Part III, I wholly endorse such efficiency and conservation policies as absolutely necessary in the fight against energy obesity.

Climate-change policies differ greatly from region to region and from country to country. Moreover, they are in a state of seemingly unending evolution and refinement. Many erudite books, reports, and government policy papers have been written on the variety of rules, regulations, and schemes designed to reduce overall emissions. It's not my place to challenge that body of knowledge and expertise. All I'm highlighting is that energy obesity causes emissions; not the other way around. So let's frame the problem that way so that we tackle the problem going with the grain of causality rather than against it.

If solving causality is the answer I'm shouting vainly from the rooftops, I need to admit something else first; namely, that this task is not easy. But thinking big never is. If we are going to solve the many different and unhealthy consequences of energy obesity, I believe we need to think more broadly than emissions and start thinking in terms of a realistic, scalable menu and a trimmed down, healthier appetite. The formula is straightforward: reduce our energy appetite and we reduce our carbon footprint and a whole host of other problems too! I believe that's the relationship, the causality, and the approach that governments, corporations, and concerned citizens should apply as they endeavor to bring about sustainable change in our energy use.

Chapter 9

The Maddening Allure of the First Principle

Remarkably, between 1979 and 1985, energy consumption in the United States dropped even as collective wealth grew. The economic expansion may not have felt as spectacular and uplifting as in the 1950s and 1960s, or even the first part of this century, but there was growth over the period nevertheless. To the best of my knowledge (and according to all the data I have analyzed), this six-year period was the only era in peacetime history in which the First Principle of Energy Consumption has ever been convincingly broken in the United States.

It was a significant event. Raw energy appetite went from a peak of 63 BPY in 1979, down to 56 BPY by 1985—a 13 percent reduction. Meanwhile, by the end of the same six-year period, average standard of living as measured by real per capita GDP grew by 10 percent, though the first three years of the 1980s were admittedly choppy.

Working under significant pressure, the most industrialized society on the planet was on a path to challenging the First Principal—an achievement not witnessed since before Orata gave the world the hypocaust. And then, as is human nature, that accomplishment succumbed to temptation. Like a dieter with the best of intentions can attest (or anyone trying to break a difficult addiction), adherence to discipline is easily trumped by the irresistible and often maddening allure of indulgence.

That 70's Show: A Sitcom We've Seen Before

We need not blame ourselves. The First Principle lures us back too easily. In the simple calculus of economic growth, if a better quality of life is readily attainable at a cheaper cost, the more energy we voraciously consume. In the petroleum market, for instance, the pressure lessened in the 1980s as we developed substantial oil reserves in Prudhoe Bay, Alaska, and in the North Sea off Great Britain. And as soon as the price of oil dropped and that reduction in prices became prolonged, we resumed—with great relief and increasing eagerness—our appetite for cheap energy.

In his 1974 State of the Union address, President Richard Nixon spoke about the difficulties the United States was facing because of the Arab Oil Embargo, begun in 1973. Promising to "break the backs of the energy crisis," Nixon acknowledged that the end of the embargo would not mean an end to America's energy shortage. He praised the contributions that Americans had been making to alleviate the emergency through voluntary conservation efforts and he called for new urgency in improving public transportation. "Let this be our national goal," Nixon stated, "At the end of this decade, in the year 1980, the United States will not be dependent on any other country for the energy we need to provide our jobs, to heat our homes, and to keep our transportation moving."[1] To meet this objective he pledged $10 billion, or 0.7 percent of GDP in public funds ($42 billion in real 2007 dollars), for research while claiming that private enterprise would be likely to invest an additional $200 billion in pursuit of those aims.

Watergate may have interrupted Mr. Nixon's efforts, but energy policy was also a profound concern for his next-elected successor.

President Carter understood the nature of an energy break point, describing as early as 1977 the way that massive global demand would soon no longer be met by ever-depleting reserves. As he put it, "We must look back in history to understand our energy problems. Twice in the last several hundred years there has been a transition in the way people use energy." Once, according to Carter, was when we switched from wood to coal, the second time was when coal got displaced by oil and natural gas. In this third iteration, by his count, we would need to adopt a policy of strict conservation and prepare for permanent renewables like solar power. "Conservation," Mr. Carter declared, "is the quickest, cheapest, most practical source of energy." The oil we were wasting by throwing it away on inefficient devices and lifestyles was oil we didn't need to drill. To that end, sacrifices like reducing the miles driven and the size of vehicles would be necessary, though painful. By 1985, Carter pledged that Americans would reduce the annual growth rate in energy demand to less than 2 percent and reduce gasoline by 10 percent below then-levels of consumption.

Those sacrifices were profoundly difficult to accept. As Carter acknowledged in his infamous "Crisis of Confidence" speech, "For the first time in the history of our country a majority of our people believe that the next five years will be worse than the past five years."[2] The year was 1979, the eve of the mark President Nixon had given for achieving energy independence. Carter echoed that call, and twinned it with an effort by the United States to shake off its malaise. "On the battlefield of energy we can win for our nation a new confidence, and we can seize control again of our common destiny." He declared that, "I am tonight setting a clear goal for the energy policy of the United States. Beginning this moment, this nation will never use more foreign oil than we did in 1977—never." If Carter's words sounded like uncomfortable déjà vu to anyone recalling Nixon's pledge, then President Obama's commitment in January 2009; "It will be the policy of my administration to reverse our dependence on foreign oil while building a new energy economy...," must sound like a flashback to a bad sitcom.[3]

To freeze consumption of foreign oil and lessen our energy burden, Carter again advocated for expanding our conservation efforts, displacing oil from the power generation market and replacing it with abundant coal, and seeking out new sources of oil and new alternatives. He spoke about tapping the massive amounts of domestic oil found in oil shale, increasing consumption of coal, producing oil from plant products, and investing in solar power. By 1983, the efforts made to reduce the growth rate of energy consumption by less than 2 percent (as outlined in Carter's 1977 speech) had been exceeded. Americans had actually reduced total energy consumption by over 4.0 million BOE a day, or 10.5 percent, relative to 1979 levels.

Even though America's economy actually grew during that period, it was the inconvenience of lifestyle sacrifices that ultimately defeated such efforts. Many didn't like driving slower, getting into smaller vehicles, and tightening belts. There was a preference for lifestyles that were open, full of potential, and enticing. It's human nature to embrace the First Principle. We consume more energy because it lifts our standard of living and grows our wealth, providing an ever-expanding list of comforts and luxuries.

President Reagan embraced this optimism and the energy formula behind it, declaring that America's best days were before her. It was an easy message to buy into. The Fuel Use Act was repealed in 1987, as was the Emergency Highway Energy Conservation Act that capped highway speed limits at 55 miles per hour. When was the last time you willingly traveled 55 mph on the highway? If you were so inclined, chances are you were nearly driven off the road by impatient commuters racing home to distant suburbs.

By the mid 1980s, Americans began to buy heavier cars again and lost their concerns for fuel efficiency. The cities hollowed out in the sorry circumstances of urban blight, white flight, and soaring crime. Developers invested in a new kind of suburb, specifically designed for the easier use of cars. Over the next 20 years distances from work and entertainment districts grew. Investment in highways surged as investment in public transportation became a disdained afterthought. Even simple visits to the corner store or the neighborhood playground, in North America at least, could hardly be accomplished without turning over the ignition. Houses got bigger and more luxurious. Gradually—and then rapidly, as personal wealth and suburban infrastructure investments catalyzed prominent social changes—lifestyles became more energy intense again. By 1989 individual appetites in the United States were back up to 60 BPY.

This all took place in the context, post-1985, of twenty years of relative calm on the energy front. Yes, there were moments of uncertainty, such as when oil prices blipped upward after Saddam Hussein invaded Kuwait in 1990. The image of Kuwaiti oil wells burning in uncontrolled fury symbolized our vulnerability to the kind of crisis that could be generated by madmen. But order and the flow of oil was restored quickly and effectively.

Later in the decade, in 1998, the so-called Asian flu—a collapse of currencies accompanied by economic turmoil in the economies of the Asian Tigers—caused oil demand to fall simultaneously when top-producing countries like Saudi Arabia were bringing big capacity additions to market. It was that confluence of events that led to oil prices dipping to a momentary low of $10 per barrel. In sharp contrast to the dire prophecies of the 1970s and 1980s, and the alarming proclamations that the world was running out of its most desired resource, this was a convincing sign that all suggestions of an apocalypse were alarmist nonsense and cheap oil would be with us forever.

Over the course of the next few years, aided by oil that held its price around $20 per barrel and a surge in investments in information technology, we saw one of the greatest wealth booms in history. Psychologically, the $20 price tag seemed to matter. Notwithstanding any temporary fluctuations, between 1986 and 2000 the price per barrel always snapped back to that magic number and the price at the pump held to an easy-to-calculate $1.00 per gallon, give or take.

Fast-Forward to Today

As the calendar turned to the twenty-first century, seasoned oil professionals saw some worrisome data on the progressively divergent trends between supply and demand. The first yellow flag was noticeable when the price of oil briefly trended into the mid-$30/B range without any discernible catalyst such as war or political turmoil to justify the rise. In fact, I remember working hard in late 2002 to convince directors of an energy company that an oil price higher than $27 per barrel was sustainable. Industry veterans who'd seen many ups and downs in the previous decade were cynical that the latest jump to $30 was anything other than an arbitrary and temporary event.

The skepticism around that board table, and around many others like it throughout the world, was replaced by growing concern over the subsequent five years when steadily higher thresholds got breached and left behind. The price of $40 per barrel, first seen in July 2004, was quickly followed by $50 in October of that same year. Then we surged past $75 per barrel in September of 2007.

The administration of President George W. Bush considered the twin threads that weave uncertain oil markets—tightening supply and lingering geopolitics—and established an energy task force in 2001 to assess and make recommendations for America's future energy needs. The task force, headed by Vice President Cheney, was the target of much suspicion because of the secrecy of the meetings and the involvement of Big Oil executives. But the recommendations on the supply side were basically sound, if the intent was to perpetuate the First Principle. The task force called for increased production of domestic oil (especially offshore and in Alaska), and massive investment in nuclear, hydroelectric, oil- and coal-fired power plants, as well as natural gas pipelines. Cheney stated that renewables looked promising, but were still too far in the future to make a meaningful difference. Most infamously, he dismissed the idea that Americans should curb their energy appetites or cut back on their desires for a higher standard of living. In his words, "Conservation may be a sign of personal virtue, but it is not a sufficient basis for a sound, comprehensive energy policy."[4]

By the time the Bush Administration's second term began, President Bush acknowledged that conservation could play a role in reducing energy needs but insisted it wasn't going to be enough compared to other, better options like improved efficiencies, new technologies, biofuels, and offshore drilling. Policy was forthcoming; amidst intense partisan politics, the Bush Administration finally passed the Energy Independence and Security Act of 2007. Philosophically, the tone of the Act was very much in tune with keeping the First Principle alive and well: 11 of 13 action items in the Act were biased toward figuring out how to deliver more energy.

In 2006, as the price of oil breached $65 per barrel the national conversation about energy was beginning to become more urgent. But a new motivation for that conversation shifted to our changing climate. Evidence of global warming, and Al Gore's documentary, *An Inconvenient*

Truth, began to have an effect on how we thought about carbon-based fuels and what we needed to do to reduce greenhouse gas emissions. Investments in renewables suddenly looked more vital. People and organizations started to talk about changes to lifestyles and operations that could reduce a carbon footprint.

When oil prices broke through the important psychological barrier of $100 per barrel in January of 2008, people's mental capacity to digest the flood of confusing news was approaching overload. On any day of the week you could watch a TV morning show host with an expert guest discuss the need to rid America of foreign oil, or read about the urgency of climate change in the paper, and finally at the end of the day, on your congested commute home, sympathize with a talk radio jock relaying hard luck stories about how high gas prices were pushing family budgets into the red zone. How was all this related? Who was to blame for all this mayhem?

After lambasting oil and auto companies for the rising price of oil, finger pointers found yet another constituency to blame: rogue investors, or speculators. The implicit accusation was that people with money to invest couldn't distinguish between reckless opportunism and looming scarcity as a consequence of several billion people on the other side of the planet ratcheting up their energy consumption. Though I enjoy such debates, I don't want to drag us into the endless conspiracy theories about the culpability of Big Oil, Big Auto, or Big Money. I am not defending any constituency here, but I do want to acknowledge one important thing: When we are faced with a major problem or crisis, it's easier to point fingers than to look in the mirror and accept that the problem reflects on all of us.

That's how the world stood in 2008, just before the biggest economic crisis since the Great Depression. A lot of confusion, anger, and blame churned around the issues of energy as we were faced with a series of closely related problems exhibiting all the symptoms of the condition I call energy obesity. For Americans, despite the suffering of the 1970s and trumpeted proclamations and policies going back 35 years, the nation was no closer to achieving its goals of energy independence or alleviating its oil addiction. In fact, because of the growth of that addiction, the scale of the growing appetite in WantingWorld, and the greater competition over progressively scarcer primary energy supplies, the situation was actually far worse than the 1970s. Perversely, the financial crisis that started in 2008 magically made our energy problems disappear through the reduced consumption that accompanies recession. But in fact, none of our energy problems were solved.

What Next?

Addressing energy obesity is not easy. Any practical and meaningful solution set will require a mix of behavioral change, good policy, new technology, and new magic bullets. I've talked about the limits of these elements as stand-alone solutions in the preceding chapters. We'll need to put them all together to get the right recipe. But we will also need to throw in a healthy dose of crisis and high prices, stir vigorously, and sustain. Unfortunately, memories are short and when the crisis wanes, so goes the motivation. That's what happened in the 1970s. And now we're back there again, as though watching a bad TV show we've seen before.

We know that this time the public won't readily accept a president in a cardigan sweater admonishing them for a crisis in confidence while comparing energy consumption habits to moral failing. In North America—and the majority of societies around the world—negotiating or rolling back enthusiasm for an ever-improving standard of living runs counter to reality. We are hard-wired to be "perpetually wanting," as Maslow so astutely pointed out.

Any solution we arrive at must acknowledge that economic growth and quality of life needs to increase while we reduce our energy appetites to sustainable levels. We don't need moralistic admonishments or calls to cut back. We need enticing potential for wealth generation to make our efforts attractive from the start. Otherwise, the vagaries of energy price fluctuations, our ability to adapt to new circumstances, both good and bad, and our shortlived learnings from past crises will undercut our aims. If that happens, as it has in the past, we'll be talking about the same issues less than ten years from now, with even more dire consequences at stake.

To avoid that, we're going to have to break the back of the First Principle and end energy obesity once and for all. As I'll show you in Part III, it can be done.

Part III

THINKING OUT OF THE BOX

Chapter 10

The Asymmetry Principle

I f you've ever discussed the meaning of life over a late-night bottle of Scotch you might have been inclined to reference the works of twentieth century German philosopher Martin Heidegger, who spent a large part of his career thinking about the reason for our "being" in the universe. I'll spare you any of the trite conclusions or epiphanies I've ever come to in such moments and focus instead on something Heidegger had to say about the energy we use here on planet Earth.

In the mid-1950s, Heidegger reflected on the historical progression of society as it developed from simple water wheels to massive hydroelectric dams. On one end of the spectrum, he suggested, we are at one with nature, living a simple agrarian existence. A modern hydroelectric dam demonstrates how we've challenged nature with technology on a large and complex scale in a way that strains any notion of being in harmony with our planet.

Surprisingly for such an existential philosopher, Heidegger concretely described the causality of energy stemming from the powerful flow of a river: "The hydroelectric plant is set into the current of the Rhine. It sets the Rhine to supplying its hydraulic pressure, which then sets the turbines turning. This turning sets those machines in motion whose thrust sets going the electric current for which the long-distance power station and its network of cables are set up to dispatch electricity." This cascading causality led to Heidegger's final observation about the dam: "In the context of the interlocking processes pertaining to the orderly disposition of electrical energy, even the Rhine itself appears to be something at our command."[1]

Imagine that a river as mighty as the Rhine, flowing over 10,000 cubic feet of water every second through Germany, is something at our command. Heidegger recognized that we've developed our energy infrastructure and technologies to complexities and scale beyond what was fathomable in our agrarian days. Now, a trivial flick of a light switch can influence a mighty energy source like a dam on a river hundreds of miles away.

Let's put on our own philosophical hats and play around with Heidegger's notion of causality. If the mighty Rhine is at our command when we turn on a switch, it is also at our command when we turn off a switch. If turning over the ignition in our car demonstrates our control over oil found in the depths of the earth, then not turning over the ignition demonstrates the same principle, only in reverse.

In fact, the amount of power and influence we have over those energy sources is much greater in the reverse than we realize. I call this influence the Asymmetry Principle of Energy Consumption: *"A unit of energy saved at the consumer level cascades into multiple units of energy saved at the source."* Indeed, the size of the savings multiplier, depending on the intended end use for that energy, can be many times over. Let me describe why the Asymmetry Principle is so significant, and how the proper application of it will provide the leverage we need to help end our energy obesity.

Our Mind-Set at Our Command

Each energy crisis brings us to a solutions crossroads: find more or use less. The latter path has seldom triggered excitement, so our periodic quests to reassert control over our energy needs have always been highly biased to chopping more wood, chasing more whales, shoveling more coal, damming up more rivers, putting up more windmills, splitting more atoms, or drilling for more oil and gas.

President Obama has made energy an early priority in his term, recognizing that security, affordability, and sustainability will again intertwine to form a tight noose around American society if not addressed. I totally agree, yet early indications are that a lot of the new administration's thinking is still mostly on the supply side. President Obama's choice of Nobel prize-winning physicist Stephen Chu as Energy Secretary is laudable, because science and technology does have a big role to play in boosting pathetic system efficiencies and addressing issues of environmental sustainability. Yet appointment of some sociologists may have been equally powerful, because the Asymmetry Principle teaches us that real leverage is in the psychology of using less, rather than the technology of using as much or more.

Being supply side biased is not exclusively an American phenomenon. As Heidegger might have observed, most nations are still trying to assert their command over nature by bidding it to deliver more power to their people. As I discussed in Parts I and II, as a global village we're stoking economic growth with greater amounts of nonrenewable fuels that strain under scarcity. When supplies tighten, prices rise, and geopolitical tension asserts itself, we look for miracle fuels, miracle technologies, or miracle sources to augment our appetite. Implicitly, and for very good reasons, we believe that the First Principle has served us well because "more energy equals more comfort." Now, with almost 7 billion people increasingly striving for a better quality of life, the logic of "more" has never been so vital to challenge—especially after I show you how much of that more goes to waste.

Don't get me wrong: I don't deny that the scale of our looming energy issues requires that we bring greater sources of supply into our diet. We must do that too, and to that end I will discuss pragmatic, scalable sources in Chapter 14, but it's also true that the extent of our energy predicament requires us to overturn old prejudices and assumptions. Not only do we need to better manage and rebalance our energy diet, we need to rebalance our mind-set, too. Crucially, our leaders must challenge all of us to think harder about how to control our energy appetites rather than always promising us a bigger and bigger smorgasbord that leads to bigger and bigger waste.

Is it possible to resolve our energy issues going forward with a framework that deemphasizes "more supply" and shifts attention to moderating energy appetite? I believe the answer is yes, especially if we're shown the improved lifestyles that are available in return for the sacrifice. But first let me show you how much power we actually command when we turn the light switch off instead of on.

An Absurd Yet Compelling Offer

Think of a time that you were in a store, agonizing over whether or not to buy a special item for yourself—something that you didn't really need, but would have loved to have, maybe a gadget, tool, or purse worth $100.

In a demonstration of amazing self-restraint, you make up your mind abruptly: "What am I thinking, I don't need that!" Walking out of the store you feel good, even euphoric for a brief moment. In the complicated and emotional logic of personal finance you are filled with self-satisfaction, because by not spending that $100 you are now $100 richer than before.

In fact, your decision was a symmetric proposition. The amount you "saved" was equal to the amount you were about to spend. But what if the weighting of the choice was very different? What if the deal presented to you in the store was as follows: "Don't spend $100 on that thing you don't really need and your benefit will be $600." In other words, put the C-note back in your billfold, and you get five additional hundred-dollar bills to go with it. It's safe to say that your decision under this proposition would require little debate. Most of us would gladly forfeit a single purchase if it benefited us six times over.

Of course, a six-to-one offer is an absurd fantasy in the real world of commerce. Yet in the currency of energy, this amazing offer is real. And it represents the biggest opportunity to make a meaningful impact toward breaking the First Principle of Energy Consumption. When you choose not to put energy to work, you save multiples of energy at the point where the primary fuel was sourced. Put another way, the amount of energy saved by not flicking on the wall switch does not translate into an equal amount of energy saved at a coal mine. The leverage up the inefficient supply chain of energy is such that multiples of that energy is saved in terms of the coal not needed to generate your electricity. For instance, for an incandescent light bulb the multiplier is not the mere six-to-one savings I demonstrated in my retail example, but approximately 50-to-one. A conscious decision to forfeit one quantum of light energy in your home means that 50 times that amount of primary energy is conserved at the source. Heidegger was right; we do have tremendous power at our command!

Not all examples are as dramatic as lighting, but the multipliers are still very large. For example, one unit of energy saved by not driving a car translates into about six times the amount of energy you no longer need to pump from a wellhead. In other words, the energy equivalent of one barrel of oil saved by not turning wheels means that we can avoid drilling between six and seven barrels of oil in some politically charged, environmentally sensitive, or geographically extreme location.

How does this formula work? The Asymmetry Principle turns one of our deepest problems—inefficient energy use—into our greatest lever-age. I've already described in Chapter 7 how shockingly little of the energy we procure from a source like a wellhead or a coal mine actually gets applied in terms of useful work—driving cars, turning on lights, heating homes. I'll go over those numbers again to bring the point home. The dismaying reality of inefficiencies all along the supply chain means that we throw away most of the energy we secure at the source. But if we reverse that process, we can see how little energy we actually need to conserve in order to save large amounts of primary energy like coal, wind, or oil. In other words, we turn a dismal and intractable problem into a hopeful and positive solution.

Wasted Kernels

Whether it comes from a hydroelectric dam, a big nuclear generator, a coal or gas-fired power plant, or a renewable source, electrical energy follows a similar path through our power distribution infrastructure to meet our needs. Let's chain through the main steps from the source to our sockets, to our end use.

When we want to turn on the TV or the light switch, a primary source of energy like coal, natural gas, or wind is fed into a device that performs a conversion to high voltage electricity. That electricity is then transmitted along large high-tension wires to a neighborhood substation, where after stepping down the voltage, the electrical current travels down smaller wires on the final leg of its journey, either underground or on poles, into your home, typically to a socket in the wall, where it is available for further conversion into the work that you desire.

As electricity consumers, we're almost completely oblivious to that behind-the-scenes process. The power only becomes real when we plug in a blow dryer, vacuum cleaner, light bulb, or television set and convert the electrical energy into useful work. We're also largely unaware that along the supply chain, there are massive energy losses everywhere. At each stage of conversion or transmission a substantial amount of energy is thrown away, mostly as unused heat.

Back to my food metaphor; imagine a typical cob of corn in a farmer's field. Husking the cob will reveal the ear with about 800 kernels arranged neatly in 16 rows. Think of the waste if only 200 of the 800 kernels made it to your plate, and the rest, including all the other parts of the cob, disappeared completely unused somewhere along the way. The waste is even more pronounced if you don't eat all that is on your plate, which is another symbolic vignette of how poorly we make use of our energy supply. Indeed, the magnitude of the waste we indiscriminately tolerate is such that in most electrical applications less than 10 percent of the original primary energy is actually "digested" for useful purpose. And that's good considering where we've come from.

The process of converting the rotating energy in a spinning shaft into electricity has been with us since Michael Faraday, a British chemist, demonstrated the principle of electrical induction in 1832. Faraday's electromagnetic dynamo became a break point innovation when Edison set up the first commercial power plant on Pearl Street in New York. In Edison's power plant, a coal-fired steam engine turned a crankshaft that spun a dynamo and generated electricity. According to Charles L. Clarke, the chief engineer of the Edison Electric Light Company, "The men financing the enterprise. . . desired that a complete operative system be installed on a suitable scale for testing the economy of the system and uncovering weak spots if any existed inherently in mere bigness, before they should risk much money in commercially exploiting it."[2] The distribution of the electricity generated at Pearl Street laid the foundation for the modern electric grid.

Edison may have proved to his backers that his electrical system possessed benefits well worth the investment, but it's striking how a system with such pathetically low energy efficiency could produce such compelling utility and customer desire. By the time the electricity left Pearl Street Station, I estimate that less than 1 percent of the original energy contained in each pound of burned coal was used to light a small room. The balance of the energy was lost to the heat of combustion, the heat of friction in the machinery, and the heat of electrical resistance in the wires and light bulb. Back then, only eight of the 800 kernels on a cob of corn made it to the banquet table.

Stepping through the Asymmetry

Today's progressive power generators are far more advanced than those in Edison's time, but the energy lost is still substantial. Let's get more specific with numbers and think about how power generated from a primary fuel like natural gas is put to work.

After being piped in from a distant gas field in Texas or Oklahoma, natural gas is fed into a big stationary turbine, similar to a jet engine bolted to a floor. The gas burns and spins a shaft that is attached to an electrical generator—the modern incarnation of the dynamo. Modern as it is, this primary process is still only able to convert about 40 percent of the energy contained in a cubic foot of natural gas into electricity (United States average). The other 60 percent gets blown out the exhaust as unused heat. Innovations have been made over the past couple of decades and new "combined cycle" generators can now recycle a portion of that wasted heat through another turbine to generate more electrical power in a second stage, bumping up overall efficiency to the 50 to 55 percent range.

Some countries, like Denmark, advance the practice of minimizing waste further by taking even more of the unused heat and putting it to valuable work other than just making electricity. Channeled through a grid of insulated pipes, excess heat is made accessible to nearby buildings for interior climate control. Making good use of both heat and electrical power makes logical sense, driving down waste to 20 percent or less in this first major step of energy conversion.

In reality, achieving average efficiency greater than 50 percent across an entire fleet of natural gas-fired power plants still looks distant in the United States. There are around 5,500 gas-fired power generators across the nation[3] and not all of them are state of the art. Old plants drag the average efficiency down. Nevertheless, progress is being made; since the late 1990s there has been a major buildup of new high-efficiency generators. This modernization has led to a significant improvement in the overall fleet efficiency.

Figure 10.1 shows that less than 10 years ago only 36 percent of the energy in natural gas was converted to electricity, but that the average has now risen to over 40 percent. This four point efficiency gain is significant: I estimate that the positive trend has mitigated the need to bring on close to 1.5 billion cubic feet a day of new natural gas supply. On average U.S. power plant consumption of 18 billion cubic feet of gas every day (2008), this appetite curtailment represents a clear example of how efficiency gains have the potential to help mitigate energy obesity on a large scale.

While it's nice to put a positive spin on this story about natural gas efficiency gains, let's not get carried away, because the sorry truth remains that 60 percent of a nonrenewable fuel still goes unused at the power plant, never to be available again. As for coal-fired power plants, there isn't even a positive trend to cheer. Figure 10.1 also shows efficiency gains—or rather, lack thereof—for electricity generated from burning coal. It depends on the type of coal being burned, but on average the efficiency of generating electrical power in U.S. coal plants has stalled at 27 percent since 1995, meaning that 73 percent of coal is wasted at the generator—and the journey from the power plant down the wires to the wall socket in your living room has not even begun yet.

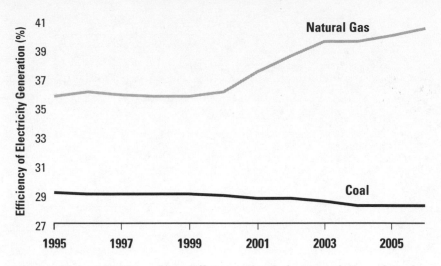

Figure 10.1 U.S. Power Plant Efficiency Trends for Natural Gas and Coal: Electrical Energy Out Divided by Source Energy In
Source: ARC Financial Research, U.S. Energy Information Administration.

As electrons flow down wires, like water through a garden hose, more energy is lost. Those enormous high tension power lines on big metal towers manage to transmit most, but not all, of the electrical energy generated at the power plant. Between 8 and 12 percent vanishes to "line losses," mostly as heat generated by the resistance of the copper wires. Then, before the electricity is distributed to your home or your business via neighborhood wires, the voltage has to be "stepped down" where yet more losses to resistance ensue. The net result is that only about one-third of the electrical energy generated coming out of a power plant whether it's fueled by coal, natural gas, wood, or wind, makes it to your home.

The electricity is now at your wall socket, ready to power a myriad of devices. Once again, let's consider the simple but enduring incandescent light bulb. The stark reality of the numbers will amplify the extent of our inefficiency, but also underscore the magnitude of the potential leverage at our command.

The original bamboo-filament light bulbs lit up by Edison's Pearl Street Station had an efficiency of 3 percent. That means that only 3 percent of the electrical energy coming out of the wall socket went to illuminating a room for your eyes to see. Through a series of innovations, most notably the coiled metal filament, the incandescent light bulb had

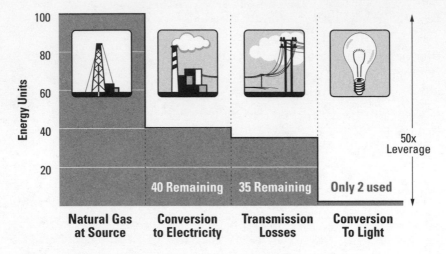

Figure 10.2 Asymmetry Diagram for Natural Gas to Light
SOURCE: ARC Financial Research.

evolved by the mid–1930s into a mature lighting device that hasn't changed much since. Note that during the winter an incandescent light bulb is actually 100 percent efficient, because the unused heat radiating from the lampshade can serve to provide a small portion of household warmth and comfort. On the other hand, in the summer, the waste heat of all the bulbs forces the air conditioner to work harder to cool down the home, which is doubly wasteful.

Let's chain all these efficiencies together with the asymmetry diagram in Figure 10.2 that catalogs the cascading energy losses that accrue by the time you flick on the light switch. To simplify, I assume that we start with 100 units of energy in the form of natural gas, which is represented by the bar furthest to the left of the diagram.

Big downward steps through the process in Figure 10.2 represent how many units of energy are left after each stage, and illustrates that the way we put fuels to work is exceptionally wasteful. After the first stage—making electricity through an average U.S. natural gas-fired power plant—only 40 units of the original 100 are left. The next step-down in Figure 10.2 reflects power line transmission losses, which eats about 5 of those 40 units, leaving only 35 for use in the home.

While we value light bulbs for their illuminating properties, they perhaps should be more appropriately appreciated as heaters. Ninety percent of the electrical energy a light bulb uses goes to making heat.[4] The other 10 percent produces light. But our eyes can only see just over half of that light, because our retinas are tuned only to a certain portion of the light spectrum that a bulb emits. That's why a light bulb is only about 6 percent efficient at taking electricity from the socket and brightening up a room. So at the end of the process, Figure 10.2 shows that only two of the original 100 units of natural gas accomplished the desired task: lighting the for your eyes to see.

The news is even worse if you use coal instead of natural gas because Figure 10.1 shows that coal-fired power plants are, on average, 27 percent efficient in the United States (modern high-efficiency coal plants can achieve close to 40 percent). Accordingly, the first step-down in the asymmetry diagram is much larger for coal, down to 27 units. In the end, what it means is that for every 100 pounds of coal burned, only 1 pound, 7 ounces is ultimately put to use when lighting a room.

My use of the name asymmetry diagram becomes clearer now, because you can see that the amount of energy actually put to work at the point of consumption is far less than the original quantity used at the source. In fact, for most energy processes the difference between the potential at the source and the actual use at the end is incredibly lopsided, or asymmetrical.

Our Asymmetrical Roads

As you might expect, the asymmetry diagram for vehicles, shown in Figure 10.3, is not inspiring either.

Let's start with 100 barrels of oil. By the time the gasoline is refined, distributed to the gas station, and put into your tank, 12 units have been lost. But the real beating takes place inside your engine, that break point innovation that Henry Ford established as our world standard over a century ago. Of the 88 units available after refining, the engine devours 63 and passes through only 25. Finally, another 8 units are lost between the gearbox and the wheels, leaving only 17 units left to move your vehicle. Additional units are used up when the vehicle is heavier, when you do more stop-and-go driving, and when you have a lead foot and drive too fast.

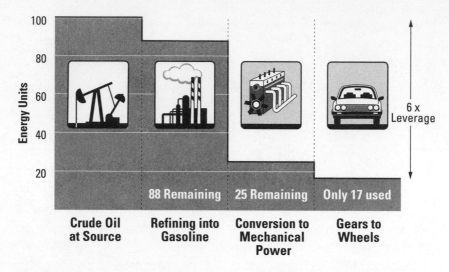

Figure 10.3   Asymmetry Diagram From a Barrel of Oil at a Wellhead to the Wheels of a Vehicle
SOURCE: ARC Financial Research, Argonne National Laboratory.

Engineers have been able to improve well-to-wheels efficiency over time but the scale of innovation is hardly remarkable, as shown in Figure 10.4. The numbers I calculated use actual road data so they include all the factors (vehicle weight, driving habits, speed, and so on) that govern how much of the energy is lost and how much actually makes it to moving you. Between 1983 and 2003, well-to-wheels efficiency improved from 8 percent to 17 percent, meaning that 83 percent of the original barrel of oil was lost out of the chimneys of refineries and the tailpipes of cars. From 2003 until 2007 there was no improvement in vehicle efficiency whatsoever. Compared to a Silicon Valley metric like Moore's Law, the pace of innovation and advancement in road transportation is pathetically slow. If progress in computer processor power paralleled that of autos we'd still be using our Apple IIs.

Two primary factors have stalled gains in vehicle efficiency. First, the automobile industry has seen the marked impact of the rebound effect I mentioned in Chapter 7. Any gains we've made have been offset by the move to bigger vehicles, the amount of time we spend stuck in traffic, and the number of inefficient electrical gadgets that sap engine power. Second, it should be acknowledged that improvements

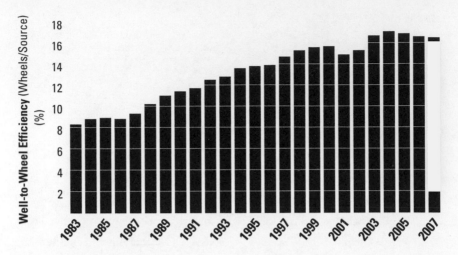

Figure 10.4 U.S. Well-to-Wheels Energy Efficiency Trend for all Passenger Road Vehicles (1983–2007)
Source: ARC Financial Research, U.S. Department of Transport.

to engine efficiency are becoming increasingly difficult because of limits in the laws of physics. The thermodynamics of an internal combustion engine impose inviolable limits on how much efficiency is possible as fuel enters the gas tank and applies itself to the engine. For example, the theoretical efficiency of a gasoline-powered, spark-ignited engine is only 25 percent. Today, our efficiency number is already close to 21 percent, leaving little room for improvement.

Obviously, then, a gasoline fed internal combustion engine is not the place to look if we want to leverage major gains in efficiency. Unfortunately, there are also few gains to be made at the refining level, where processes are already highly optimized. Switching to different fuel sources won't do as much as people think, either. The Argonne National Laboratory outside of Chicago has compiled extensive well-to-wheels analysis of all the different fuel-engine permutations.

A quick 2008 snapshot of the source-to-wheels efficiencies of a sample of different vehicle types in Figure 10.5 shows some interesting facts. At the low end is ethanol, which has a crop-to-wheels efficiency of only about 10 percent—in other words only 10 percent of the energy in a cob of corn actually makes it to turning wheels. An engine burning natural gas is marginally better than gasoline-from-oil at 17 percent. Diesel

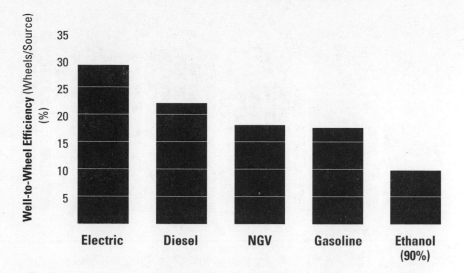

Figure 10.5   Source-Energy-to-Wheels Efficiency for Various Vehicle Types
SOURCE: ARC Financial Research, Argonne National Laboratory.

engines are notably more efficient than gasoline, and represent a real opportunity for quick efficiency gains using readily available technology and infrastructure. Europe embraced the opportunity long ago, but the diesel bug has yet to hit North America. Finally a pure electric vehicle charged by electricity that has been generated by the typical blend of American power-generating fuels[5] does show the best overall use of energy at 29 percent (measured from primary sources all the way to the wheels). It's almost twice as good as a gasoline-powered car, but let's be frank, losing 71 percent of the original energy is still not something to rejoice.

The best thing to do is to figure out how to drive less and exploit the leverage offered by the Asymmetry Principle. As I'll show you in Chapter 13, it can be done.

The Alternative Energy Source of the Future

Our societal issues reside with our energy at the source; for example, the politics of oil, the environmental issues of coal, the scalability and cost of renewables. There is no leverage; in other words, there is no multiplicative benefit, to merely adding more supply at the front end of

what sustains our society. But that's what we've always done to supply our way out of past energy predicaments and avoid harder choices. Whenever 100 units of fuel have run out, we've sought and found another 100 units, or we've adopted a different kind of fuel to get those 100 units from an alternative source.

The real leverage lay at the consuming end, where the forfeiture of relatively small amounts of energy multiplies into large savings where our biggest problems exist—the source. This is what the Asymmetry Principle teaches us, and this is our real alternative energy source of the future.

I showed how the efficiency stats are dismal. But like the absurd offer I described earlier, we can turn the losses between source energy and consumed work into our greatest opportunity. To do so, we need to start thinking about the causality from the opposite direction that we're accustomed to: from the light bulb toward the coal mine instead of the other way around, from the wheels to the oil well, from the TV set to the wind farm, the furnace to the gas well, and so on.

Looking down a cascading asymmetry diagram like Figure 10.2 a 2 percent end-to-end efficiency from gas-fired power plant to a light bulb is pathetic, but looking at it in reverse the 50-to-1 leverage is spectacular! That means for every unit of energy not used in lighting, 50 units are forfeited at the gas well.

Figure 10.3 highlights the 6-to-1 leverage of not driving. Simply put, saving energy that's equivalent to one barrel of oil at the wheels, translates into six barrels that don't need to be found and produced at the source (often a politically charged source).

Even solar power, a limitless green energy source, is incredibly inefficient. If fact, getting energy from sunlight to the light bulb in your house is the most inefficient of all mainstream processes, because a solar panel is only about 5 percent efficient at the primary conversion stage. Cascading 5 percent efficiency at your electrical socket through a 6 percent efficient light bulb, you get a process that only yields 0.3 units of useful work out of 100 units of exposed sunlight. The multiplier here is over 300 times! While sunlight is admittedly plentiful and free, land required for larger-scale solar farms is not. The more solar energy the consumer end user comes to rely on translates into more land we need for solar farms and other space. But if we can find ways to reduce our energy appetites—especially the amount of energy we consume that serves no useful purpose, for example, unnecessary lighting—the Asymmetry Principle provides a framework of how we can meaningfully cut multiples of that energy at the source, regardless of whether that fuel is green or black.

Looking at all major energy processes in society and ranking the multipliers can serve as a priority list of where the greatest gains can be made. There is not enough space in this chapter to do so, but my purpose here is not to focus on minutiae, rather to stimulate holistic thinking and methodology. In doing so, we will realize that the magnitude of the inefficiencies in our energy supply chains hands us a unique opportunity to manage our renewable and nonrenewable sources. Boosting system efficiencies (with the caveat of controlling wasteful rebound effects), and reducing end use consumption is far more logical, and has much more potential, than just looking for the next 100 units of energy at the source.

Indeed, because there will always be inefficiencies in our energy processes, no technological advances within the energy industry will ever provide us with as much leverage for solving our energy problems as reducing consumption.

Asymmetry on Walden Pond

Perhaps the most introspective place to think about efficiency and the Asymmetry Principle is just down the road from Concord, Massachusetts, cradle of the American Revolution, where lies Walden Pond, a small picturesque body of water that takes little effort to row across. I have visited Walden on a few occasions, most recently in the summer of 2008, taking a moment to consider the experiences of its most famous resident from the past, Henry David Thoreau. A prolific writer, philosopher, and scholar, Thoreau was perhaps one of the first Americans to be concerned about sustainable development of modern society.

In July 1845, Thoreau, determined to experience life like a pioneer, moved into a small shack on bucolic lands owned by fellow author and poet Ralph Waldo Emerson near the shores of Walden Pond. There he set out to conduct a two-year personal experiment in voluntary simplicity, the discipline of shunning wealth and consumption. It was then and there that he wrote his classic book *Walden,* a naturalist manifesto that augmented his many other writings on ecology and environmentalism.

Musing about the direction society was heading and presumably unimpressed with the way nearby Boston and other communities were rapidly developing, Thoreau wrote metaphorically about waste and in-efficiency: "Where the citizen uses a mere sliver or board, the pioneer uses the whole trunk of a tree."[6]

After landing on the shores of Plymouth, those who pioneered America in the seventeenth century were living off the land in such difficult circumstances that they had to conserve their resources and use their materials with utmost efficiency—in other words, they had to make use of the entire tree trunk. Over time, as hardened pioneers became established citizens living in structured templates of towns and villages, society became less mindful of conservation and efficiency.

Today, the template that defines our modern society uses only mere slivers of the energy contained at the source, wasting the rest. I am not suggesting that we all embrace voluntary simplicity or go back and live like pioneers, but it is realistic to think that our pioneering spirit, our amazing ability to innovate and adapt, can help us leverage our foibles and end our energy obesity for the benefit of all who follow us. As you'll see in upcoming chapters, we're now developing technology and behaviors in areas outside the energy realm that will enable us to wrest control of our insatiable energy appetite.

Chapter 11

Beyond Nostalgia

S tudying the Asymmetry Principle shows us that only a small fraction of the primary energy makes it to its intended use and that using less energy at the consumer level mitigates our need many times over for energy at the source. It's a simple and powerful idea, made even more tangible when we compare the rate at which our consumer energy demand is growing against the potential *reduction* in primary energy sources that could be attained if we got our appetites under control.

What strategies can we adopt to exploit this concept? Simply put, if the Asymmetry Principal is the map, how do we get ourselves moving in the right direction? In fact, there are three paths on the solutions map: one of which is well trodden, one that obliges us, and one that is most effective. Here they are in that order.

Path 1: Keep adding more energy. As I discussed in the previous chapter, installing more upstream energy capacity has historically been society's favorite solution. It's worked in the past, but going forward taking this path is not only unimaginative and void of multiplicative benefit, but is highly uncertain as well. At the margin, bringing on more energy upstream—renewable or nonrenewable—requires a tremendous amount of capital on a growing base of consumption. For example, in the fall of 2008, the International Energy Agency estimated that $26 trillion in capital spending will be required to satisfy the world's energy needs by 2030 (that's assuming we continue to tackle our energy problems in this old-school way). The root problem is that upstream energy is an idea-starved industry where the boundaries imposed by the laws of physics make it increasingly difficult to introduce novel systems that demonstrate compelling utility over entrenched infrastructure and processes. Consequently, change is slow to occur, because market penetration rates are low, especially for things that are only marginally better than what is already in place. Despite these criticisms adding more energy at the front end will still be necessary going forward as I will discuss in Chapter 14, particularly for the purpose of changing our energy diet to healthier alternatives. Nevertheless, we can no longer chart this route in isolation.

Path 2: Reduce waste by increasing efficiencies. My asymmetry diagrams showed you the shocking amount of source energy that never gets put to any useful purpose. Concentrating on maximizing the amount of useful work out of our energy conversion devices makes imminent sense; at an absolute minimum, there is moral obligation to be more prudent in the use of our resources. In Thoreau's simple environment, being more efficient meant using more of the tree trunk, rather than just being satisfied with using small splinters and then chopping down more and more trees (which leads us back to Path 1). The urgencies of energy security and climate change are waking us up to the need to make our energy systems more efficient—from power plants to light bulbs. I'll reiterate in the final chapters of this book that it's a path we must take, because with discipline and incentive, small efficiency gains spread across a whole system can lead to multiplicative benefits in reducing our appetite. But this path only works if, as I discussed in Chapter 7, we don't squander those benefits by being wasteful with the work we gain or use the dollar savings from those gains to gorge on other unattended inefficiencies in society.

Path 3: Reduce energy appetite (especially by targeting wasteful consumption). Using fewer splinters means a lot fewer tree trunks need to be cut down. Mitigating consumer demand for energy is where the big leverage lies. For innovators and entrepreneurs it's this last option where things are going to get really interesting over the next 10 years, where break point innovations *outside* the realm of energy will engage society—especially if incentives are presented to pursue this path. In the era we're entering, entangled trends in high technology and societal behaviour are actually expanding our energy options in ways we may not yet grasp.

The Technology Bug

Perhaps you're a gadget person, like me. I've enjoyed the technological changes of the last few decades wholeheartedly. Some might call me a geek or an early adopter. Truth be told, I'm one of those people who occasionally stands in line for the next big thing, buys it when it's still expensive and novel, gladly suffers the pains of installation, and enthusiastically gushes about its potential. In recent years and with varying levels of satisfaction, I've been on the forefront of digital photography, high-speed Internet, high-speed computing, GPS, HDTV, Blackberries and iPhones, Blueray, and Skype, to name but a few. I've had meetings with peers around the world in dedicated telepresence boardrooms that feel like something out of a science fiction movie. I've replaced the furnaces in my house with more energy efficient models and swapped most of the incandescent bulbs in our rooms for CFL lights, some even with LED. I'm equally enthusiastic about old technology. I collect antique light bulbs, ever in search of ones with unique bases or screw-in fixtures, and I own a number of whale oil lamps from the pre-incandescent days. I derive great pleasure marveling at the intersection of creativity and science; especially when their combined magic emerges in the marketplace to meet consumer needs and change lifestyles.

I first came down with the technology bug in 1972, the day my father brought home an electronic calculator. It was a sleek, black Commodore, a little larger than the book in your hands. For me, the LED display was a calming and inviting blue. My father was a budding entrepreneur and he was always bringing paperwork home. We were used to his old, mechanical adding machine, and had grown accustomed to the "chunk-chunk-whir" sound you heard whenever you hit a button. I often helped him with the books but I disdained how the numbers spewed out as washed-out digits on rolled paper. Now, with the calculator on the table before us, my dad and I marveled at how quickly and silently the numbers could be added, subtracted, multiplied, or divided, right there on the narrow screen. We did the work with delight that evening, as if we'd stepped into a new and improved future.

And yet it seemed that it was only a matter of days before the novelty of the new calculator became routine. That's an emotional letdown many will recognize. I no longer felt the tingle of thrill as I flicked it on and saw that blue LED glow. It was as though that minor miracle had always been with us. The books and my father's entrepreneurial adventures were still interesting, but the calculator was now just a tool that I used to accomplish a simple task, no different really than the adding machine, though much quieter and faster. I didn't appreciate its newness anymore; infected by the technology bug, the digital calculator had become an essential and expected part of my life.

Although we've enjoyed many novelties in the past 30 years, hardly noticing the magnitude of the impact along the way, it's worth contemplating the dynamics of embracing new technology. In 1964, science fiction author and futurist Arthur C. Clarke wrote an astonishingly prophetic piece for *Life Magazine,* in which he reflected on technological developments already seen, and outlined the shifts to come. Clarke was a little early in his predictions—that's the danger of such a business—but he was amazingly prescient about the impact satellite communications systems would have on our lives.[1] As he wrote:

> *No one in 1900 could ever have dreamed that the internal combustion engine, via the automobile and the airplane, was about to transform society. Looking beyond the next decade, we can dimly glimpse the shape of another revolution—one not of transportation, but of communication. We can see instantaneous mail delivery and a few planetary newspapers ... flashed on home screens.... Within another 10 or 15 years men at the higher executive levels will be able to do most of their business without stirring from*

their homes. Their personal communications console will incorporate a phone, closed-circuit TV, a datahandling filing unit, and an electronic secretary-computer to deal with appointments, incoming calls, expense accounts and unwelcome clients.[2]

By the late 1970s, satellite television had arrived, the first cellular communications system had been developed by Bell Labs, and personal computers were about to make their way into offices and homes. Today, we can barely imagine a world without such life-altering devices. My generation may be the last one to remember how mainframe computers had to be programmed with punch cards, or to have heard the peculiar, screeching sound of a 14.4kb dial-up modem making a connection. Today we hold tremendous computing power in the palm of our hand every time we scroll through a list of songs, text a message, or take a call, only to be connected silently and effortlessly to an infinite web.

That's the thing about the technology bug, particularly with new electronic devices. As we adopt something that offers more ease, speed, quality, or usefulness, we quickly dispose of our old devices—the slide rule, the clunky record player or Sony Walkman, all those VHS tapes, our worn-out Rolodex, and other relics of past routines. When everybody gets the technology bug we all become infected in a positive manner and change the way we do things—we call this *progress*—and then get seamlessly absorbed into a different way of living, one that typically uses more energy than before.

iPhone versus Prius

We've experienced numerous examples of rapid and widespread adoption of electronic goods over the past 20 years. Digital cameras are now more compelling than film cameras, and considerably cheaper too. Cell phones have become more compelling than landlines. Digital music purchased and played over wireless devices becomes more compelling than music on CDs, which previously supplanted records and tapes. What's more, we're switching to new electronic offerings at an increasingly rapid pace.

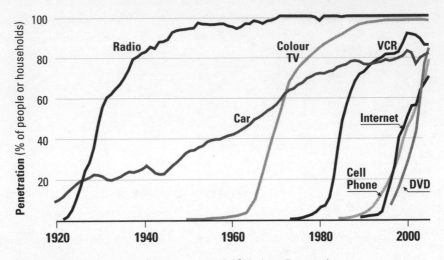

Figure 11.1   U.S. Market Penetration of Various Innovations
SOURCE: ARC Financial Research.

Figure 11.1 shows adoption curves for a number of technologies that have changed our lifestyles over the past 100 years. An adoption curve measures the percentage of individuals or households that buy or adopt a new device; the steeper the market penetration, the faster the rate of adoption in a society.

Starting with radio all the way to DVDs, the "steepness" of high-tech product adoption rates is quickly apparent. Radio made it into most homes in 30 years. Once the color TV bug infected consumers' imaginations in the early 1960s, it only took 20 years before 90 percent of all households in America had one. Moving closer to recent history, VCRs, cell phones, Internet connections, and DVD players all became ubiquitous within 10 to 15 years. That's the way it is now: new, irresistible, compelling high-tech products take the market with all guns blazing in 10 years or less. An individual product like Apple's iPhone (with compelling improvements over traditional cell phones including a touch screen, an accelerometer, GPS, and 3G web browsing), grabbed 1.1 percent of the worldwide cell phone market in only 18 months.

Now compare the adoption rate of the iPhone with the Toyota Prius. The patent for a hybrid engine design was first filed in 1974. In 1994, Toyota engineers began to look at ways to use those ideas to develop a car that was highly fuel efficient and environmentally friendly. Much of the hard work of making such a technology practical centered around the challenge of developing a battery that had a sufficiently long life span. In 1997, the Prius was released in Japan. In 2001, it was sold in the United States and around the world. By 2008, one million Prius cars had been sold globally, 60 percent of those in North America. Socially, the Prius has made a significant mark—its adoption symbolizes that we can alter the paradigm of obese gasoline-consuming cars. In terms of market share, however, the Prius only amounts to 0.25 percent of the 230 million U.S. vehicle fleet after 12 years. Hybrids in general have only penetrated 0.40 percent over the same period; a complete market failure by high-tech standards.

Why so slow? The advantages of a hybrid seem obvious in the context of the triple threat to our way of life: environmental challenges, high gasoline costs, and concerns about energy security. But while the hybrid represents a reasonable advance in fuel economy (1.5 times better than a car of equivalent size and weight), to the average driver it isn't significantly different than a regular car on other dimensions, and most notably a hybrid is more expensive. William Davidow, in his book, *Marketing High Technology*,[3] named a whole chapter "Slightly Better is Dangerous," meaning that to succeed, new products must be significantly different than what is already in the marketplace, and no more expensive on top of it all. The Prius may look cool, demonstrate social responsibility, and have lots of cultural cachet. But if a hybrid could deliver five times the fuel economy, drive three times the range, and put out twice the horsepower of a standard vehicle—and be two-thirds the price—then it would start to sell like an iPhone.

The fundamental problem with new energy technologies today is that they are only slightly better than what's already out there. New high-tech products, on the other hand, are constantly demonstrating tantalizingly superior performance and utility with each successive generation. An important question follows: where should we be looking for faster solutions to our energy problems?

Nostalgic Innovation

It's worthwhile to further explore the pace of change in the high-tech world versus the pace of change in the energy industry, because it highlights the low leverage that we have by placing too much emphasis on Path 1 (Keep adding more energy). I had yet another reminder of that disconnect in the summer of 2008 when I traveled to the Cape Cod area with my family. Of course, all our reservations for flights, ferries, rental car, and accommodations were made online. We picked up a car in Boston, plugged our destination into the GPS system, and headed out. (Actually, I miss unfolding a map and plotting a course, but GPS is so compellingly convenient, helpful, and available that it's almost impossible to avoid using—a point that's germane to this chapter.) Late in the morning, we took the ferry to Nantucket Island, where fishermen once sailed floating factories to harvest the sperm whale for its illuminating oil. It was a great day for a walk, so we set out for the Old Mill on the hill above town (see Figure 11.2).

There was a tour guide on-site, but I took the initiative to pull up information off the Web with my iPhone. An early example of our energy evolution, the mill was built in 1746 by a Nantucket sailor who'd studied the technology in places like Holland. It was 50 feet high, could be rotated to align with the direction of the wind, and had a simple system of wooden cogs and teeth to grind corn and grain. Impressed by this still-functioning device, I was at the same time struck by how little our energy technology has changed in the interim centuries. Today's monolithic steel and carbon fiber turbines, elegant and beautiful in their own way, are far more efficient in the work they do. However, the concept of harnessing wind to do work, for all the sleekness and the computer-power behind it, hasn't changed that much since 800 A.D., when the first windmills were reported in Persia.

Indeed, these days it almost seems as if the energy industry is experiencing a sentimental bout of nostalgia. We're putting sails on large freighter ships as though we were back in the days before steam. We're assessing the economics of turning coal into oil or gas, even though such refining of coal was developed in the 1920s and used by oil-poor Germany and Japan during World War II. We're becoming enamored by biofuels that were popular in the early days of motorcars. We're resurrecting the electric car, another echo of the distant past; the highly anticipated Chevy Volt is expected to be launched in 2010—a date that will mark nearly a century since Henry Ford eclipsed the electric vehicle industry with his more compelling Model T. We're switching our incandescent bulbs for compact fluorescents—devices that are only a coiled

Figure 11.2   The Old Mill on Nantucket Island

version of a fluorescent lamp developed by GE in the 1930s, itself based on innovations made by Peter Cooper Hewitt in 1901. We're putting radiant heating under our floors, but that only brings to mind the luxury promoted by Gaius Orata in Ancient Rome.

I'm not suggesting at all that reverting to past processes is a bad thing, especially if the revived and improved utility justifies the comeback. I'm only highlighting that the scope of thinking and innovation in energy technology is confined to a fairly limited box. On the other hand, the high-tech realm, with its compounding pace of innovation, is still very much open-ended and set to change our lives in ways that we will quickly take for granted. Break point innovations and moments, like those experienced in the days of Ford and Edison, are imminent yet again. And this time we'll be given the opportunity to break the First Principle, not perpetuate it.

If new high-tech innovations are channeled creatively, under ripe circumstances, then radically new products and processes can be developed to take advantage of the third and most powerful path mapped out by the asymmetry principle: cutting consumption, especially the wasteful type. Let's look at a handful of some relevant nonenergy trends.

Four Nonenergy Energy Trends

You may not find the following trends particularly new or enlightening. My list is far from complete, and if you are even somewhat technically oriented the discussion is going to sound cursory. You can read plenty of other books, blogs, and publications about the dizzying advances being made in countless other areas of science and technology, including but hardly limited to nanotechnology, biotechnology, material science, and wireless communications. My main purpose here is to continue giving you a flavor of the incredible pace of change in the high-tech world, which is measured in orders of magnitude, not mere multiples. Also, consider the following discussion a rudimentary primer to get you thinking about what new lifestyle-changing products can emerge as a consequence of the convergence of these trends. Then in the following two chapters, I'll give you a futuristic peek to show how these trends can significantly change our energy paradigm.

The Internet Talks to Itself

If you haven't noticed, today's Internet is different from even a few years ago. Our understanding of what works and what doesn't on the Web has become more sophisticated, and many new systems, programs, and ways of communicating have evolved to capitalize on that awareness. That second generation of the Internet is often referred to as Web 2.0—and it largely involves enhancements that improve human-to-human communication frameworks. Sharing is the mantra of Web 2.0. Instead of providing all the content and data like a television production channel provides a complete broadcast, Web 2.0 applications give us the ability to share and distribute content, evolve networks and knowledge, and expand the way we interact socially and economically. Facebook, eBay, YouTube, Craigslist, PayPal, Wikipedia, Blogware, NING, and even iTunes are among the businesses, services, or software accelerating collaboration, social networking, and peer-to-peer commerce.

All of that is very exciting, and the potential for new businesses, services, and networks to proliferate and serve mass market demands is probably limitless. But there is another iteration of the Internet on the imminent horizon. To date, the Internet has largely been a medium that facilitates human-to-human interaction. The next step will be human-to-device and device-to-device interaction.

Fundamentally, human-to-device interaction is nothing new. Every time we flick on a light bulb, we're interacting with a device. The electrical system behind the light bulb awaits our input and instructions: on/off. An extension to that rudimentary power is the ability to control a light bulb from our computer or cell phone. That's possible today. In fact, the technology to remotely control all sorts of appliances, devices, and alarm systems using cell phones or computers already exists.

All computers and related devices that are connected to the Internet have a unique internet protocol, or IP, address. Now devices are starting to get unique IP addresses, too. Though it's going to take time for standardization to occur, appliances like refrigerators, stoves, lighting tracks, video cameras, and furnaces will be accessible through their IP addresses. Once you know the digital address of a device, you can communicate with it through a computer or handheld device. What's more, devices with digital IP addresses can also learn to communicate with each other through computers. This means you will be able to instruct your air conditioner or stove to modulate its energy consumption, and your air conditioner and stove will be able to talk to each other too, to optimally balance energy use in your home (perhaps they can complain about you as much as you complain about them). In the near future "smart" homes and buildings, and all the smart appliances within will be able to "think" about how to save energy and get that 50x leverage from the Asymmetry Principle when you don't.

A Superhighway with 500 Lanes

In mid-2008, I was told that the number of downloads of YouTube videos had reached a billion per month and was growing exponentially. What makes that number even more staggering is that an average 10MB YouTube video contains as much digital information as a thousand text-only e-mails, and the ratio is growing with progressively higher video resolution.

Thankfully, bandwidth, or the capacity to transmit all those videos and movies, is growing at a staggering pace, too. There are potential problems with this growth, most notably congestion. Nevertheless, history tells us that the ability to transmit more and more information—whether by cable, optic fiber, or the wireless ether—has been able to keep up with demand. In fact, the more bandwidth we get access to, the more we fill it up. That's analogous to the rebound effect of building bigger freeways—more lanes do not alleviate congestion but typically invites more traffic.

The growth trend in transmission capacity, shown in Figure 11.3, is striking. In fact, it's so rapid that I've had to plot the bandwidth data on a logarithmic scale, where every vertical increment grows by 10 times. What the straight line broadly reveals is that bandwidth has been

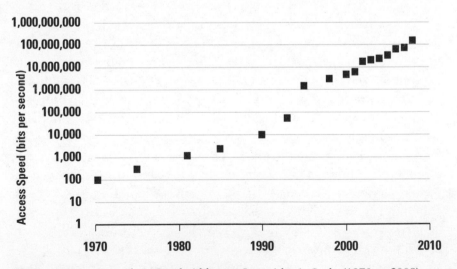

Figure 11.3   Growth in Bandwidth on a Logarithmic Scale (1970 to 2008)
SOURCE: ARC Financial Research, Cedarville University.

increasing at an uninterrupted, exponential rate (a linear trend on a log scale is exponential on a uniform one).

This fantastic growth in our ability to transmit more and more digital information is described in the literature as Nielsen's law, which states that the speed at which bits of data can be transferred to a high-end user is growing by 50 percent a year. In the mid-1990s, we used to call the system of wires and optical fibers the "information highway." If the Internet were a physical highway, a four-lane road constructed in 1994 would be almost 6,000 lanes wide in 2012!

Nobody lent their name to a mathematical law describing the rapid proliferation of roads, highways, and freeways in the twentieth century, but the resultant network of streets, avenues, and interstates has provided anyone with a car the freedom and ability to access anyone else attached to the system. Much as that has radically changed the way we live, Chapter 13 shows that the growth in digital highways will create a new outlet for "meeting" with others—one that actually has the potential to partially obsolesce asphalt and the car.

Moore's Law Does a Teraflop

Doing a single computation on my dad's first calculator seemed lightning fast. Thirty years later, that execution seems snail-paced. It's well-known that the general rule of thumb for improvements in computational power was first observed by Gordon Moore, one of the cofounders of Intel, in 1965. Moore conjectured that the complexity of integrated circuits, which are the building blocks of computers, would continue to double every year without an increase in component costs. By 1975, Moore's formulation was adjusted slightly. The relationship was lowered to a doubling of complexity (and, in particular, speed) every two years while size and cost are cut in half over the same period. This new formulation has proven true for over 30 years. Though the technological approaches to enhancement are changing, the computer industry's ability to deliver products that can process numbers at twice the speed every 24 months shows every sign of continuing. And digital memory capacity is growing by approximately the same rate too.

Extrapolating Moore's trend, in the next five to ten years computer-processing power will pack eight to sixteen times more capacity. People that I have spoken to in Silicon Valley confidently tell me that early next decade personal computers will routinely be able to crunch over one trillion numbers per second, or one *teraflop*. To understand the significance of that number, you should know that supercomputers used for tasks like predicting weather patterns and simulating nuclear explosions only broke through the teraflop barrier in 1996. Of course, we don't need a teraflop of processing power to write e-mails, deliver PowerPoint presentations, or shop on eBay. Instead, expanded bandwidth and faster computing components will enable us to experience breakthroughs in things like two-way video.

To transmit high-quality interactive video, massive amounts of information need to be processed in real time with specialized graphical processing. If you want to preserve the fine resolution that makes an HD image look so real, you need more computing horsepower. The ability to do that in real time has already taken a step-jump. Breaking the teraflop barrier will turn high definition and even finer transmissions into everyday miracles.

I bought my big screen LCD panel TV because I couldn't resist the clarity and size of the images. The transmission of high definition images to come will make my LCD panel seem as though we're shifting from the age of black and white TV to the age of living color. Soon you will be able to walk into a room in your house and see a wall-sized unprojected screen that looks so real you will feel as though you are in the presence of interactive images on the other side. Your mother, your client, or your favorite football team will be standing in front of you, reacting in real time. At the moment, the prospect of such technology is tantalizing and cool; in the not-too-distant future it will change the way we live and redefine how we use "transport" ourselves.

The Plugged-In Nervous System

We live through our five senses. Sight, touch, smell, hearing, and taste are the ways in which the human nervous system interacts with and understands the world outside our bodies. Increasingly our physical surroundings are developing a nervous system too. In addition, we are developing the capability to plug our own nervous systems into devices and virtual landscapes.

Have you noticed that some things can react to our presence? Rudimentary sensors and motion detectors have long been put to use in energy saving ways. In public restrooms for example, it's often the case that toilets flush after you leave, taps turn on, and driers dispense paper towels or warm air automatically when they sense our presence. In some public places, especially in Europe, room or hallway lights only go on when a sensor detects our motion.

Great strides have been made in low-cost, practical sensors in the last decade, driven largely by the security industry. It's just the start; many different sensing devices will become mainstream in homes, offices, appliances, and devices in the near future.

Small, ultrasensitive sensors are already allowing us to become more integrated with our gadgets too. Nowhere is this more obvious than in the latest generation of smart phones. Aside from "hearing," with its basic telephone function a smart phone today can sense touch on its touch screen, precisely sense the magnitude and direction of your movements with its accelerometers, recognize your voice commands and the name of a musical tune you may be listening to, "see" with its built-in camera, and on top of it all know exactly where you are and where you are going with its GPS receiver. Smart phones have yet to taste and smell, but no doubt those things are in the works too.

The list of new-generation sensors and their applications is long, but the point is that we are on a path to be able to interact with devices, and they will interact with us and with themselves in ways that put the "real" into virtual reality. In the simplest applications, sensors will be able tell us when we're wasting energy; in later evolutions they will be able to reduce the waste without us even knowing it.

A Car Is Still a Car

An important thing to think about when seeking novel solutions to our energy problems by improving energy technologies or developing new energy alternatives is that such measures do not change consumer behavior. A hybrid car is still a car. The compact fluorescent light bulb still lights our rooms or offices—and is probably still being left on hours longer than necessary. A new, greener power plant is still generating electricity. Right now, our energy obese lifestyles are being supported by new energy technologies, not changed by them. Most in North America still drive in a car through traffic to work in a large office tower, shop at mega grocery stores loaded with produce, and live in large houses in the suburbs.

In dramatic contrast, new electronic devices have shown their ability to transform our lives very quickly and thoroughly. Two decades ago, you still needed spare change in your pocket to use the phone. Good luck finding a telephone booth on any big city street now. Two decades ago, unless you were a shortwave radio ham or a serial postcard writer, your network of friends was limited to the people you interacted with physically on a regular basis. Now you can exchange messages and updates more or less constantly with people all over the world through services like Facebook. Even a decade ago, long-distance calls were expensive; now when I'm traveling on business, I see and talk to my family on Skype for free.

Because of radical advances in a wide scope of technologies—computing, telecommunications, and information to name a few—we now connect differently, shop differently, get our news differently, play games differently, schedule our lives differently, find ourselves on a map differently, and hang out with friends and work differently. Societies around the world are being radically altered and it seems we've barely noticed the shifts. And yet the potential impact of those changes on our energy appetite is enormous, because such technologies are changing the way we live, work, and play, just like the light bulb and car did a century ago.

Chapter 12

Conservation 2.0

Whenever I travel, whether on business or with my family, I'm drawn to local antique shops to see what energy-related collectibles I can find on some dusty shelf or in the dark corners of a creaky back room. In 2006, on a narrow street in Stockholm, Sweden, a strange device in a shop window caught my eye. I couldn't immediately identify it, but I knew it had something to do with a candle. Stepping inside to speak with the proprietor, I learned that the device was an automatic candle snuffer from the eighteenth century. Here, I thought, is one of the earliest examples of an energy conservation device. We struck a deal and I walked back to my hotel with a new treasure (see Figure 12.1).

As an energy-consuming device, candles have been very successful. For many centuries, they were the primary means of illumination throughout the world. Cheaper candles of past centuries were made from rendered animal fat or tallow, and they burned with a weak light while sputtering grease and giving off dirty, foul-smelling smoke. Higher quality candles were made from beeswax or spermicetti. They were

Figure 12.1   Eighteenth-Century Automatic Candle Snuffer

sweet-smelling, relatively smokeless, and provided bright and pleasant light, but were also quite a bit more expensive.

The good candles, then, were not something to waste. Unless your wealth was bottomless, you didn't burn them indiscriminately. And yet candles have a quiet way of melting down to nothing without being noticed. You can picture a merchant's wife in the 1800s reading a Jane Austen novel or the latest issue of *Punch Magazine*, and dozing off to sleep, only to wake up and find that the expensive beeswax candle (because, seriously, who can stand the smell of tallow on a pillow?) has melted all the way down to the brass holder.

That's where my automatic candle snuffer came in. The pewter device could be clamped onto the neck of a candle, a desired distance below the wick (left photo in Figure 12.1). When the candle burned down to that level, gravity acted on a mechanical lever that could no longer be held up by solid wax and the snuffer swung down to put out the flame (right photo). The merchant's wife could drift off to sleep, secure in the knowledge that the expensive candle would be there in the morning, a little shorter, but preserved.

I don't know who invented the automatic candle snuffer, and I don't know the degree to which its technology caught on. I haven't noticed any references to the device in any books about candles or candleholders. But I suspect that, based on the economics of candles, it would have been a sound investment. The owner of such a contraption would be able to conserve a relatively high-cost fuel without much effort or thought.

On our own, without automatic devices, human beings have proven themselves to be woefully poor conservers of energy. Though our intentions are often good, the effort of paying conscious attention to the dwindling candle seems to be too great for our distracted brains to handle. We like to take our energy sources for granted, largely because they are cheap. In times of scarcity or high prices, when we have to carefully ration or conserve fuel, we feel a sense of constriction and discomfort. We'd rather enter the house, turn on all the lights, turn up the heat, flick on the electric gadgets, and bask in the splendid glow, even if that means forgetting to turn off all those switches when we enter another room. This behavior seems so common I can only call it human nature. Anyone who has children knows how difficult it can be to get them to turn off a light, close a refrigerator, or shut the front door. It seems that no amount of haranguing, threatening, or rewarding can make them change easily.

It's for such simple human reasons therefore, that conserving energy is quite difficult. In the 1970s, when oil prices soared, we adopted the behaviors of conservation, individually and collectively, but as soon as the pressure of scarcity, high price, and regulatory restrictions lessened, we rushed back to the comforts of wanton and thoughtless energy consumption. Most of the long-term plans that could have eased or prevented future crises were summarily abandoned. This on-again-off-again energy dieting is a dynamic I call Conservation 1.0.

That's why the automatic candle snuffer, or its twenty-first century equivalent, is a necessity going forward.

The Resurrection of Personal Virtue

When Vice President Dick Cheney dismissed conservation as a "personal virtue" in 2001, he was alluding to the fact that few of us, absent forceful economic or regulatory reasons, willingly participate in such altruistic efforts. Without high prices to drive our conservational efforts, most of us metaphorically forgot to turn off the lights and close the front door throughout the 1990s. Indeed, we bought bigger houses, more gadgets, and larger cars—as though cheap oil was never going to run out, and the environment could withstand any amount of emissions. In contrast, Japan and a number of developed nations in Europe kept a measure of regulatory and price pressure and prevented energy consumption from rising as steeply.

Most nations need to do better than the on-again-off-again conservation approaches of the 1970s. An energy diet will not stick if we constantly long for foods that are tantalizingly available. We need awareness and information about costs and benefits to make the right decisions. We need other, healthier alternatives to be more appealing than what we're used to. And we need automation, incentives, and a measure of policy to help support those better approaches and turn them into everyday habits. Because of the technological trends I discussed in the previous chapter, we now have the ability to use energy far more intelligently—and virtuously. That's what Conservation 2.0 is about.

A Price for Everything

When American gasoline prices rose above $4.00 a gallon in 2008, some people started hypermiling, vanpooling, or taking public transit. It's true: whether it's a gallon of gas, a carton of eggs, a song on iTunes, or a tank of heating oil, consumers respond to changes in price.

One of the problems with electricity consumption, especially in North America, is that individual consumers seldom ever know the price. Electricity streams into the house through a box tucked away in the utility room. We plug our many devices—refrigerators, TVs, coffeemakers, exercise machines—into the wall sockets, and have almost no knowledge of what costs more or less to operate. We may get a monthly bill for the aggregate electricity we consume in the home but we don't know when prices were high or low, and any association between the amount of electricity we consumed and what we did to consume it is tenuous at best. That's especially the case if you're on a direct deposit plan where the utility automatically withdraws from your bank account without you really knowing when or how much. Most people don't bother to read their statement details—they just breathe with relief or frown with dismay depending on the number.

In 1984, when I was a graduate student in England, I lived in a small flat where I had to buy electricity credits manually whenever I wanted to turn something on. This was done through a small coin-operated meter mounted behind a hinged panel in the wall. A 50 pence coin (worth about $0.70 back then) would credit the little dial on the meter with enough electricity to buy a day's worth of lighting, refrigeration, and TV. For the first time in my life, I became truly aware of my electricity use. If I was cooking on the electric stove, I could watch the meter run down like water from a leaky bucket and became conscious of every coin the meter needed. If I forgot to plug the meter and was out of change, I would need to run down to the pub on the corner and order a beer. (Not a bad excuse for a grad student.) Dropping those coins into the slot of that meter made me smarter—or at least more informed—about my energy use.

Though the character of the electrical current and the scale of distribution have changed dramatically, the basic premise has been the same for 125 years. The grid delivers electrons to our homes, offices, factories, and places of entertainment. Those electrons don't carry any information about how much they cost or what kind of power station they came from or what to do if there's no need for them. But that system is about to change.

Imagine if we could put a bar code on electrons that delivered us information as well as electricity. By doing so we'd learn some interesting things; first and foremost, we'd discover that not all electricity is created equal. For one thing, its price is highly variable throughout a 24-hour cycle.

When we wake up in the morning, flick on the lights, turn on the coffeemaker, put bread in the toaster, turn on the TV, and blow-dry our hair, our use of power starts rising. Then we go to work, turning on office lights and factory machinery. In the evening when we come home from work, turn on all the appliances, open and close the refrigerator door repeatedly, and throw the laundry in the dryer, we're using more power collectively than we do in the middle of the night when consumption is limited to streetlights and late-night TV.

In general, the high consumption hours in a city are between 7:00 A.M. and 7:00 P.M. with peak electricity demand occurring just before noon. Simple economics tells us that electricity should cost more when demand is highest, especially if supply is constrained. Yet, 125 years after Edison's grid, we in North America still don't differentiate between high and low periods of energy demand. By virtue of tradition and long-standing regulation, the price of electricity doesn't change other than for heavy industrial users. Instead, we pay a flat fee regardless of time of day.

However, new technologies, wired and wireless, are now making it possible to transmit real-time price information about the electrical energy to consumers. This is a big component of "smart energy" or the "intelligent grid." Market penetration is in the very early stages, but gaining momentum. In British Columbia, Canada, a pilot program has been in place since 2007, where smart meters have been installed in homes, allowing people to know how much electricity they are consuming at different times during the day. In a province where electricity is cheap enough to breed apathy, the average reduction in household electricity at the test sites was still an impressive 10 percent. In Britain, a plan is being developed to install 46 million gas and electricity smart meters in every home in the nation, and in the United States, Boulder, Colorado is set to become a "Smart Grid City," with $100 million worth of new technology.

You can actually go buy such a meter yourself from the local hardware store. I bought one myself, made by Black and Decker, for around $80. An external sensing device that attaches to our home's electrical meter transmits our consumption data to a small receiver, about half the size of this book, that mounts anywhere inside. I punched in our local electricity rate and the display turns kilowatt-hours into dollars and cents. Now I can point out to my kids what we pay in real time—especially when all the lights get carelessly left on.

Once such meters are in place, awareness about electricity consumption is raised. Then the next step will be to allow utilities to charge more during peak periods and less during times of reduced demand. "Dynamic pricing" is not really a technological barrier today, but a regulatory or policy hurdle. The technology is not really the hurdle, but can we break out of entrenched templates and invest in new ones? It's likely we'll need leadership, education, more crises, or all of the above to motivate the shift. Once that happens, however, consumers will be able to make individual decisions about how much they value their electricity. Remember when long-distance telephone prices varied widely depending on the day of the week or time of the day? That knowledge affected telephone calling habits. Similarly, with dynamic power pricing, it's likely that you'll be operating your washing machine late at night, when power demand is low, not during dinner when it's high. You'll be turning off unneeded lights and appliances. You might actually get out the instruction manual and set your central air system to power down when you're not home during the day. You'll be motivated to do so because doing nothing will mean that you're throwing money away.

Knowing the price of anything is key to understanding its value and making decisions about usage. It works for gasoline; it will work for electricity too.

Clever Homes

One of the simplest, and most intriguing, devices that has become available is an energy orb, an oblong piece of plastic that looks like an escaped bubble from a lava lamp.[1] The idea behind this device was first articulated in 1995 by the head of research at Xerox PARC (Palo Alto Research Center), who described a new principle called "calm technology."[2] The premise was that digital information, which we receive through computers, e-mails, cell phones, television screens, and so on, is so intrusive, ubiquitous, and frenetic that it can numb our perceptions and cloud our decision-making ability. Calm technology interprets the data storm for us, allowing us to physically feel or view information and thus understand it more intuitively. The researchers at PARC weren't sure how calm technology would be used, but they knew that there were many potential applications.

Around 2001, a company called Ambient Devices developed an orb that they programmed to react to information about stock prices. Anyone who has ever worked in front of a stock quote machine or traded online knows how all-absorbing and yet distracting and confusing (and stressful) value fluctuations can be. The data is difficult to absorb on an intuitive level and yet you feel caught up in each uptick or downtick. The Ambient Orb makes soaking up data a calmer experience. You no longer need to pay attention to each number—each flying bit of data—but can instead watch the orb out of the corner of your eye for simple changes in color. When your stock portfolio is increasing in value, the color stays green. When prices drop the color shifts to purple. That's when you know you need to look up from your other work and pay attention.

The orb can be programmed to interpret any kind of fluctuating information—the weather forecast, polling data, the playoff chances of your favorite sports team. In 2006, a programming engineer working for California Edison hacked an orb and reconfigured it to interpret energy consumption relative to energy prices.[3] He had become frustrated with the ineffectiveness of various direct means for informing customers to dial back their energy consumption during peak times. Text messages, e-mails, and automated phone calls didn't work. The energy orb, on the other hand, was a big success. When energy loads were at a peak, and customers were consuming too much energy, the orb glowed red, which encouraged customers to make some kind of immediate change, turning off appliances, lights, or air conditioning units until the orb's color returned to a calmer green.

Smart meters, while more technical than energy orbs or other ambient devices, allow us to make more precise decisions about our home energy use. When I think of the potential of smart meters, I think of how much easier it is to record television programs today compared to 20 years ago. In the late 1980s and much of the 1990s most of us used video cassette recorders (VCRs) to watch movies or record television programs. Remember the blue "00:00" time flashing on the VCR display? That was the default setting the VCR time display reverted to after it was unplugged or the power went out. That blinking string of zeroes was symbolic of the gap between the promise of easy TV recordings and the reality of VCR use. We should have been able to program our VCRs to record TV shows and movies whenever we wanted, but even resetting the clock was a nuisance. For many, it was simply too complicated or time-consuming to dig out the instruction manual, get down on their knees, and hit the cryptic sequence of buttons.

DVD-R players were a little more intelligent, in that their clocks reset automatically. Digital video recorders (DVRs)—or personal video recorders (PVRs) attached to satellite or cable—on the other hand, have given TVs an IQ; digital signals deliver the program content, as well as information that is captured in easy-to-access menus about shows and schedules. In fact, over time, some DVRs can learn your recording preferences and actively seek out shows you might like. Its ability to do so accurately can be surprising. Through all that, DVRs allow you to get control of your viewing habits and not waste time watching commercials and crummy shows. "Get control" and "not waste"—sounds like things that can be applied to energy obesity, no?

The thermostats in some old houses are reminiscent of the recording abilities of VCRs. The interface is not intuitive. Setting times for the heat or air conditioning to go on or off is complicated and time-consuming. Similarly, programming lighting systems to go on or off at set times is something that most of us can't be bothered to do because the steps involved are too cumbersome and there is no price motivation anyway. In contrast, smart meters are like DVRs, offering a simple and intuitive digital interface to monitor and control energy expenditure in the home. Climate and lighting times can be easily scheduled. Every energy-consuming device in the home can be monitored for the amount and cost of the electricity used. Energy use can be tracked over a period of time. Homeowners can get automated tips for ways to improve energy efficiency and apply those ideas with the tap of a screen.[4] Currently in the United States, there are only about 500,000 smart meters in use. It will take a committed effort on the part of utilities and policymakers to get smart meters into as many as 50 million homes within the next five years, which is the desired objective some experts are talking about.

What's really interesting is that the kind of monitoring and feedback that smart meters provide can help prevent us from the direct and indirect rebound effects I discussed in Chapter 7. In other words, if we've made the effort to assess, monitor, and save energy we'll be less likely to squander.

Working in tandem with smart meters are smart appliances and the mechanisms by which these energy-consuming devices communicate with each other. One of the biggest problems with the rise of electronic gadgets and appliances is the tremendous amount of collective energy they consume. What's worse, much of that energy is being consumed when our appliances and gadgets are providing no useful work. Every computer, television, or cell phone recharger siphons electricity, even when not in use; just go around your house and count all the little red, green, or blue LED lights that are on—all the way from your toothbrush charger to your PVR. It's estimated that between 5 and 10 percent of a household's electricity consumption is now attributable to phantom load or leaking electricity, and that percentage is growing. Add up all the trickles of electricity from vampire gadgets ranging from refrigerators to the base chargers of electric toothbrushes and you have the equivalent of a garden hose of power turned on 24 hours a day, gushing water into the street from every hosuse in the neighborhood. If each of the 112 million households in the United States could cut their phantom load in half it would save 44 billion kWh of electrical energy in a year. Now run that number backwards up the asymmetry principle and it works out to the equivalent of 12 million tons of coal or 79 billion cubic feet of natural gas that Americans wouldn't need to burn every year.[5]

The "One Watt Initiative," sponsored by the International Energy Agency in Paris, is pushing for all appliances manufactured by the year 2010 to reduce stand-by power use to a single watt. Soon we'll be buying appliances and gadgets that sip energy when needed rather than spill it all the time. In addition, those devices will be able to communicate with a smart meter in a home to modulate energy consumption without our intervention. We'll provide the instructions, probably through a web page that directs traffic in our networked home, and our fridge, kettle, and blow-dryer will do all the monitoring and work.

Human behavior is mostly unreliable. Even when presented with clear signals from smart meters and smart appliances, we're still likely to be lazy, inconsistent, or distracted about our energy use. But smarter sensors communicating with each other can supplement new behaviors and overcome our natural tendency to consume energy unnecessarily. In the not too distant future, by marrying sensors and network technology, our dwellings and workplaces will come alive with the ability to automatically control and optimize energy consumption.

Traditional sensors leave something to be desired. If you've ever waved your hands impatiently in front of a public restroom tap to make the water flow, you know what I mean. Sensors that light up a room after motion is detected can be similarly annoying. You only need to sit on the couch and pause for a few minutes with a book before you're suddenly blinded by the dark. Because of such inconveniences, few of us install or keep using the sensor systems in our homes or workplaces.

New generation sensors on the other hand, will be able to do much more. Special tags in our clothes can be preprogrammed with our personal characteristics and inform sensors of our presence and needs as soon as we enter a room. If that's not appealing (or your tag ends up in the washing machine), other types of sensors will be able to detect voice, face, body shape, gait, temperature, and exhaled carbon dioxide. In short, the room will know who you are and "learn" what you like and don't like.

These sensors will communicate with the gadgets and appliances, adjusting them to our particular needs: more light, less heat, the TV on, the computer off. At one level, none of this is different than the "Clapper" we once used to turn lights on and off. But sensor technology and device-to-device communication is approaching a level of utility that will make such integration seamless and comfortable, offering us a much leaner template for consuming energy. It's early to say how much leaner, but discussions that I've had with industry experts suggest that 20 percent reductions are realistic. The beauty of being able to sense, measure, and control is that targets can be set, and lightweight control is the key to reducing energy obesity.

Of course the thinking need not stop at the household level. Smart grids and networked homes, notwithstanding security considerations, can be expanded to the neighborhood level and up. During times of heavy electrical usage, utilities could call on networked homes to dial down their power consumption by a few percentage points. Asked through the smart grid, your system could intelligently decide where in the home and how much consumption can be sacrificed, probably without you even knowing or feeling it.

You may think that all this is science fiction, but it's not. Innovative high-tech companies and utilities are working on such systems for new homes and buildings, and also for easy retrofit into existing ones. If I told you 10 years ago that a computer would be choosing your movies and music and delivering them to your home without a plastic case you would have scoffed then too.

Combine all this awareness, potential automation, and new behaviors with smart appliances, green building standards, and an intelligent grid, and we'll soon be living and consuming energy differently than before—while feeling as though the day of *The Jetsons* has finally arrived.

Smarter Roads, Too

Outside of the house, when concerned people worry about conserving energy, they think about transportation—especially gasoline-powered cars. But to tackle our car problems, most of the hyped attention has been directed to the kind of fuel our engines use, or the type of engines. I've already shown you in Chapter 10 that improving well-to-wheels efficiency is tough, and that realizing big gains in the entrenched vehicle fleets of the world are going to take many, many years. Not to say it shouldn't be done, but it's a slow moving rate of change.

Again, technologies that are exogenous to the energy or auto industries can help improve well-to-wheel efficiencies faster, though by how much has yet to be quantified. But the numbers are potentially big, because in the United States, where gasoline consumption is 400 million gallons a day, even a 1 percent improvement in well-to-wheels efficiency—from 17 percent to 18 percent—can potentially save 22 million gallons of gasoline from the refinery every day, courtesy of the asymmetry principle.

For example, just as a smart grid can help us smooth load levels and optimize energy use, a smarter road system can help us smooth out traffic congestion and improve fuel economy by avoiding the tap dance between the accelerator and the brake. It's already happening. Awareness of traffic patterns and the resulting optimization of traffic flows show a lot of promise. Big Brother can see and control more than we think with video systems that monitor flows and manage lights. But that's not all; in many areas we're now able to foresee congestion on our GPS enabled devices, including our smart phones, and take advantageous time- and fuel-saving detours.

Transportation engineering is a huge subject and there is no way that I can do it justice in this chapter. But I don't really need to, because what's most important to recognize here is that new-age technologies (that have nothing to do with energy) are triggering behavioral change that's helping to reduce fuel consumption. That dynamic is where the leverage lies.

A Future That's Already Here

Ten years ago, the advances I've described in this chapter would have seemed like science fiction. Now, RFID (radio-frequency identification) tracking tags, sophisticated sensors, wireless networks, congestion detection, and smart meters are everyday commodities we barely notice. But these and other innovations are also starting to provide us with awareness of energy use, feedback about prices, and enough automation to change our behaviors in ways that can reduce energy consumption in a meaningful quantity and time frame.

Though sci-fi technologies are seductive, what I've really started talking about in this chapter is how new break point innovations outside the world of energy have the potential to aid in the reduction of energy at the social level. Conservation 2.0 will work by leveraging off the gadgets and systems that are already painlessly weaving their collective way into our lives. We're embracing them, adopting them, and being changed by them because we like how they make our lives easier and more comfortable.

Were they alive, Ford and Edison would have been pleased.

Chapter 13

Dissolving Distance

There wasn't much question, when I was growing up in the 1970s, about where to live. If you had a certain middle-class income and family structure—and there were many tens of millions of us across North America—then you resided in the suburbs. Urban neighborhoods weren't appealing for a number of complicated reasons. I'm sure crime statistics and perceptions about lack of space had a lot to do with it, but the best deal for your real estate dollar was offered in subdivisions beyond the inner city core. For a reasonable price you could get a nice-sized home with a garage and a yard, amidst many other similar families in the same neighborhood. Even in Canada, it was the epitome of the American Dream.

Yet we know from Part I of this book that the American Dream constitutes a template of energy consumption that demands at least 60 BPY, and that a significant contributor to that obesity are the intertwined issues of car dependency and sprawling suburbanization. In this chapter I will explore how a seemingly rigid societal template like the modern North American city, with all its freeways and cars, may be redefined without moving a single building, conserving large amounts of oil in the process. Distance can be dissolved well beyond the boundaries of cities too, lessening the need for air travel and jet fuel.

The North American suburb, as a modern phenomenon, started in the 1920s as skyscrapers rose and pushed people out of the cities, and new highways made distances smaller. But the suburban lifestyle really picked up momentum at the end of World War II. Several critical federal programs helped tip the balance. The U.S. Federal Housing Administration and the Veterans Administration created loan programs for returning soldiers, encouraging them to buy newly built homes—and those homes tended to be found outside the cities. The Federal-Aid Highway Act of 1956 catalyzed the next wave of development of highways and roads connecting these new living spaces, basically under-writing one of the biggest costs of a suburban lifestyle—the need to drive everywhere.

The more peculiar characteristics of the modern suburb, however, were the result of zoning laws. One of the major principles in zoning is to create distinct spaces for working and living. This made sense during the Industrial Revolution, when building row houses next to toxic factories could be harmful to the public health. But the principle had unintended consequences when applied to the suburbs during the new era of white-collar work. When urban centers and villages grew organically they evolved according to the principle of mixed use. You lived, worked, went to school, and shopped in the same basic area, and were often able to walk from one activity to another. Suburbs broke that down and made every activity à la carte. Because of zoning regulation, you lived in a neighborhood of cul-de-sacs. You worked in an office park some distance away. You shopped not at the corner store or the butcher or baker, but at the Shopping Center and Supermarket, surrounded by parking lots. To go to school or a sports facility or even a playground you took a bus or got your mom to give you a lift.

When people criticize suburban life, it's the sense of homogeneity and isolation they are usually talking about. Because of zoning, income levels are roughly the same, unlike in the city, so there's less variety among types of people. There's lots of space but little of it is accessible or livable. The streets have gentle curves and the houses vary slightly but there's a mind-numbing consistency to the overall patterns. You need to drive to get almost anywhere. Even things that are nearby can be hard to reach because of busy roads or fences.

And yet, despite all these downsides, I actually liked growing up in such an area. When I think back on what made my childhood enjoyable, the pleasures seem accidental. I liked the dirt road that went through farmland to another subdivision. I liked exploring the forested ravine down by the river. The local shopping mall was a handy escape, and had a library, a bookstore, and a food court. Now it seems to me that suburbanization has grown more extreme, and those little accidents have been smoothed away. In my childhood neighborhood, the pleasant dirt road is now a six-lane highway. Access to the ravine has been cut off. The shopping mall has been refurbished and modernized, but also seems more sterile and anonymous.

For the office worker, too, the commute from the suburbs to the office park or city skyscraper has only gotten worse. At the end of the long congested drive, you're faced with another kind of suburb, the cubicle farm. For suburbanites who don't work at an office or who work from home, the subdivision neighborhood may feel like a trap. The conveniences are handy but the quality of life has its cons. In particular, the paucity of social interaction is something Daniel Boorstin noted in his classic 1966 essay, *Television: More Deeply Than We Suspect it has Changed All of Us*. As Boorstin put it, "When a colonial housewife went to the village well to draw water for her family, she saw friends, gathered gossip, shared the laughs and laments of her neighbors. When her great-great-granddaughter was blessed with running water, and no longer had to go to the well, this made life easier, but also less interesting. Running water, electricity, mail delivery, and the telephone removed more reasons for leaving the house. And now the climax of it all is Television."

The expansion of suburban living was one of the social convergences that made the adoption of television so rapid and widespread. For many people, Boorstin concluded, television was emblematic of the way electronic technology alienates us. Living color gives the semblance of the real world but it's still a poor substitute. The television screen is a one-way window rather than a two-way portal. Indeed, much like television, technologies like the radio, the telephone, our many household appliances that run on electricity, and the all-important car, are conveniences that have given us just enough connection with the outside world to make life in the suburbs possible, while also isolating us physically and socially. At the same time, such technologies have formed the template for our energy obese lifestyles.

Breaking that paradigm is one of the most significant things we can do to get our appetite permanently under control. Skeptics can be excused for believing that more technology will only make matters worse, but there's a step-jump in connection coming through new technological advances that have the potential to make our neighborhoods more social, stimulating, and convenient places to be. If we adopt those technologies, we will be able to reduce our need for travel and for congregating in large office buildings, shopping malls, and places of entertainment. In essence, we've spent 50 years trying to escape suburbia in cars and planes or through television sets, in the process consuming vast amounts of energy. Now, we need to bring the world into our homes to make our energy-consuming lifestyles more sustainable.

The Great Mash-Up

The difference in information technology today is that it's intensifying two-way, organizational, and social connection.

We've come a long way from the flashing zeros on the VCR and the shoe-box-sized cell phone. Take a smartphone like the iPhone as an example of the new platform at which we're beginning to live, work, and play. Like all cell phones now, it's not tethered to lines, cables, or your home address, and has almost no geographical limits. The most immediately striking feature may be the multi-touch screen, which lets you physically navigate a surface that once required you to use up-and-down key strokes or a mouse. But inside, the iPhone has the digestive capacity of a large whale. It has swallowed your iPod or MP3 player, which previously swallowed your stereo, your entire music collection, and your radio. It has largely swallowed your computer, which means it can do most things the computer can do, including access the Internet, send e-mail, perform calculations, watch videos, and shop electronically. And it has swallowed your portable digital camera and your car's GPS transponder, too.

Then come the mash-ups. My loose usage of that term will probably offend techno-geeks, but I see the concept as a metaphor for what we're now beginning to experience. A mash-up is a combination of unrelated things that gives birth to something new. In IT terms, it's basically an application that combines information, services, or abilities from more than one source to provide you with some different but enhanced new option. For example, GPS is intended for navigation, the cell phone is intended to make calls, and Twitter is a social networking service that allows you to inform your friends what you're doing in 140 text words or less. Using your iPhone, you can now locate yourself in the city, determine that your girlfriend is nearby through her "pings," find a nice restaurant online, access the phone number to make reservations, text message your girlfriend to meet you there in 20 minutes, take a picture to commemorate the occasion, and announce to the world—or at least your social network—that you've asked her to marry you. None of that, except the marriage proposal, was possible a few years ago.

What does my little Apple commercial have to do with reducing energy consumption? Nothing in particular, but it's a small and perhaps clunky example of the ways in which we're becoming integrated, connected, and networked to the world around us. The Apple App Store is a business version of what's taking place. The App Store provides a relatively open marketplace for software developers to offer all kinds of integrated services for the iPhone. The other smart phone producers, especially Google, are incorporating that capability, too. The gamut of options is impressive, but the metaphor of mashing doesn't stop with the smart phone. A very odd collection of services, technologies, and applications are being mixed together to create new recipes, new tastes, and new appetites, like some delicious Indian masala. We now have the contents of all the world's books, movies, or music at our fingertips. We can speak to and even see each other online, anywhere and anytime, for free. Soon products on store shelves will helpfully inform us of their nutritional value or energy costs. We may even wear our electronic devices since new flexible screens with incredible clarity will enable us to put interfaces anywhere, accompanied by circuits that stretch like rubber and react sensitively like skin. We can go portable like never before with batteries that can be recharged by the bending of our knee when we walk or the vibration of our car. We can keep in touch through photos that are automatically linked with GPS coordinates to where those shots were taken. We can immerse ourselves in video games or training programs that let us react bodily over any distance in a virtual world. I don't have the imagination or mind-mapping capacity to guess where all of that might take us, but I know it's leading to a new lifestyle. The connections, the conveniences, the comforts, and the costs are simply too good to ignore.

Where will we live, work, and play in the world that's almost upon us? Anywhere we want. The sense of connection and communication that the radio, the telephone, and television promised but never quite delivered is now available in a high-definition/high-touch version. Looking ahead, ongoing advances in technology are going to make more lifestyle choices possible than we can imagine. Most important of all, the paradigm of physical space will be altered as distance is dissolved.

Virtualization

Radio, it has been said, was the Internet of its day. The first station began broadcasting in 1920, and it took several years before it really caught on and began to change people's habits and behaviors. Music, news, and events transmitted over thousands of miles into the small set in your home was a wonder of technological advancement. Suddenly, hundreds of thousands of people all over the United States could listen to a boxing match or political convention in Madison Square Garden, a church sermon from Pennsylvania, or a live orchestral performance in Chicago, and feel in touch with the happenings of the larger world. It was all part of a general sense of great technological possibility. As noted by an advertiser, "What an age. Photographs by radio. Machines that think. Lights that pierce fog.... Vending machines to replace salesmen.... The list of modern marvels is practically endless."[1] Not surprisingly, the stock of radio broadcasting companies rose and rose as the bubble of the roaring twenties stretched.

The hype was a little premature. Radio had its limitations, not least of which was that the signal is one-way. We couldn't radio back. Other than a little dabbling in ham or CB radio in the 1970s (for those old enough to remember those crackly two-way radio communication systems), the first time that I felt as though I could interact with people at some distance was when electronic bulletin board systems (and a different system called Usenet) became available in the late 1970s and 1980s. You needed something called a modem to go with your computer, and unless you were in the same area as your BBS (Bulletin Board System), you paid expensive long-distance charges to make the connection. This encouraged "communities" of local users. But once you were connected, you could enter spaces that were devoted to particular subjects of interest, read what others were thinking and saying, and text your questions or your thoughts about issues. It was pretty cool stuff.

The Internet made that kind of congregating easier and more expansive. BBS's turned into forums or chat rooms, and e-mail zipped back and forth between people. The notion of communicating in such a way migrated from the bedroom computer to the office desktop and became part of the way we worked. You could observe the sea change as the old men on Mahogany Row (a staid reference to the ranks of top corporate executives behind wooden desks), started communicating via e-mail. A few years before, their secretaries typed every memo or letter for them to sign. By the time the BlackBerry came around, they were as hooked as teenage boys in 1980 were with their first Atari game console.

The Internet forum idea reconfigured itself, in my view, with the rise of such social networking sites as Friendster, MySpace, hi5, and Facebook. A generation of young people, predominantly college students, have become hooked on social interfaces. (Facebook itself has 120 million users worldwide.[2]) They can connect with friends, grow that network to include others they've never actually met, see what all those friends are doing, post updates about themselves, share photos, videos, links, and interact on areas of common interest. What's more, the barriers between isolated social networking sites and the Internet in general are breaking down. A new application on Facebook, called Facebook Connect, permits users to log onto other sites using their Facebook identification. Accordingly, friends can see what other friends are doing online, and web sites, advertisers, and other businesses can follow that traffic, too, and respond with new products and services accordingly.[3] As Daniel Boorstein might appreciate, applications such as Facebook are increasingly becoming the new "water wells" of the twenty-first century.

None of this, to a mature and privacy-concerned adult from a generation past, seems particularly healthy, wise, or productive, but that's missing the point. A *New York Magazine* article called that ease with personal exposure and constant connection the "biggest generation gap since rock and roll."[4] Beyond the divide of that gap is a population of young people who have a mind-set for communicating online in ways that develop very real connections and relationships. When I was a teenager we did this in the hallways or cafeteria at school, in our basements, cars, or over the telephone, but always within close physical proximity of those people we called our friends. Now, distance is no barrier and networks self-propagate by design, expanding exponentially.

In the process, the Web is becoming more social than ever, and that sense of connectivity is taking on economic ramifications. Social networking, like computer use and e-mail in past eras, is migrating from the noneconomic realm of play and becoming essential to work. We've already seen evidence of the way social networking can serve other purposes besides gossip and self-expression. There are many variations that expand knowledge, spread ideas, stimulate understanding, and generate other kinds of activity, ranging from social activism to job-related networking to commerce. Digg, Wikipedia, LinkedIn, YouTube, eBay, Twitter, and Flickr are just a few services encouraging social networking that I've come to rely on or experiment with—and remember, although curious, I'm on the wrong side of that generation gap, so my knowledge is limited compared to a twenty-something. The important thing to realize is that anyone under 40, as rock and roll songs once drew the dividing line, will be completely open to the idea of working on sophisticated and long-term group projects without any physical proximity. They'll think it's natural to interact online with customers, suppliers, colleagues, and even competitors—wherever those people are—in an open-source fashion.

And static social networking sites may seem primitive as "virtual worlds" become more populated and active among mainstream users. What was first imagined in the late 1980s and early 1990s in novels like William Gibson's *Neuromancer* and Neal Stephenson's *Snow Crash* has today become an everyday reality with advances in computer processing power and graphics that I described in Chapter 11.

Virtual worlds are graphic-based, computer-generated environments that participants can inhabit as avatars. An avatar is a 2D or 3D graphic depiction of a person's physical form. Many players choose to embody avatars that depict themselves as physically different from their real-world forms, a kind of extreme self-expression, designed to shock or intrigue, that reminds me of body-piercing or tattooing. Probably the most popular or commonly known virtual world is Second Life. With masked identities and the freedom that comes from a simulated environment in the company of strangers, there are plenty of unsavory and questionable activities going on, as there are all over the Internet, but there are many interesting developments too. Participants from anywhere in the world can inhabit the same social space online in a 2D or 3D form. They can interact with each other and with their virtual environment through movement, text, expressions, sounds, and even a kind of physical bumping. They can get to know one another socially, attend an event like a concert or a political rally, and even trade goods and services in the local currency. In fact, the virtual world itself is largely user-generated. The landscape has been established but the features, including buildings, storefronts, rooms, and events are created by the participants.

Personally, I initially found the experience too game-like and unpredictable to enjoy. But looking ahead, I believe that many people will be comfortable in such a world—indeed, perhaps more comfortable than in this world—and are at ease with the interactions and commerce of that animated daily life. I also believe that the experience is going to become more real, and will increasingly serve real-world purposes, as I'll describe in the next section.

We're already seeing the tip of the iceberg with the latest generation of virtual reality game-consoles like Nintendo's Wii. If you've had a chance to try one, you've probably enjoyed the playfulness that comes with making movements in the real world and seeing them happen to your avatar on the TV screen. Wii achieves that interactive ability by incorporating accelerometer and infrared sensing technology into what's essentially a wireless handheld joystick. But the spin-offs from games to other activities are what's really interesting. Using a Wii you can participate in virtual exercise programs, much like going to the gym and getting an aerobics workout. Virtual training and virtual physical therapy are around the corner. And the experience is becoming increasingly real.

As scientists in Sweden recently showed, with the right cameras to simulate perspective and a certain amount of sensory physical interaction, the human brain can be fooled into having an "out-of-body" experience.[5] Someday, our virtual selves may feel surprisingly real.

Telepresence

Middle-aged that I am, I still have issues with the verisimilitude of virtual worlds and avatars, but I have no such problems with telepresence. Because of the astounding degree of reality and the potential of the practical applications, telepresence is where distance, in my view, dissolves most convincingly. I've been lucky to participate in a number of telepresence meetings using Cisco's TelePresence system. Let me try to describe my experience.

You walk into a simple conference room with a standard, 12-person boardroom table. The five people sitting around the table look up when you enter. You make eye contact and smile as you normally would, and then you realize that three of the five people are not actually in the same room with you; they are images on a series of three large screens spanning one-half of the table. Your brain tries to understand why they look so real. Perhaps it's because they are life size and extremely clear. But there's also a near-physical sense that you're in each other's presence. When they speak, you see their lips move and hear their voices without delay, directionally correct, just as you would if they were actually sitting before you. When you walk across the room, their eyes follow you naturally. It's all happening in real time.

In fact, during my first experience sitting through a telepresence meeting, I found it hard to concentrate on what was being said, as if some portion of my brain were trying to rewire itself and adapt. I realized that the illusion of presence was generated to some degree by simple cosmetics. The room I was in and the room on the screens across from me were consistent in color and tone, as if the half table I sat at was extending into another space. But this illusion was amplified by the clarity of the images and the synchronized fidelity of the sound. There was simply no comparison to that primitive ancestor, the videoconference. I've found videoconferencing to be a convenient, if somewhat cumbersome, way to have a conversation with people who are far away. But you hold no illusion that you're physically meeting with someone when you talk. You speak into a camera. You tend to watch yourself on the TV monitor. You need to restrain yourself to deal with the delays of transmission. It's the difference between a low-touch experience and a high-touch experience. Cisco's Telepresence engaged enough of my senses simultaneously to be convincing.

We're seeing similar advances in 3D movies right now. Like most people my age, I'd grown up with a low opinion of the gimmicky quality of 3D movies. The awkward paper glasses with red and green lenses seemed to obscure more than they revealed and gave me a headache as a bonus. The horror and science fiction movies using the technology were extra-schlocky, as if making fun of the mediocrity. Objects that flung themselves at you from the screen or hovered in mid-air were amusing and startling but hardly realistic. Compare that to 3D technology now. In 2007, I went to my local theater and saw the 3D concert movie, U23D, and the experience was quite impressive. The visual quality of the images was life-like, and the sense of reality was enhanced by the full spectrum of sound that a modern movie theater can deliver. The crowd shots, in particular, were interesting because it felt as though I were sitting in an audience of standing, cheering people, even though all of us were sitting down. The *New York Times* reviewer observed that, "The very idea of self-contained screen geography is thrillingly reconceived."[6]

The same kind of 3D technology has also been used to film football games between NFL teams. In December 2008, the NFL showed a live game between the San Diego Chargers and the Oakland Raiders on movie screens around the country. For the select viewers, the experience was reportedly even more intense than watching an actual game from expensive seats close to the field. Indeed, people felt as though they were *on* the field and in the middle of the play. Whether that's a terrifying or a thrilling thought probably depends on your view of football.

From 3D images coming out of a 2D screen, the next logical leap is 3D holography. In fact, that's a step up that's already been taken. If you caught some of the 2008 Presidential Election Coverage on CNN you might have seen a segment where Anderson Cooper spoke to a holographic image of an election reporter. That image was smaller than life-size and shimmered slightly with a pale blue glow around it, reminding me, and probably many other viewers, of Princess Leia asking Obi Wan Kenobi for help in the original *Star Wars*. I've seen more impressive presentations with a technology called On-Stage developed collaboratively by Cisco and Musion Systems. Cisco CEO John Chambers is standing onstage at a speech in Bangalore when he calls on two of his senior people from California. They join him from stage left and the three men converse. Only Chambers is actually present, but the liveliness of the interaction is very convincing. The men are the same size. Their conversation is natural, and without delay. But it's the sense of their gestural communication that makes you appreciate what the technology provides. The men are reacting to each other's body language—sometimes with ease, sometimes awkwardly, as we do when we're in the physical presence of another human being.

I believe it won't be long before Telepresence screens are a fixture in offices and even in homes. In fact, the screen technology is improving so rapidly that we'll soon be able to "wallpaper" our rooms with high definition displays that utterly obliterate the "self-contained screen geography." Furthermore, 3D and even holographic image technology are about to break out of the boundaries of the cinema and become possible in the office and home. Mash all that with improvements in infrared sensors and accelerometers and you've got the capability to turn relatively flat and cartoon-like virtual worlds into Telepresence-quality images of the "real world" that you can step into and interact with. Imagine walking into a meeting room on the other side of the world, exploring the Louvre from your own local community museum, or visiting the International Space Station.

That might seem like science fiction to some readers, but it's coming soon. I estimate that telepresence systems are in their adoption cycle where color television was in the late 1950s.

Referring back to Figure 11.2, color TV really started to take off in the early 1960s. Then, a couple of timely social events accelerated sales momentum. When the Gemini space launches began and the Pope visited America in 1965, those historic occasions were broadcast on TV sets around the country and announced as taking place "Live in Color." The demand for the color viewing experience became more insistent. Color television had suddenly become more compelling than black-and-white TV for the masses, and few could resist.

Like color television and countless other break point innovations, there is no question that telepresence systems will get better and better and eventually become part of mainstream life. But a timely social event like an energy crisis may bring it to us sooner than we think.

Virtually Everything

In a series of essays comparing the Industrial Revolution to the Information Revolution, Peter Drucker offered some brilliant insights about how our society shifted in the industrial era and predicted what's likely to drive change in our era. According to Drucker, rapid industrialization had a limited impact on people's lives in the first 40 years after Watt's steam engine, while it was the steam locomotive—an unanticipated offshoot— that really altered the game. As Drucker points out, "The railroad was the truly revolutionary element of the Industrial Revolution, for not only did it create a new economic dimension but also it rapidly changed what I would call the *mental geography*." From the railroad came different ways of living, working, buying and selling, and organizing the state.

When Drucker applies that kind of thinking to the information revolution, he observes that computers didn't really change much about our world for around 50 years. Even as they became quite powerful at processing, computers basically allowed us to do the same things we'd always done, only faster and more accurately. For example, we automated the routine processes of inventory, finance, and supply chains. But then came an unanticipated offshoot, or more accurately, a long-awaited one. According to Drucker, "E-commerce is to the Information Revolution what the railroad was to the Industrial Revolution—a totally new, totally unprecedented, and totally unexpected development. And like the railroad 170 years ago, e-commerce is creating a new and distinct boom, rapidly changing the economy, society, and politics." Drucker went on to note, "In the new mental geography created by the railroad, humanity mastered distance. In the mental geography of e-commerce, *distance has been eliminated*. There is only one economy and only one market."[7]

Drucker's sentiments remind me of a comment that Lou Gerstner made when he was CEO of IBM. In the late 1990s, most major corporations were trying to stake out territory on the Internet by establishing web sites, though few seemed to know exactly what to do with that space or how to make any money being there. Indeed, some companies, in their haste and enthusiasm, gave away services online that they charged for in the brick–and–mortar world. Gerstner was shown the GE web site with all its bells and whistles, but instead of being wowed he asked, "Where's the 'buy button'?"[8] That challenge to the presumed economic value of the online model cut through a lot of fuzzy thinking.

We have a buy button now, we've gotten used to paying for stuff online, and the adoption of those behaviors is making our lives that much more digital, if not virtual. Of course, there is a limit to how many products can go digital, but there is no limit to how digital we can go. We can even digitize ourselves with incredible realism.

Like what Gerstner did with online services in the 1990s, inventors, innovators and entrepreneurs are going to cut through a lot of the fuzzy thinking surrounding today's virtualization technologies and bring compelling value propositions to society over the next few years. And like break point innovations of the past, some of our most intense energy-consuming habits will change as a result—except this time our energy obese habits have the potential to retreat.

Tele-office

With virtualization, the office complex and business travel itself are also becoming relics of the industrial age. Some might be doubtful about that statement. We've heard lots of noise about telecommuting before, and it's value has failed to stick. The idea became resurgent in the summer of 2008 when gas prices at the pump breached $4.00 a gallon in the United States. Why not work from home? Some companies and government offices began to encourage it. Stay home one day a week and "dial" in. Not only are individuals saving gas by avoiding the commute, but the office is saving power: fewer lights and terminals, less concern about the air conditioning or heat. Although such talk has retreated significantly since the financial crisis destroyed energy demand, the cat is out of the bag. Hopefully, common sense, competitive advantage, and good policy will prevail and there will be no going back.

After all, how functional and productive is your office experience? If you're like me, the commute to the office is becoming increasingly pointless. I enjoy my coworkers and fellow partners immensely—we have a great team. But I rarely actually see people on the other side of the floor on an in-person basis. In fact, although we are often physically just down the hall from one another, we typically communicate by e-mail, telephone, or instant messaging. Most of my work is done with people outside the office via e-mail, telephone, Skype, or Cisco's Telepresence, and through an unfortunate amount of business travel. My office is just a place of work, not a place I need to go to work. Much of the collaboration on this book, for instance, was accomplished by using Skype video; there was communication between Central Europe and Western Canada, with intervals in the midwestern U.S., New York City, and Hong Kong, and Singapore.

We've talked a lot about the technological advancements that are making telework possible. The critical question is whether the social and organizational advancements are also happening. Some who worry about the downside of telecommuting are concerned about the loss of watercooler time at the office. This is the metaphor for that aspect of the work experience that gives us social pleasure, deepens personal connection, and builds organizational culture. And I agree—we are social animals. One of the benefits of work, one of the reasons it's worthwhile, is the pleasure we take in each other's company. But I also think the office watercooler has largely gone virtual. If you have an active account on Facebook you might understand what I mean. All of the banter, the spontaneous time wasting and interaction, the questions of concern, the non-work-related topics, the sports talk, the relationship talk, and the checking in time, can and does take place vigorously through such social networking sites.

A bigger impediment may be the mind-set of the organization, and principally, its executive leadership. Some organizations, despite lip service to flex time and irregular career paths, are stuck on the industrial model of working, like the stubborn physicist clinging to his slide rule. Arriving early, leaving late, attending lots of meetings, and traveling like a road warrior are badges of merit equating time served with performance and productivity. Part of this may be generational. At plenty of organizations, the leadership is older than 50, with lives even less enmeshed in Web 2.0 than mine. Tell them that social networking applications can accelerate communication and decision-making speed and they stare blankly at you while puffing on their metaphorical cigars. But of course, physical age is not always indicative of openness to new ideas. My point is that while adoption of social networking and telecommuting tools is likely to be a grassroots phenomenon at many organizations, visionary leadership can make an immense difference. And assessments of energy demand, globalization, and productivity show that working virtually is going to be a critical competency in cost-efficient and strategically competitive organizations of the future.

Cisco Systems is one company that has the technology—a broader suite of it, in fact, than I've alluded to already—and is walking the talk. With a white-collar workforce of around 60,000 people around the world, half of whom travel for business, it made sense for Cisco to apply its technology for its own use. At the beginning of 2009, Cisco had 320 Telepresence units in 135 cities in 40 countries for corporate use, and plans for more deployments. More importantly, those Telepresence sites are being heavily used. According to the people I've talked to at Cisco, the utilization of old generation video conference call systems that are ubiquitous in most organizations is around 3 percent. But the allure of Cisco Telepresence—the quality of the interaction experience, and the convenience and productivity afforded by it—is such that suites are booked more than 48 percent of the time, based on a 10-hour business day. Cisco has scheduled almost 215,000 Telepresence meetings since its launch date in October 2006 up to January 2009.

By proliferating its Telepresence network internally, with customers, and even with the general business public, Cisco believes it's creating momentum for mass adoption. In support of this view is Metcalfe's Law, which holds that a network's value is proportional to the *square* of the number of users connected to the system. One telephone doesn't do anyone any good. Two is fine, but limited. Put ten telephones in the mix and you ramp up use and reliance exponentially. Same goes for Telepresence systems.

To a surprising degree for a technology hardware company, Cisco is also highly aware of the soft issues involved in shifting the behavior of employees to embrace distance-dissolving technology tools such as Telepresence. It has needed to instill changes in workflow, organizational culture, business processes, management practices, and the way it measures performance and productivity. For a global business, this makes sense. The less you have to travel from California to hold important meetings with colleagues in Dubai (or anywhere else), the better.

To reduce business travel, Cisco has framed its efforts as a corporate mission to reduce greenhouse gas emissions. To do so, the organization has a goal of reducing business travel miles by 20 percent. I'm trying to nudge them toward thinking in terms of energy appetite. As I've said many times already, if we reduce appetite, we reduce emissions, while also solving our other problems with energy supply.

Telepresence is a huge advantage for Cisco right now in those efforts, and one that not every company has access to—although, if Cisco is right about the market demand, a significant percentage of companies will access it in the future.

But there are other technologies that enable people to dissolve distance in their work. Some of them are basic, like WebEx collaboration tools, web-based seminars and conference calls, and Skype. Others are slightly more alternative. Instant messaging is more immediate and interactive than e-mail, and allows you to know when recipients are at their computers and available. Twitter also helps people keep track of and stay in communication with one another, particularly when away from their desks. Facebook's friends feature allows you to develop a work network within your organization and beyond; and its News Feed feature gives you instantaneous updates on what everyone in your network is "doing," which can be invaluable to keep track of the status of a project. Second Life has a new platform called Grid, geared specifically toward hosting meetings in virtual space for businesses, government agencies, and educational institutions. Other companies like HP and Nortel are following suit with systems for corporate virtual worlds.

Together these distance-dissolving technologies are helping to break the paradigm of commuting and business travel. Do we really need office parks or office high-rises anymore? Consider the net energy that can be saved if we commuted to our neighborhood tele-office rather than spending 90 minutes in the car twice a day. Do we really need to travel hours by plane to have an hour-long face-to-face meeting? Suburbanization, commuting, and business travel are major reasons why the United States is the largest consumer of oil in the world, guzzling 20 million barrels a day, 13 million of which is imported. Half of every barrel goes to powering cars, SUVs, and pickups around our vast network of roads and freeways. Another 17 percent goes to air travel, rail, and sea transport.

I showed in Chapter 10 that taking oil from a deep hole drilled in the earth and flowing it through refineries to engines, gears, axles, and tires is an extremely inefficient societal template that is only 17 percent efficient at best (Figure 10.3). Combined with suburbanization it's led to an energy obese lifestyle, one with an appetite that burns up 400 million gallons of gasoline every day in the United States. That's the bad news. But it's also the good news, because of the six-to-one leverage up the chain of inefficiency. Stressing the importance of this powerful concept again, saving the energy equivalent of one barrel of oil at the wheels (by not driving) means that six barrels of oil are no longer needed at the source.

In this context, consider the potential of virtualization as a disruptive energy technology. If for only one day a week the herd of stop-and-go business commuters was allowed to telework from home or from a net-worked satellite office near their neighborhood, over 30 million gallons a day of gasoline would be saved.

Similar calculations can be done for air travel in the United States. If every corporate meeting junkie were to substitute telepresence for one in five business encounters that requires air travel, I estimate that 100 to 200 thousand barrels a day of jet fuel could be saved.

Although I did not attempt it in my calculations, it should be noted that the numbers presented don't include indirect savings accruing from multiplier effects; for example, less frequent tire changes and engine maintenance. Nor do they include the benefit of productivity gains coming from avoiding time wasted in airports and congested freeways. In short, intelligent investment on conservation-enabling, lifestyle-changing technologies will lead to the easiest barrels of oil society can find.

In the business arena alone, by reducing marginal land and air commuting by 20 percent, the United States can cut fuel use by about one million barrels of petroleum products a day. At 5 percent of the nation's oil demand, this is a very meaningful number and the environmental impact of trimming such energy obesity is significant too just the reduction in land travel cuts CO_2 emissions by over 100 million tons per year. This is equivalent to taking 27 million vehicles—almost exactly the entire number of registered vehicles in California[9]—off the road! And that's in the United States alone. Consider that in 2008, it took the worst financial crisis since the Great Depression to slow down all western economies enough to rein in a mere two million barrels per day. As a consequence, oil prices sold off sharply, falling from a record $147/barrel to $35/barrel. Using $50 per barrel as a reference price, curtailing one million barrels of oil per day is like not burning $1.5 billion per month—or at least cutting the U.S. trade deficit to foreign suppliers by the same amount.

The Next Productivity and Entertainment Miracle

Ironically, the same kinds of communication technologies that encouraged us to move away from the city core over half a century ago have the power to collapse suburbanization and reduce our energy appetite today. Through virtualization, social networking, and many yet-to-be-imagined mash-ups, we'll be able to reconfigure the paradigm of suburb, commute, office building, and business travel.

I also believe that we'll generate wealth in the process. Economic prosperity of the kind we experienced in the mid-1990s seems like a faded dream from the rearview mirror of 2008. But it's interesting to remember that the tremendous growth of the 1990s was built on the basis of incredible gains in productivity. The early 1990s were a period of recession, as major corporations reengineered and reorganized, laying off tens of thousands of white-collar workers. What seemed dire at the time turned out in retrospect to be fortuitous. Overnight, many of those tech-savvy white-collar workers found themselves freed from a stifling blue-suited environment. Supported by the information technologies that enabled them to work from home or from smaller organizations, they helped to establish a wave of entrepreneurial businesses and services. In the wake of that disruption, the so-called productivity miracle was under way, though we only recognized it as such a half-decade later.

Virtualization could very well make those productivity gains look pale in comparison. Consider the time saved by drastically reducing commutes and business travel. Imagine, instead of traveling for a week to three cities for three separate meetings, you could hold those three meetings and more in a single day. Imagine the speed of interaction and decision making that will come when social networking becomes an intracorporate tool, not just something we do in our spare time. Our ability to be "friends" with 20,000 other colleagues, to quickly data-mine their backgrounds and skills for the tools and knowledge we need, to virtually assemble experts and experiences in a half day instead of a half year, will transform the way we work and generate wealth.

And the rewards will not just be with work but with quality of life, too. We'll get to enjoy more time with our friends and family and have more time for our personal interests—a novel, potentially richer, variety of experiences and interactions. Virtualization doesn't mean losing social connections or real experiences. It means being able to manage them on our own terms, the way iTunes helps manage our music catalog, TiVo helps manage our TV watching, and Amazon's Kindle helps organize our books. We'll still meet with friends and family face-to-face, but we'll also get to spend "real" time with loved ones who are far away, more often and more conveniently. We'll still take real two-week vacations to exotic parts of the world, but we may take "day-trips" ten more times a year to places that are otherwise out of reach.

I play the piano and I learned recently that Yamaha has an Internet-connected piano that can be played at a distance. I immediately thought of the ability to sit in my living room and listen to a great pianist like Maurizio Pollini as he plays in Carnegie Hall, the keys on the piano before me moving to his fingers. Indeed, there's no reason why Pollini himself couldn't be sitting there before me in Telepresence or holograph, and all of it happening in real time. That's a world I'd like to experience and share with my children.

Chapter 14

A Low-Carb, Highly-Scalable Diet

Throughout this book, I've focused on the most practical options that provide us with the highest leverage for resolving our many-tangled energy problems. Some readers, ardent in their hopes for totally green energy solutions, may be uneasy with my dry-eyed assessment of the necessary, but limited potential of renewable energy solutions. Other readers, dismissive of any solution that is not black and tar-based, may roll their eyes at the role break point innovations in information technology will play in reducing energy demand.

But both the history and economic principles of energy markets teach us that those options that provide the most *value* per dollar are the ones that end up winning. Value, as I've discussed in Chapter 6, is assessed on the basis of how compelling a solution fulfills its attributes; and to the degree that fate factors into the equation, value is also governed by how well a solution converges with the specific social trends of the day.

Recall from Chapter 11 that I outlined three possible paths to tackle energy obesity. I would be remiss if I did not discuss value propositions under Path 1: *Keep adding more energy*, before the end of this book. Though it's the least exciting and most hackneyed solution set, the enormity of our energy needs is such that we must also identify as many high-leverage solutions as possible at the source in order to balance out our energy diet. Ending energy obesity does not mean eliminating our energy appetite—it means reducing it to levels that are more healthy and sustainable. In addition, like good dieters focused on nutritious alternatives, we must cut back on the "bad carbs" and digest more "good carbs" as much as possible.

In dietary terms, carbohydrates are the most abundant of the biomolecules we ingest to nourish our bodies. Not all "carbs" are created equal, however. Bad, or "simple," carbs like those found in sugar and highly processed foods constitute a poor diet and lead to health and weight problems. Good, or "complex," carbs are those found in whole grains, vegetables, and fruit. Doctors tell us to avoid bad carbs as much as possible and insist that good carbs are essential for a healthy lifestyle.

In the realm of energy, what constitutes a good carb? The fuels we rely on, such as oil and coal, are energy rich because they contain—much like the carbohydrates we eat—chains of hydrogen and carbon molecules. Some fuels have very complex hydrocarbon compositions, while others are simpler. The thicker fuels have the longest and most difficult to break chains of hydrocarbons. Crude oil, for example, has many different kinds of hydrocarbon chains mixed together. Through fractional distillation or chemical processing we separate crude oil into distillates like fuel oil, asphalt, tar, gasoline, or kerosene. Some of those fuels have as many as 70 carbon atoms for every hydrogen atom. Others are "lower carbs" with as few as eight carbon atoms for every hydrogen atom. From an environmental point of view, the "high carb" fuels are poor choices because upon combustion they create more undesirable emissions.

To meet growing appetites around the world and address the need to shift to a healthier energy diet with the greatest leverage possible, we need to identify a fuel that is low carb, plentiful, scalable, and affordable. As fate would have it, we are very fortunate that such a fuel is emerging and is already being added to our diet in greater proportion, especially in North America. Actually, it's an old fuel, but we're finding new ways of accessing and using it. We used to call it "nature's gas."

The Diet of a Distant Past

The basics of how North Americans burn gas in their homes isn't much different today than it was nearly 200 years ago, though the sources of that gas have undergone many changes. The full story of natural gas shows that innovation in delivering greater quantities of primary fuels hasn't hit an end-point yet. In fact, we're now entering a third era.

In the nineteenth century, gas came from coal. Through a series of chemical processes, coal was converted into "coal gas," also known as "manufactured gas" or "town gas." The first commercial American coal gas plant was built in Baltimore, Maryland in the early 1800s. Within a hundred years, it's estimated there were 52,000 localized plants within municipalities all over the country. At first, manufactured gas was piped from plants into the homes of the wealthy, but as the compelling quality of manufactured gas was realized, the infrastructure expanded to include middle-class homes, factories, and streetlamps. If you've spent time in an old East Coast neighborhood you might have noticed the remnants of that system: elegant old lamp stands on sidewalks that are straight out of Dickens' day, ornate metal fireplaces in brownstone apartments that have never seen firewood, and abandoned plots of land where, to this day, nothing can be built because the ground is too poisoned by the toxic residues discharged into the soil and watershed.

When Edison's incandescent system came along, we finally had a convenient and scalable alternative for lighting. And yet, despite the fact that light bulbs were safer than gas lamps, our energy diet continued to include manufactured gas for some time. The reason? We'd become quite dependent on it. Many household appliances like stoves, furnaces, and even bathtub heaters were operated with manufactured gas, and such comforts were not eagerly sacrificed.

In our rush to use oil for transportation we neglected a form of gas that did not need to be "manufactured." So-called "natural" gas was found in similar geological settings as oil. Indeed, natural gas is commonly found near oil, with oil, or even *in* oil, dissolved in solution like the carbonated bubbles in soda water. When oil is pumped to the surface through a wellhead, the associated natural gas is liberated, similar to opening a soda can.

For much of the twentieth century, oil was so prized that natural gas was ignored or deliberately wasted. An extensive and complex distribution system of trucks, pipelines, and tankers was developed with oil in mind. But natural gas was difficult to store and transport and was considered an unwanted, uneconomic by-product that was cheaper to dispose of than to bring to market. During the early twentieth-century oil boom, when wildcatters drilled a well that produced only natural gas and no oil, they considered the find a failure and capped it. Until the 1920s, any natural gas produced with oil at the wellhead was usually piped a short distance away and allowed to blow into the atmosphere. Later, natural gas was simply burned at the top of a tall pipe in a process called flaring. At night, the flames of natural gas flares from a field of oil wells would light up the darkness with an eerie glow. This practice still occurs in countries like Iran and Russia where solution gas is abundant with oil production, yet "stranded" with no access to the market. The flares are so big in northern Siberia and the Persian Gulf that at night they can be seen clearly in satellite pictures.

Such waste only emphasizes the extent to which a fuel must be compelling before its value is even perceived.

The Beginning and End of the Euphoric Era

Perceptions and, more importantly, the fundamental economics of natural gas, began to change in the late 1920s and 1930s as a break point innovation arrived on the scene. New high-pressure welding techniques made it possible to build long-distance pipelines. For towns that already had an infrastructure of pipes for transporting manufactured gas, the sudden access of natural gas from distant fields was a windfall. Soon, natural gas producers and manufactured gas producers began to consolidate. Cheap and clean natural gas was piped into an existing distribution system, in the process rapidly supplanting manufactured gas. The new era of natural gas had begun.

An August 1930 article in *Popular Science* could barely contain the excitement over the potential of natural gas use in the home. "Chicago is going to get natural gas. San Francisco already has it. New York may get it . . . [and natural gas is] likely to make radical changes in the daily lives of millions of Americans who live in, or near, those cities." The authors commented on how standards of living would improve across the income spectrum, noting that, "with cheap natural gas, such rich man's luxuries as heating a home with gas, all winter, begin to look practical."

And scarcity was no issue, at least across North America. Oil drilling had already validated 52 great gas fields spanning from the Appalachians to Texas and across to California. In Canada, large quantities had also been found. On a trip to the Wild West that took him through the prairie town of Medicine Hat, Alberta, the famous poet Rudyard Kipling saw that natural gas burned in streetlights 24 hours a day. Amazed at the huge reserves that must have existed beneath the city, Kipling wrote that Medicine Hat had "all Hell for a basement."

Throughout most of the twentieth century, economics dictated that most of America's natural gas came from conventional fields in West Central and Southern regions, notably Texas and Oklahoma, followed by the mega-offshore fields in the Gulf of Mexico.

There have been six important periods in the history of U.S. natural gas use since the industry began in earnest in the 1930s (see Figure 14.1).

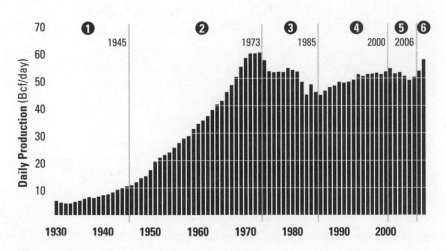

Figure 14.1 Six Eras of U.S. Natural Gas Production (1930–2008)
Source: U.S. Energy Information Administration, ARC Financial Research.

Between 1930 and 1945, natural gas was heralded as a scalable, clean new source of energy that could replace manufactured gas in homes, and an aggressive phase of pipeline construction resulted. World War II slowed some of that growth, but then the new home building that began with the rise of the suburbs and the arrival of the Baby Boomers encouraged real estate developers to tout natural gas as a modern necessity. As one builder expounded in a 1966 advertisement in *Life Magazine,* "After building 12,000 homes we know that gas heat makes satisfied homeowners."

The big decline in the demand and production of natural gas started in 1973. Shaken by the oil shocks of 1973 and 1979, homeowners made more effort to insulate their walls and attics. In addition, President Carter's Fuel Use Act of 1978 encouraged more nuclear power and coal in the electric power generation market to conserve oil and gas. As we've already seen, this strategy significantly rebalanced the U.S. energy diet. By 1984, the use of natural gas had declined 25 percent from its peak in 1973.

As oil prices eased in the mid-1980s, North Americans increased their appetite for oil, natural gas, and, indeed, all energy commodities. Between 1985 and 2000, new technologies gave the ability to expand cost-effective exploitation of larger reservoirs, especially in the Gulf of Mexico. But by the early 2000s, natural gas production from conventional reservoirs started to "mature." After 70 years, the easy reserves of natural gas were becoming increasingly difficult to maintain at prevailing prices. Even if natural gas production had been rising, the ability to take market share from other fuels like oil, "clean coal," and nuclear power was limited because there were no compelling reasons for North Americans to change their energy diet.

Game-Changer

So what's different now? As I've suggested a few times already in this book, the widespread adoption of new devices and new fuels is never due to one impetus or reason. Instead, a convergence of many factors is necessary for a sea change to occur.

Since 2002, coal and oil have increasingly become *disadvantaged* fuels. That's what happens when a fuel confronts one or more challenges and its utility becomes compromised. Both coal and oil are now disadvantaged, though for different reasons.

Society wants to turn away from coal because it is a high carb fuel. The emissions of CO_2 and other greenhouse gases are becoming less and less acceptable. With pressure for businesses in the West to reduce carbon emissions, coal's position as a dominant fuel in our energy diet is being challenged.

Geopolitics and price are a double set of challenges for oil. When oil crossed the $100 per barrel threshold, U.S. politicians began an outcry for "energy independence." After all, the U.S. imports 65 percent of its most vital commodity from foreign sources, a strategic vulnerability that is increasingly viewed as untenable.

Together, oil and coal represent 60 percent of the U.S. energy mix. Between the forces of price, environmental advocacy, geopolitical tension, and national security, the conditions are ripening for a change in diet. After all, the geopolitical issues surrounding oil and the environmental "baggage" associated with burning coal will not disappear when the financial crisis eases—instead, they are likely to be amplified.

I've discussed how renewables on their own will not be able to take up enough market share to reduce the pressure of the break point—they cannot be brought to scale cheaply enough to make the difference needed over the next two decades. Similarly, nuclear power is frequently touted as our modern-day magic bullet and the most likely candidate we can scale up to alleviate our problems, but long construction times, high capital costs and the established resistance of people in WealthyWorld to having nuclear power generated anywhere near where they live make that a harder sell than many acknowledge.

Until recently, few considered natural gas as a viable third way. Perceptions are partly to blame. The high prices of natural gas from 2000 to 2007, especially during some particularly cold winters, conditioned people to believe that the United States is running low on natural gas, too. Even Fed Chairman Alan Greenspan was prejudiced by this development, and in July 2003 told the House Committee on Energy and Natural Resources that, "Today's tight natural gas markets have been a long time in coming, and distant future prices suggest that we are not apt to return to earlier periods of relative abundance and low prices anytime soon.[1]"

Fortunately, Alan Greenspan was wrong.

The Unconventional Third Act

In 2008, as if out of nowhere, U.S. natural gas supplies started soaring (refer again to Figure 14.1). The reason? Eighty years ago America transitioned from manufactured gas to natural gas. Now the shift is toward "unconventional gas."

Everyday consumers of natural gas have no idea of the transition taking place behind the scenes. After all, homeowners still heat their homes using the same fuel. In fact, unless you spend your time avidly reading petroleum geology journals, you're unlikely to be aware of the shift within the industry. But the changes that have taken place reflect a new era for natural gas that is no less significant than the transitions of the past.

Both conventional and unconventional gas is obtained by drilling a deep well that penetrates a geological formation. The piercing of gas-rich rock provides access to a treasure that's been hidden for millions of years. The subtle distinction between conventional and unconventional natural gas lies in the source rocks where the gas is found.

Imagine a sand castle on the beach. Though tightly packed, the upside-down bucket-shaped cones of sand are quite porous. If you gently pour water on top, that water is easily absorbed by the sand and passes through almost immediately. Visually, that kind of porous sand makes a good image for a conventional gas reservoir. The weight of several thousand feet of rock pressurizes the gas. When a drill bit penetrates the formation, the gas easily flows up the well to the surface, where it is ready to be pushed through a pipeline network.

Unconventional reservoirs, by contrast, comprise many geologic types including shales, tight sands, and coal beds. The primary feature of these gas-bearing rocks is that they are much less porous. Nature's gas is plentiful but not all of it is eager to stream easily into a well bore. As such, more effort and new innovative techniques are required to "stimulate" the rocks and force a free-flowing, steady stream of gas to the surface.

Geologists have known of the existence of unconventional gas for over a hundred years. But that gas has been more expensive to liberate, and there was no economic motive for applying greater resources to a costly source of gas when another source, packed in porous rock, has been readily and abundantly available. But the game is changing now. Because conventional resources are maturing, extracting unconventional sources makes bottom-line sense.

Equally important are new innovations for making it cheaper to liberate a unit of gas from tightly packed rock. Those who love big machinery will revel in the technology that has been introduced in recent years. Massive hydraulic pumpers inject hundred of thousands of pounds of fluids and special "proppants" at high pressures down well bores. In this way, precisely targeted rock formations are fractured and pinned open, thousands of feet below the Earth's surface. After being fractured (or "fracked" in the industry vernacular), the once tightly packed gas comes gushing up the well in great volumes, eventually settling to a long stable flow that can last for decades.

In fact, hydraulic fracturing is nothing new. The practice started in 1946 and has become progressively more advanced over time. But the break point innovations in how to stimulate and fracture deep well bores have taken place in the last ten years. This new technology is converging with present needs and economic circumstances to make unconventional gas a highly desirable and timely fuel.

The U.S. production trend—absent the effects of the 2008 financial crisis, which severely restricted the spending ability of gas companies—speaks for itself. Between 2005 and 2008 the United States added as much *new* natural gas production in 18 months as the entire proposed Alaskan oil pipeline is supposed to deliver (if and when it's ever built). The oil and gas industry is still in early days of proving how much unconventional gas can be economically exploited, but those in the business already know that the reserve potential is enormous. Geologists are busy recalibrating the numbers based on the new capabilities, but numbers being thrown around now is that over 1,000 trillion cubic feet (Tcf) can be exploited economically in the United States alone. That's the equivalent to 166 billion barrels of oil! To appreciate the magnitude of that number, the north slope of Alaska, where so much political attention is now being paid, has only a few billion barrels of oil.

The elephant oil field recently discovered off the coast of Brazil—the largest field in the world in the past 20 years—has only 10 billion barrels, all of it much harder to tap than energy from unconventional gas.

The Low-Carb Substitute

Finally, what makes natural gas so compelling relative to high carb fuels is its molecular structure. If you care to remember your high school chemistry, natural gas is actually methane, which contains one carbon atom for every four hydrogen atoms. That differentiates natural gas from coal or oil, which have very long chains of carbon molecules that, when burned, release a great deal of CO_2 and other undesirable organic compounds. On an energy equivalent basis, Figure 14.2 shows that burning one unit of natural gas energy produces 30 percent less CO_2 than burning oil, and 45 percent less CO_2 than burning coal.[2] That makes natural gas a "good" carb. Further, as I described in Chapter 6, the EROEI of natural gas is very attractive at 18:1, better than any other fuel we currently depend on, except light sweet crude oil. (Refer back to Figure 6.5.)

If the objective is to reduce CO_2 emissions quickly, the most compelling large-scale substitution is replacing coal-fired power plants with

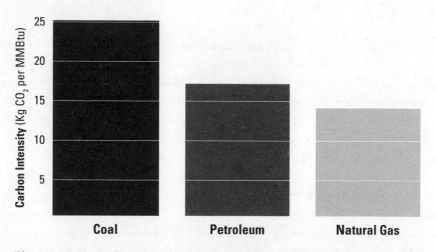

Figure 14.2   Carbon Emissions per Unit of Energy for Primary Fossil Fuels
SOURCE: ARC Financial Research, U.S. Energy Information Administration.

natural gas units (though the coal industry would be none too happy to acknowledge it). A modern gas fired power plant requires 30 percent less energy to generate a unit of electricity than an existing coal equivalent.[3] Combining that with the fact that natural gas emits almost half the emissions as coal per unit of energy consumed (from Figure 14.2), you end up with the cascading result that emissions can be cut by about 75 percent!

By carefully pairing and optimizing the use of natural gas with renewables—like solar, wind, or biomass power—we can reconfigure our electricity generating system to deliver high-quality, high-efficiency, low-carbon energy, day or night, in good weather or bad. If the economic, geopolitical, and social conditions are ripe and we have the right sense of urgency (or crisis) driving us forward—as I believe we will—then natural gas and renewables *together* promise to rebalance our energy diet in a way that will provide us with much greater security in the future too.

Centralized electricity generation is the large end of the scale. On the small, decentralized end of the scale, natural gas is also flexible enough to power a car. The biggest opportunity for natural gas will be if it can penetrate the transportation market. When you look objectively at the way we live today, it's quite shocking how overwhelmingly dependent we are on a single fuel for transportation. Henry Ford's self-contained fuel system is still largely powered by oil, and it has been more successful for far longer than perhaps he or Thomas Edison could ever have imagined. Rebalancing our energy diet in the area of transportation is a critical task.

To a small degree it's already happening, as natural gas vehicles have been commercial for a long time and buying one is about the same cost as those that run on gasoline. Vehicle fleets are the easiest place to start, and the switch to NGVs (Natural Gas Vehicles) has been mandated or adopted in some areas or municipalities. For example, Los Angeles Airport is a natural gas-only zone. But vehicle fleets and buses represent only a small fraction of our overall road transportation needs. Getting natural gas to the mainstream is a bigger challenge, because the utility of gasoline-powered cars is so difficult to beat. For example, the horsepower ratio of natural gas is not as good, and for those of us accustomed to harsh winters, natural gas engines are harder to start if left out in the cold. If you think about it, these are somewhat minor inconveniences when balanced against a desire for energy security and lower emissions. In the end, it is all a matter of how determined the citizens of a nation or region are in wanting to change their energy diet to become more lean, secure, and flexible.

Another impediment to NGVs is that North America doesn't have a widespread fueling infrastructure, though a system where vehicle gas tanks could be filled in home garages is now available for early adopters. In fact, NGVs are not as much of a novelty as you might think. Several countries, such as India, Pakistan, and Argentina, already use natural gas for individual transportation.

It's true, and I've said it before, that the entire fleet of vehicles in the United States and around the world is so large that it would take many decades to replace them all. But we don't need to go so far so soon. We just need to get started by getting into a mind-set of change. Diversifying North America's energy diet in road transportation to natural gas can have a long-term, meaningful impact on a cleaner and more secure future.

Fuel of the Future

Canada and the United States have been leaders in the rapid adoption of unconventional gas technologies. However, elsewhere in the world the geopolitics of natural gas are as unstable as that of oil. The three largest reserve holders of conventional gas—Russia, Iran, and Qatar—recently announced their intention to possibly form an OPEC-like natural gas cartel. Russia's near-monopoly of natural gas in Europe is like a prong-collar leash in the region and the country hasn't been shy about tightening the leash in the middle of winter to exert influence. For all Europeans, it's a major energy security concern.

But oil service companies that are big innovators in exploiting unconventional gas are starting to diffuse the technology around the world, including the North Sea and Eastern Europe. The worldwide reserves are potentially astronomical, and are more widely distributed than any other primary fuel. If the North American experience in the early twenty-first century is any indication, other regions of the world, including places like China, will be entering the unconventional third act too.

Promising as all of this sounds, it is important to remember that natural gas is not the ultimate answer to our energy needs, whether in America or the rest of the world. There is no one answer, and in my opinion the really intriguing solution sets still lie in figuring how to cut our energy appetite while improving standard of living. But if we're looking for the highest leverage solution on the supply side, natural gas is the fuel of the future.

Chapter 15

The Energy Health Craze

The Hula Hoop has been around for thousands of years, as far back as ancient Egypt and Greece. Whether rolling it along the ground, tossing it gently through the air, or spinning it around the waist, human beings of all cultures and eras seem to universally enjoy the magical sense of motion that a circular hoop around 36 inches in diameter can create. Over its history, the simple hoop was often made of vines twisted together or carefully shaped wood. Bamboo was actually the best natural material for making a hula hoop because that natural wonder-fiber is almost as flexible and light as it is strong. In fact, the relatively consistent quality and size of bamboo allowed for a certain amount of mass production of hula hoops.

But there wasn't enough bamboo to keep up with demand once the hula hoop fad hit. As a somewhat mystifying mix of social, marketing, and technological trends came together in the middle of the twentieth century, the hula hoop took off. First it happened in Australia, where a million hoops were sold in a country with a population of a little over nine million. Then in 1958, a U.S. toy company called Wham-O (which actually coined the name "Hula Hoop"), began making the hoops out of polyethylene, the polymer now used in everything from plastic bags to toys. With plastic, supply could keep up with demand, and the fad became an outright craze. Within four months, around 25 million hula hoops were sold in the United States. Within a year that number reached 100 million. Adults gave it a whirl at parties or in backyards. Children learned how to wiggle and spin so that the hoop crawled up and down their bodies or traveled a distance away and zipped right back again. Competitions were held in small towns and state fairs, and popular magazines like *Newsweek, Life,* and *Time* chronicled the crescendo of interest as though it signified some major new development.

In fact, the hula hoop craze faded nearly as quickly as it erupted. People stopped spinning and buying. The Wham-O toy company was fortunate in that it had another trick up its sleeve: the Frisbee. But for the rest of us, the hula hoop got squashed in the back of the family room or garage somewhere near the forgotten Yo-Yo's, Bolo Bats, and Pogo Sticks of other bygone eras.

One of the nice side effects of wiggling a hula hoop around your waist is that it actually gives you a pretty good workout. It takes stamina and a surprising amount of muscular coordination to keep a hula hoop spinning, and people in the 1950s found that they lost weight giving it a whirl on a consistent basis. It's no surprise that the Ancient Greeks were onto that idea from the beginning, and regularly incorporated hula hoops into their exercise regimens. To my mind, the great thing about such a device is that it's playful. Unlike a treadmill or a stationary bicycle, you don't plod diligently toward your allotment of exercise time, but have a little fun instead.

In order to develop good energy-consuming behaviors going forward, we need a health craze of our own, preferably enjoyable. As I've mentioned throughout this book, we know we can cut our energy consumption if we simply cut back on work, travel, shopping, entertainment, and some comforts of modern life. During painful recessions and oil shocks, this kind of retrenchment actually takes place, but no one enjoys the feeling or longs for the benefits to continue. So in breaking the First Principle in a sustainable fashion we need to focus on habits and changes that are going to be embraced eagerly, or that will be easy to adopt and difficult to neglect. Virtualization technologies and smart devices will help much in this regard.

Most of all, unlike the hula hoop, Yo-Yo, or Frisbee, we need our energy health craze to be lasting. So let's look at what that will take, and where it's already happening.

Shining Lights

I burned plenty of calories myself, and much midnight oil, in the analysis of economic data to identify any industrially mature countries that have meaningfully broken the First Principle already. In other words, I'm looking for countries that have leveled off or cut their energy demand, while still having grown their long-term standard of living.

In that search, I identified just three nations that have done so over the past 20 years: Japan, Denmark, and Switzerland. Looking at their accomplishment, others can learn a lot about what it takes. Over the past 20 years, each of those three WealthyWorld nations have shown the following.

1. Positive, long-term trends for wealth creation as measured by real, per person GDP growth, even if slow.
2. A trend showing flat or reduced energy appetite (adjusted for off-shoring) after aggregating all primary fuels.

To grasp that visually, let's look at the charts. Figure 15.1, panels a, b, and c, illustrate the First Principle dynamic for Japan, Denmark, and Switzerland, respectively. The bold lines show real wealth per head from 1965 to 2007. The grey lines show energy appetites as measured in BPY. In each case, offshoring of energy associated with manufactured goods—the dynamic I discussed in Chapter 3—has been factored in, so whole energy consumption per person is properly attributed.

The trend lines of personal energy appetite for the three countries of interest are essentially flat. Japan's appetite has leveled off to approximately 30 BPY, Denmark's is around 27 BPY, while Switzerland's is 28 BPY. All three countries are below the adjusted OECD average of 40 BPY, which for now I'll define as "normal."

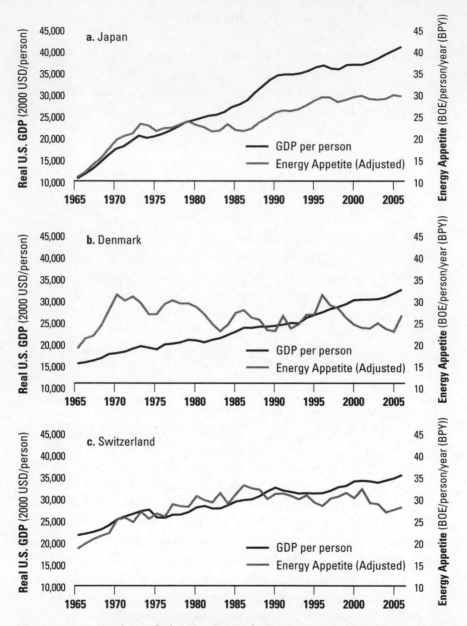

Figure 15.1   Analysis of The First Principle: Japan, Denmark, and Switzerland
SOURCE: ARC Financial Research, BP Statistical Review 2008, IMF.

Top Runner

The Japanese chart in Figure 15.1 tells a very interesting story. As shown by the bold line, Japan's standard of living, as measured by real per person GDP, has increased fourfold over the last 30 years. Notwithstanding the long-term trend, the *pace* of growth has been anything but constant. Throughout its "miracle" growth years of the late 1960s and 1970s, coinciding with its rapid industrialization, both Japan's economy and its standard of living increased at an annual average rate of between 9 and 10 percent! Growth slowed to a still-robust rate in the 1980s, before leveling off to a mere 1.2 percent during the Lost Generation decade of the 1990s and early 2000s. After that, up to the financial crisis of 2008, Japanese economic growth revived slightly, growing around 2.4 percent per year—a rate more typical of a mature WealthyWorld country.

Japan's corresponding appetite trend follows a different trajectory. After rising almost in tandem with standard of living during the miracle growth years, energy appetite fell off in the early 1980s, even as per capita GDP increased. I've already discussed this historical episode at length in the preceding chapters as the aftermath of the 1979 oil price shock, during which WealthyWorld nations—with Japan at the helm—were *forced* to reign in their energy demand through a series of energy-saving rules, measures, and legislation. We already know that it's difficult to keep such discipline. After oil prices fell in the mid-1980s, Japan's chart shows a recoupling of energy demand and standard of living. The two trends continue to move in lockstep into the Lost Generation decade, during which we see a significant slowing of *both* energy demand and standard of living. Although this lends support to our First Principle, which works in both directions, it's not a period to boast about: the ultimate goal of a society has to be to reduce energy demand *without* compromising quality of life. To that end, the final segment of Japan's chart, from 1996 onward is noteworthy. Since then it appears that Japan has managed to create wealth while keeping its energy appetite constant. Could it be that this island nation with a dearth of domestic energy resources has learned the secrets of, and is on the road to, breaking the First Principle permanently?

Japan looks at its overall consumption of energy very deliberately and holistically. It has implemented comprehensive policies, and it has hard goals and constantly evolving efficiency targets. Unlike the United States where any truly holistic national energy plan has been elusive, Japan has a target to reduce its energy intensity relative to its GDP growth by at least an additional 30 percent by 2030. During the same time frame, it aims to reduce its oil dependence within the transportation sector to approximately 80 percent of today's levels.

One of the innovative ways Japan is directing itself toward such targets is by chaining responsibility for energy conservation to all segments of the economy, thus addressing what is referred to in the economic literature as the "principal-agent problem." In an energy efficiency context, principal-agent problems emerge when the party responsible for designing or producing energy-using equipment is not the party that pays for the energy use. For example, an appliance manufacturer may not care much for designing the most efficient coffeepot, because they are ultimately not the one paying for the electricity to boil a pot of java. So without some responsible stake in the end use, the manufacturer has no incentive to improve the energy efficiency of his or her product.

The Japanese government identified the principal-agent as a major problem affecting its large vending machine industry. The situation existed because although vending machine owners would lease space for their machines from building owners, it was the building owners who were responsible for paying the entire energy bill. A few years ago, Japan mandated that the machine owner who leases space from a building owner face the electricity bill indirectly, as his contract must now include an electricity component in addition to the location rent. Between 2000, when the program was introduced, and 2005, the performance of vending machines increased 33.9 percent. That's the kind of benefit holistic policies can bring about.

The centerpiece of Japanese efficiency policy, known as the *Top Runner Program*, was first implemented in 1988. Under Top Runner, energy efficiency performance targets for many categories of machinery and equipment (including vehicles manufactured domestically or imported) are set in an interesting, market-oriented way. Products made by the manufacturer with the most efficient specifications on the market at the time of the value-setting process are taken as the new base level. For instance, the company with the most efficient coffeepot sets the standard. Going forward, all competitors that manufacture products

Product category	Improvement period	Target energy efficiency improvement (%)	Actual energy efficiency improvement (%)
Televisions	1997–2003	16.40	25.70
Video-cassette recorders	1997–2003	58.70	73.60
Air-conditioners	1997–2004	66.10	67.80
Electric refrigerators	1998–2004	30.50	55.20
Electric freezers	1998–2004	22.90	29.60
Gasoline passenger vehicles*	1995–2005	22.80	22.80
Diesel freight vehicles*	1995–2005	6.50	21.70
Vending machines	2000–2005	33.90	37.30
Computers	1997–2005	83.00	99.10
Magnetic disk units	1997–2005	78.00	98.20
Fluorescent lights	1997–2005	16.60	35.60

* The energy efficiency improvement estimate is based on a simple average of the fuel efficiency of all vehicles offered for sale. In contrast, the energy efficiency targets are based on a sales-weighted average. Please note that the effects of reducing consumption are indicated as inverse numbers because the coefficient of performance of fuel economy (km/L) is used as an energy consumption efficiency index.

Figure 15.2 Japan's Top Runner Program: Target and Actual Efficiency Improvements
SOURCE: ECCJ, "Top Runner Programme", October 2006.

covered by Top Runner must meet or exceed the new base level of energy efficiency performance in their future products. Moreover, there is a Darwinian economic incentive for a manufacturer to become the next Top Runner and force competitors to reach their high standards by the time the next value-setting round takes place.

The Top Runner Program has been very successful, regularly exceeding efficiency goals and consistently expanding its coverage of products. Figure 15.2 shows that for each product category subject to the Program, target efficiency goals were met and in most cases exceeded. In April 2007, large trucks and buses, LCD and plasma TVs, rice cookers, microwaves, and DVD recorders were added to the program list. In this way, Japan is extending the incentives for energy efficiency holistically across its economy at the end point of energy usage. By broadly covering every energy-consuming device, the indirect rebound effects I discussed in Chapter 7 are substantially mitigated.

So what's the driving force behind such innovative and comprehensive measures? Although today it seems that nations adopt new energy policies on a weekly basis, Japan gains credibility by virtue of the fact that it is actually achieving results.

Officially, the Basic Act on Energy Policy, formulated in June 2002, sets the general direction for Japan's future energy policy. It specifically identifies "securing stable supply, environmental suitability and utilization of market mechanisms" [1] as key policy directions.

Reasons to Cycle

Denmark, as a northern European nation, has a lifestyle more familiar in character to that which is enjoyed in North America, but has done much better at restraining energy appetite growth. Like Japan and many other WealthyWorld countries, Denmark embarked on an energy-saving crusade after the oil shocks of the 1970s. Unlike most other countries, which reverted to old energy habits after prices stabilized, Denmark persisted in its efforts, and has seen results.[2] Denmark's success can be attributed to a combination of tough economic measures, stringent taxes, incentives, and a nationwide push for creative energy-saving innovations.

The price of electricity in Denmark is by far the highest of any country in the industrialized world. As reported by the Energy Information Administration (EIA), the average price per kWh in 2006 was 32 U.S. cents, which was 25 percent higher than the next highest price in the Netherlands. Not surprisingly, higher prices drive conservation efforts. As we've seen before, the pressing economic incentive is often the most compelling. The average Dane uses 6,300 kWh of electricity a year, compared with 13,300 for the average American.[3] Denmark also applies direct energy taxation on devices as a means of reducing energy use. For example, the registration fee for a new car is approximately 105 percent of the car's value plus additional taxes on fuel.[4] In other words, a car with a $30,000 sticker price in Denmark will actually cost the consumer $61,500; that's a tough policy that gives good incentive to buy a bicycle!

In the 1980s, the Danish government embarked on a massive overhaul of the heating system as part of its "no-waste" initiative. To that end, Denmark developed a combined heat-and-power "cogeneration" system where heat produced as a by-product at power plants is transported to heat homes and offices. Today, cogeneration is cheaper than heating with natural gas or oil and around 61 percent of homes are heated by cogeneration.[5] To complement the new heating system the Danish government introduced a strict new building code in 1979, which is periodically tightened. According to the Danish Energy Authority, the new code lowered Denmark's heating bill by 20 percent between 1975 and 2001.

Though tough minded, such policies and cultural awareness to reducing energy consumption has led to impressive results. As Figure 15.1, panel b shows, the citizens of Denmark have enjoyed a lean energy appetite of between 25 and 30 BPY since around 1970, while their real per person GDP has doubled over the same period.

The First Principle Beaten

Switzerland has taken a somewhat lighter-handed approach than Denmark. The government's primary tool for improving energy efficiency is the SwissEnergy Programme, a predominantly voluntary, though closely monitored, nationwide program. SwissEnergy aims to reduce both fossil fuel use and CO_2 emissions by 20 percent, relative to 2000 levels by 2010. Again, the program uses and advocates a combination of taxes, regulations, incentives, and investments in emerging technologies to reach its ambitious energy-saving goals.

For example, in the area of transportation, the SwissEnergy Programme consists of a number of mandates. Legally-binding measures promote energy efficiency in transport, including harmonizing annual registration fees on motor vehicles and establishing a feebate scheme on the purchase of new cars to favor fuel-efficient vehicles. Other measures include a mandatory Eco-Drive Course, where participants learn how to reduce their fuel demands by 10 to 15 percent by optimizing their driving habits.

In the realm of heating and cooling, SwissEnergy has developed a program to promote the refurbishment of buildings to meet specific energy standards, known as MINERGIE, that are approximately half the current requirements. This program will be implemented from 2010 to 2020 and will be financed through carbon tax revenues. And

SwissEnergy has also established feed-in tariffs to promote the adoption of renewables, waste heat, and biomass for heating in place of fossil fuels. Altogether, the Swiss Government estimates that fossil fuel demand was 7.5 percent lower in 2005 than it would have been otherwise, and larger gains are expected in the future.

Swiss results are shown in Figure 5.1, panel c. It's the one country I have found where, after all adjustments, its energy appetite is actually on a gentle decline since around 1990, while real GDP continues to climb. This is a country that has truly beaten the First Principle of Energy consumption.

Different Shapes and Sizes

Switzerland, Denmark, and Japan have demonstrated foresight, vision, and practical innovation in curtailing their energy appetites, and just as important, a culture of wanting to do so. Each have their own unique approach, and what I am trying to underscore most is that these three countries have actually broken the First Principle for several years now, and they have done so by applying an interesting variety of measures, legislation, and incentives. Other countries can learn much from what has worked for them, and adopt that spirit in thinking through the nuances of their own situation.

Nevertheless, it's paramount to recognize that not every nation is like Denmark, Switzerland, or Japan. Merely copying selective policies and approaches may not work for others. Geography, availability of resources, demography, climates and importantly, societal attitudes vary widely from country to country. Japan's lack of natural energy resources and its high population have forced it to be creative and aggressive about maintaining a low energy appetite. In an even more extreme example, Hong Kong's strict energy regime shows the impact geography, population density, and lack of resources has also.

Denmark and Switzerland are small countries with relatively dense populations. This has made it easier for them to be energy lean. Compare Denmark with Norway, its geographical neighbor. At 73 BOE per person per year, Norway's appetite is 2.8 times greater than Denmark's. The reasons are not hard to guess. Norway's higher latitude makes its climate colder. Its population density is less, making its travel distances greater. It also has a large oil and gas economy and expends energy exploring and producing these resources.

Similarly, Canada has an appetite 2.5 times the OECD average. Like Norway, the climate is cold, population density is very low, travel distances are very far, primary fuels are abundant, and the economy is heavily oriented toward energy-intense, resource-based industries. It's worth comparing the United States with China, too. In the West, we may be biased toward thinking that China's energy profile resembles Japan's or South Korea's because of some commonality of Asian lifestyle, but nothing could be further from the truth. China and the United States both have large populations, large geographical and climate variations, and large distances to contend with. Accordingly, it's more likely that China's energy appetite will "grow up" to look more like the United States than Japan.

If you're going to adopt a serious, life-changing diet, it's important to know what kind of body type and metabolic needs you have and what stage of growth you're in before setting targets for a healthy weight. It's unreasonable to think that a full-grown football player weighing 275 pounds can or should adopt the dietary regimen of a 135-pound marathon runner. Both individuals may be in extremely good health, but their body types, their metabolic needs, and their optimal weights are radically different. At the same time, we need to account for differing stages of development. A high school athlete is still growing and needs a great deal to eat. A retired 40-year old football player is no longer growing and must curb the eating habits of a lifetime to avoid poor health.

Similarly, a country like China, intent on improving the lifestyles of many hundreds of millions of people has a rapidly growing appetite. Whereas a country like the United States, with many trillions of dollars invested in its transportation, industrial, and lifestyle infrastructure, has institutionalized its energy appetite to a degree that resists change. However, that's not to say that the appetite of an emerging superpower can't be optimized and the appetite of an established superpower can't be reduced. In fact, both must happen.

As a first step to understanding the United States, let's look at the many facets of the American appetite and understand its regional differences better.

American Health Check

In Chapter 3, I showed that the American energy appetite was 1.6 times that of the OECD average appetite without adjusting for energy offshoring, and 1.8 times with full attribution. So, is the United States just a strapping 275-pound football player with a large energy appetite or is it an unhealthy adult with an obese level of consumption? The answer, unfortunately, is not simple and clear. If we stick with sports metaphors, the United States is like a team in which every player (or state) has a very different "energy physique." Accordingly, one program for better health will not fit all.

Let's look in more detail. Spanning three times zones, the United States, as the largest energy consumer in the world, does not have a single energy appetite, but many. The chart in Figure 15.3 shows 2006 energy consumption per head for six key states in the Union that spans the spectrum of energy use. These numbers are unadjusted for any offshoring effects. A first look at the data shows that New York and California are the trimmest states, each with an appetite of about 35 BPY. At the other end of the scale, Texas pushes the scales at 89 BPY—a full 54 BPY more than California.

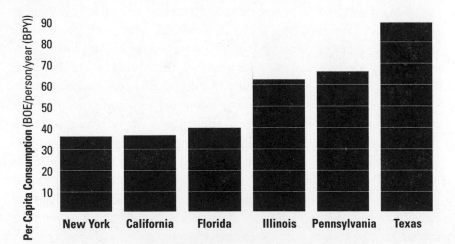

Figure 15.3 Comparison of Personal Energy Appetites for Six U.S. States: Raw Energy Appetites *Unadjusted for* Interstate Outsourcing and Global Offshoring

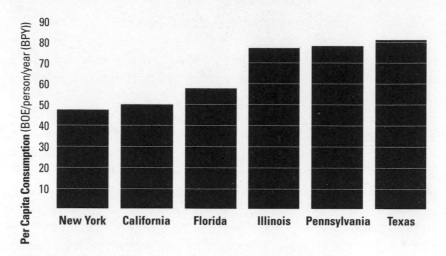

Figure 15.4   Comparison of Personal Energy Appetites for Six U.S. States:
Appetites *Adjusted for* Interstate Outsourcing and Global Offshoring
SOURCE: ARC Financial Research, U.S. Energy Information Administration, BEA.

Though the raw national average is 60 BPY, we shouldn't be too surprised by the wide regional spread. Anyone who's been to New York, California, and Texas knows that these states are diverse in their attitudes and circumstances. Just like various countries around the world, each state has evolved its own unique energy template. As mentioned, the bars in Figure 15.3 are raw and are not entirely complete; two things need to be considered.

First, within the United States there is substantial interstate out-sourcing of energy. A New Yorker buying a Dell computer assembled in Austin, Texas should take ownership of the computer and the energy it took to assemble it. Moreover, some states are much more intense in industrial activity. For example, the energy appetite of a Texan is substantially biased by the state's massive, power-hungry petrochemical industry, while a preponderance of deal making on Wall Street keeps New York relatively lean.

To remove such biases and better reflect the relative personal energy appetites of different states on an "apples-to-apples" basis, the appetites should be adjusted to account for interstate manufacturing differences. This is important because manufacturers locate their plants in the most financially attractive locations, but all Americans collectively benefit from the output.

On top of this, and as introduced in Chapter 3, global energy off-shoring has to be accounted for as well. I've already shown this on an aggregate national level. There is a Wal-Mart full of Chinese-made goods within reach of nearly every American citizen. All Americans, regardless of which state they live in, outsource about a fifth of their net energy appetite to other countries by buying their goods.

Adjusting for interstate and global factors, Figure 15.4 shows the *adjusted* energy appetites for the six states. As you can see, doing so increases the appetites of Californians and New Yorkers to 47 BPY and 49 BPY, respectively. For perspective, the leanest states have energy appetites about 20 percent higher than the WealthyWorld average of 40 BOE/person per year.

Let's dissect California, Pennsylvania, and Texas and look at trends of energy appetite and diet over time. Figure 15.5 shows consumption of all the primary fuels and renewables since 1965 on an *unadjusted* basis for each state.

Taking the numbers back to a personal level for a moment, before the 1980s California's unadjusted energy appetite was close to 50 BPY. Policies and prices cut appetite by a dramatic 20 percent over the 20 years between 1980 and 2000. Though Californian readers are sure to congratulate themselves for leveling out their appetite at between 35 and 40 BPY, the trend is actually going upward when proper attribution for outsourcing is applied. That is not to say that California's efforts should be trivialized. California's diet is worth talking about because it highlights some key issues that I have discussed at length in this book.

Commonly referred to as America's "greenest" state (and one with a temperate climate), California has managed to reduce energy consumption through a mixture of mandates, regulations, and high prices. As Denmark has one of the highest electricity price regimes in the world, so electricity prices in California are by far the highest in the United States. Perhaps not surprisingly, while the average American uses 13,300 kWh of electricity, the average Californian uses a mere 7,000 kWh. Besides high prices, California has long-standing energy mandates. In 1977, California was the first state to adopt efficiency standards for appliances. Today, the standards have been expanded to cover 21 categories of appliances, ranging from audio and visual products to ice makers and heaters.

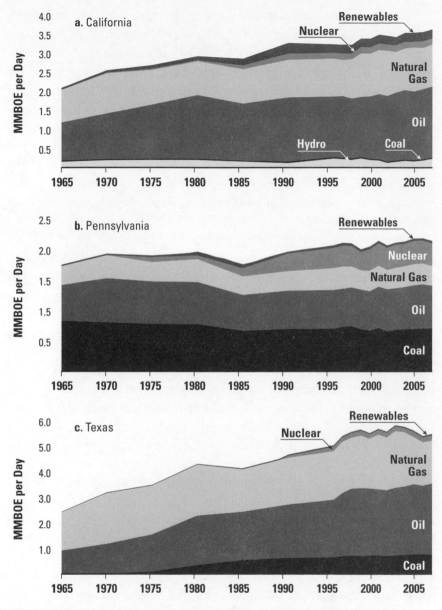

Figure 15.5 Total Energy Appetite and Energy Diet of Three States (1965–2007)

Source: ARC Financial Research, U.S. Energy Information Administration, State Energy Data System.

Perhaps even more celebrated are California's efficiency standards for new buildings. These standards, first introduced in 1978 and since replicated all over the world, have recently been rewritten, and will soon apply to all new construction in the state. The code sets targets for energy efficiency, water consumption, dual plumbing systems for potable and recyclable water, diversion of construction waste from landfills, and use of environmentally sensitive materials in construction and design, including eco-friendly flooring, carpeting, paint, coatings, thermal insulation, and acoustical wall and ceiling panels. It is America's first statewide green building code.

California also offers lucrative incentives for consumers to "go green." To qualify for a $2,000 tax rebate, homeowners must show that their homes beat building standards for energy efficiency by 15 percent or more. This is often as simple as changing the color of one's roof from black to a lighter shade. Incentives are also offered to homebuilders who integrate solar technology into their designs. Additionally, since January 1, 2007 the California Energy Council has been offering cash rebates on eligible grid-connected small wind turbine and fuel cell renewable investments.

Now let's consider California's energy diet, as characterized in Figure 15.5, panel a. Hydroelectric power is minimal in California, as rivers are at a premium in western states. Oil is the dominant fuel, which won't come as a surprise to anyone who has been caught in a traffic jam on Interstate 5. The most notable aspect of California's diet is the absence of coal. Coal is not abundant in the state and besides, using coal in California is about as acceptable as smoking in an elementary school classroom. Nuclear power is about the same proportion as hydro and other renewables in its contribution to power generation. The second largest primary fuel is natural gas, about the same proportion as oil.

California is targeting some aggressive targets for renewables going forward. The thinking behind such targets is that small-market, green fuels will substantially reduce emissions. Frankly, it's tough to see how that will happen. Renewables mostly generate electricity. Oil won't be displaced, because it's a transportation fuel and not used in power generation. There is no coal to displace in California, so renewables will mostly take market share away from the natural gas portion of the state's energy appetite, which I showed in Chapter 14 is the cleanest of all the fossil fuels. Pushing more wind, solar, and biomass into California's energy mix is a bit like swapping out already-lean turkey bacon with fruit; it's a good dietary shift, but the benefits are more marginal than most think. If reducing emissions is the goal, much more impact could be made by focusing on cutting end use energy consumption and leveraging off the asymmetry principal.

The biggest issue in California's diet, like most everywhere in the United States, is its gasoline consumption. California is justly infamous for its urban sprawl. At 25.6 BOE/person per year for transportation fuel, the average Californian consumes 1.5 times as much petroleum as the OECD average. That's 1.8 times the Japanese average, and twice that of both the Swiss and Danes.

Here is where I believe that virtualization can, and will, make a big difference in the near term. A shift to higher efficiency vehicles over the longer term will help too, of course. But if Californians could cut their commutes by 20 percent, the state's gasoline appetite would be reduced by up to 8 million gallons a day.

Other than guzzling too much oil, California's energy diet is actually pretty good. More nukes could take the pressure off natural gas, which can be seasonally volatile in price, but building nuclear power plants comes at a substantial cost and such plans are often contentious.

More than most Americans, Californians have already bought into the notion of conservation, so with a concerted effort, I believe that California could reduce its unadjusted consumption to below the OECD average, and its adjusted appetite to not much above. Achieving that would be a major accomplishment that would convincingly break the First Principle, show a cynical world that a key region of the United States can be at parity or better than its Western peers, and offer an inspirational example to other states.

Pennsylvania's diet is considerably different from California's (Figure 15.5, panel b). In a region that still evokes images of steel mills and mines, Pennsylvania's resource-rich circumstance has led to a 33 percent coal energy diet. If reducing greenhouse gas emissions is a major objective, then Pennsylvania's diet decidedly has to change. The obvious substitute fuel is natural gas. Indeed, promising new natural gas reserves in the Appalachians, in particular the Marcellus Shales that cover half of Pennsylvania, is potentially a boon for the region and could also catalyze a meaningful coal substitution, though coal companies will no doubt lobby hard to protect their interests.

With substantial commuting between cities like Philadelphia and New York, there is a big opportunity in this region for virtualization too. The population is dense and decentralized telework nodes could redefine the whole commuter paradigm with appetite reductions potentially greater than California's. The same of course would apply to all surrounding states like New York and New Jersey. Again, a mind-set shift toward controlling energy appetite, rather than just focusing on supply, can make a substantial difference.

Texas is everyone's favorite scapegoat when it comes to excess. Of course Texans like to play up the "Everything is bigger in Texas" image and they don't disappoint when it comes to energy appetite. At around 90 BPY, the average Texan's energy helping is nearly three times what you would see in Europe or Japan. Nevertheless, we shouldn't be too quick to criticize the energy-consuming habits of those in the Lone Star state, as circumstance plays a big role in how countries and regions develop their appetite.

Lacking major rivers, Figure 15.5, panel c, shows that hydroelectric power is almost nonexistent. Coal and renewables are dwarfed by the two fuels—crude oil and natural gas—that have always been abundant. Natural gas is used primarily for two purposes: petrochemicals and power generation. Both of these commodities are exported by the state for the benefit of other regions in the United States. Oil, of course, is big in Texas, too. And though oil appetite is 42.3 barrels per person, per year—almost 1.7 times California—the statistic is deceiving, because a substantial fraction of oil use in Texas goes toward industrial purposes for the benefit of other Americans. Proper attribution is key to making fair comparisons. In fact, our adjusted 80 BOE/person per year number in Figure 15.4 is probably too high for Texas, as the dynamics of interstate oil and electricity transfers are not taken into account. Also, Texas supplies much of America's overall energy needs, and as we know by now, it takes energy to make energy.

Nevertheless, one shouldn't make too many excuses. Like all states and regions Texas can do more to mitigate appetite and change its diet. The good news is that on the demand side, those with the biggest appetite often have the most opportunity to make the biggest difference.

It's almost trite to analyze the energy circumstances of a handful of states in a few short pages, when each has compiled many years' worth of work and implemented all sorts of extensive energy policies. My observations, analysis, and comments here are meant to highlight the importance of circumstance, or what I'm calling a region's "energy physique," whether it's a country, state, or municipality. I'm also trying to demonstrate that proper "apples-to-apples" comparisons require careful analysis and thinking.

It's easy to criticize countries like the United States and Canada that have big energy appetites, but the reality is that energy physique in a mature economy is difficult to alter. However, that's not to say it can't be done, as Switzerland and others have shown, albeit with much regulatory vigor. For mature economies that are fully industrialized, understanding circumstance and recognizing how appetite and diet has evolved over time is key. As I've discussed throughout Part III of this book, the trick is to apply leverage in the right places—on both the supply and the demand side—where the biggest changes can be made in the shortest period of time.

Prescreening and Avoiding the Next Health Scare

Energy obesity can be tackled in WealthyWorld, but what about WantingWorld? The scale of the potential appetite in WantingWorld is truly frightening. If the United States as a whole reduced its energy appetite from 60 BPY to 45 BPY, it would be viewed as a major accomplishment. However, from a global perspective that achievement would be more than offset by 5.8 billion people in WantingWorld increasing their appetite by just 1 BPY, from 14 to 15. Indeed, 1.3 billion people in China are projected to increase their appetite from an average of 9 BPY to 23 BPY by 2020—a 2.5-fold increase!

It would be nice if rapidly developing nations could avoid the energy obese templates WealthyWorld adopted over a few hundred years of blind progress. The best hope is that countries in WealthyWorld that adopt an energy fitness craze inspire and encourage WantingWorld to avoid excesses and target leaner energy physiques.

But do both worlds, Wealthy and Wanting, have the will to accomplish what Japan, Denmark, Switzerland, and even California have? Are the incentives tangible enough?

For all the difficulties ahead, the good news is that we are experiencing a wonderful convergence of new technologies, new science, and new innovations that, properly channeled with intelligent policies, can help end energy obesity in an even enjoyable way, like the hula hoop was to physical fitness. The sobering news, however, is that technological convergences must often be accompanied by social convergences to have truly significant impact, and the social realm is our greatest weak point, our most uncertain vulnerability.

Will we catalyze enough action on the social, political, and business fronts to step through the doorway that new technology has opened? As we saw with the financial crisis of 2008, a system that appears to be working fine, that is applauded as functioning at the highest levels of efficiency and productivity, can crumble suddenly and unexpectedly. Experts still don't fully understand why the credit crises occurred, but looking back they can see how warning signs were missed, and how opportunities to curb bad practices and habits were overlooked because of the complacency of prosperity.

The energy crisis the world experienced in 2008 can be a reminder for countries to proactively change their practices and behaviors now—or the event can be ignored. Those who pay no heed will only defer to vulnerabilities that keep recurring like unchecked health scares. Let's hope this time that our understanding of the nature of our energy problems has reached a breaking point. As Rahm Emanuel, President Obama's Chief of Staff, said shortly after the presidential election of 2008: "You don't ever want a crisis to go to waste; it's an opportunity to do important things that you would otherwise avoid." That's true for every nation on the global commons.

Leadership on the Commons

The scene is in the future. The year is 2012, over three years since the publication of *The End of Energy Obesity*. Issues relating to energy security, environment, and the economy all continued to occupy the news headlines, though often in separate stories with no apparent thread. That reality was not lost on the participants of the second annual Tri-Issue Energy Symposium, who had gathered for the opening address. Present at the symposium was Peter Tertzakian, who was anxiously waiting to listen to the keynote speaker share ideas from his book and then formally open the proceedings. All participants had been supplied with symposium materials, including a copy of Peter's book. The following are Peter's reflections on that most interesting session.

I was among the many thousands in attendance at the 2012 Tri-Issue Energy Symposium, a worldwide gathering of specialists, business leaders, policymakers, community activists, environmentalists, economists, military experts, and concerned citizens. Like everyone else, I was excited to hear the keynote speaker, who was standing on a broad stage before a backdrop of floor-to-ceiling walls that were actually gigantic screen-like panels dimmed to a pale violet color. After she welcomed us all with her youthful thirtysomething enthusiasm, and applauded the efforts that had made this second annual congress possible, she began to lay out the themes for this year's event.

I was thrilled that Kate was giving the keynote. Her new global Foundation for promoting awareness of world energy issues had really embraced many of the ideas in my book after its publication. As the symposium started, I didn't know exactly what she was going to say, but I did know that that the themes in my book would be threaded together. I was also excited because her Foundation had taken the extra effort to spice up her speech with dynamic visuals.

But for a quick moment I thought I'd arrived at the wrong hall, because Kate had suddenly launched into a lively discussion of the history of time. I'm as enthusiastic a history buff as anyone, but it took me a few minutes to understand the parallels. The walls came alive as the audience watched a series of three-dimensional images demonstrating the evolution of timepieces. We saw sundials powered by solar energy and water clocks powered by hydro. We saw complicated town hall clocks that worked as a result of the countervailing motions of gears and weights, and simple wristwatches that "self-wound" with the natural movement of the wearer's arm. We saw clocks that measured minutes and hours and the phases of the moon, and even the progression of "name days" and astrological signs.

"Throughout history," Kate declared, "human beings have sought to rationalize time. And yet for many centuries, the notion of time was an uncertain and localized concept. When someone looked up into the sky and saw the sun directly overhead, they believed the hour to be noon. But at a town or farm a hundred miles further north or south noon would be determined slightly differently because of the tilt of the earth in its axis. Indeed, noon was different at different times of the year in the same town because of the rotation of the Earth in orbit around the sun. As late as the mid–1800s, the time in New York, Boston, and Philadelphia remained minutes apart by local reckoning.[1]

"This wasn't a serious social problem," Kate noted, "until the Industrial Revolution."

Suddenly, the presentation immersed me in a railway station, on an outdoor platform, as a huffing steam engine filled the screens around us. The image was so vivid it felt as though I had stepped back in time to the early days of rail.

Kate continued, "The Industrial Revolution was catalyzed when James Watt harnessed steam power. But it was the steam locomotive that really changed the way we lived, in part because it dissolved the distances between places. This shift in our concept of geographical space made the synchronization of time necessary."

Listening to her historical dissertation, I found myself thinking about the dissolution of distance in our own era, and wondered where she would take us next.

"Robert Stephenson was the inventor of one of the first steam locomotives. Aldous Huxley, who once wrote so eloquently about the difficulty of abandoning a comfort once attained, called Watts and Stephens coinventors of the modern concept of time.[2] But it was Sandford Fleming, a Scotch-Canadian, who led the push to standardize time after he missed a train in Ireland because of a misprint on the schedule. Fleming wasn't the only person to be frustrated by the imprecision of train schedules in those days, but he persisted with his efforts at standardization beyond any political or social obstacles.

"As a result of Fleming's efforts, eight years later, on October 1, 1884, U.S. President Chester Arthur convened the Prime Meridian Conference in Washington, D.C. After nearly three weeks of deliberation and negotiation, the representative countries agreed that the world would be divided into 24 time zones, with the Prime Meridian running through Greenwich, England, and that each new day would begin at 12 midnight instead of 12 noon. Collectively, as a planet, we synchronized our watches for the first time.

"That synchronization was a key feature of the Industrial Age. Just as work became automated and precise, so the distribution of people and goods became much more efficient. The economies of the industrialized nations began to grow at a pace never before seen in human history. And our energy appetite began to surge, as the First Principle of Energy Consumption—the relationship between energy use and wealth creation—proved itself valid.

"Now, at an event much like the Prime Meridian Conference a century ago, we have gathered to grapple not with the problem of synchronizing time, but with the challenge of breaking the First Principle of Energy Consumption. And yet, synchronization is in part the root cause of our crises. Like the railroad and the standardization of time, the Internet and globalization have done much to synchronize economies around the planet. In the early 2000s, we saw the impact on global energy appetite when economies began to grow in sync. It was the broad expansion of GDP in the developed and developing nations that tightened energy supplies so dramatically, culminating in the events of the summer of 2008. Likewise, it was the synchronized nature of our global financial system that led to the sudden drop in stock prices, the collapse of banks, and plummeting housing prices when the credit crunch rippled through interconnected markets.

"Looking back a few years ago at the financial crisis of 2008, we saw how it resulted in a global recession that reduced consumer demand for goods and services. As the First Principle would indicate, that also resulted in a sharp curtailment of energy appetite. But looking ahead, as our synchronized global economy continues to expand, the 2008 financial crisis will be seen as a mere anomaly in a world where energy appetite is increasingly ravenous. It is our task this week, and in the years to come, to do what we can to reduce energy appetite worldwide and end energy obesity once and for all."

A bit of spontaneous applause could be heard, but Kate didn't allow time for it to ignite.

"I am heartened that this tri-issue conference brings together people with expertise on the troika of subjects that include energy security; environmental sustainability; and economic prosperity—each of which are normally addressed in separate symposiums."

It was great to hear her remind everyone of that important point. I was excited by the possibilities of a forum that would encourage the world to start thinking about how to solve three closely-related problems simultaneously, instead of tripping over each issue in isolation.

My wandering mind returned to Kate's speech as she raised her voice to finish up her introductory comments with an almost staccato conviction: ". . . and breaking today's energy addiction for a prosperous and secure tomorrow!"

This time the applause caught on as she took a moment to shuffle through a few notes and gather her thoughts in advance of launching into the details that the eager faces around her were now expecting.

"I'd like to present you with five core principles that are key to reducing energy appetite in WealthyWorld, decelerating energy demand in WantingWorld, and making meaningful shifts to cleaner, more diverse, and more secure sources of energy. Doing so will put us all on a path to end energy obesity.

"Though my five principles are broad, I will address how each idea affects the various roles of government, corporate leaders, entrepreneurs, financiers, investors, communities, and most importantly . . . us as individuals."

She hadn't even finished the word "individuals" when the walls faded into the full motion of a packed crowd of people, fairly affluent looking, moving slowly, shoulder-to-shoulder, as far as the eye could see. Clearly the scene was somewhere in Asia; and though I thought it was China, the throng of masses looked like what my family and I had experienced in Japan, back in August of 2007, when we attended the Sumida River Fireworks Display in Tokyo. Before I could think more about the location on the screen I had a déjà vu of when, in 2006, we stood in another mass of seemingly endless humanity at Place Trocadero, to watch fireworks blaze out of the Eiffel Tower as hundreds of thousands of Parisians celebrated their July 14th Independence Day. The claustrophobic imagery was effective in creating some discomfort and making me feel very small in my seat.

Text emerged on the walls filled with the moving people, and the speaker continued, "My first core principle is *Recognize the Scale and Scope of the Problem.*

"I have been giving speeches on energy matters for several years now and the number one thing that I feel my audiences don't have a good sense for is the scale of our energy issues. The global numbers are staggering, but even on national scales the realities of effecting meaningful change among even a few hundred million people are daunting. In my view, failure to recognize the scale and scope of energy-related issues are leading us to partial actions that are too slow to be effective.

"Then there is the big picture: the commons on which seven billion people are living is not getting any bigger, yet the number of people continues to grow. And those that have already laid claim to their piece of the commons are getting wealthier and consuming more and more energy in the process. Everybody on the commons is affected by what others are doing. And if the occupants of the commons don't break out of their old-school thinking about energy, by 2020 the world will need a third more energy than we use today; on a daily basis that's 7.6 million tons of coal, 24 million barrels of oil, 145 billion cubic feet of natural gas, among other primary sources! I question whether such volumes are at all possible strictly from a supply point of view, let alone with the caveat that all of it must be delivered with the added need to be secure, clean, and cheap. Frankly the numbers are so incredibly large that they are difficult to comprehend, but that's exactly my point.

"The scope and character of the issue needs attention too. Industrializing nations like China and India are in a different phase of societal evolution than mature countries like Germany, Japan, and the United States. This means various energy appetites and diets on the commons are different, which can lead to misunderstandings and stalemates among policymakers trying to harmonize universally acceptable solutions. Failure to recognize this variation guarantees impasse and inaction, whether the objective is reducing emissions, strengthening energy security, or preserving prosperity.

"To be blunt, made-in-WealthyWorld solutions used to have merit in bygone days, but on a globe where 88 percent of the people and nearly half the economy reside elsewhere, different perspectives and frames of reference are needed. And even within WealthyWorld there needs to be mutual understanding between countries that have their own unique 'energy physique' and circumstance."

She paused for a nervous cough, as though sensing her audience was becoming uncomfortable. But I liked her bluntness and candor. I agreed that expecting the United States to be like Europe was not realistic. Nor was it realistic to think that emerging economies could be denied their right to pursue the same standards of living we have, even if it meant burning a mountain of coal to get there. The question was could they achieve the same objective burning only half a mountain? Surely, we could help them learn from our worst—and best—practices.

Looking up, she continued. "That's the enormous and daunting story about scale. But there are two pieces of good news in recognizing the issue. First, to entrepreneurs it means the market is also huge. And second, if we can figure out the right leverage points at an individual level, that means we can work the scale to our advantage. In other words, it's all a matter of perspective. But I'll come to that in the last of my five principles."

The screens faded out and there was silence. I was glad she transitioned on a positive note about the issue of scale and scope, because I could see from faces in the audience that some were getting quite depressed about the state of the world.

Now my eyes looked to the left in the direction of new sounds and imagery. Vignettes from the world of energy were appearing: old windmills, oilmen wildcatting with wooden rigs, coal mines, and pumpjacks. As the videos took over the center of the stage I made a fleeting mental note that the speaker seemed to have disappeared. More 3D imagery began coming toward me and flowing to the right in a timeline of progressive energy stages moving faster through tighter edits, taking over more and more of the stage like an action movie: solar panels, crops, biorefineries, trucks hauling oil sands, and finally, massive offshore oil platforms that were so real I actually started feeling that I was perched on the top of the drilling tower. I saw a giant arm, spanning floor to ceiling, sweeping round and round in front of me. The drilling tower was fading naturally and then I felt as though I was at the top of a wind turbine with spinning blades. Then, the emergence of text broke the near reality of my experience: *Break Away from Old-School Thinking*. Kate reemerged as if from thin air.

"We are too entrenched in our thinking," she said firmly. "Merely adding more and more energy supplies, renewable or nonrenewable, to fulfill the growing needs of our planet's population is uncreative, undesirable, and unsustainable over any reasonable time frame. The scale and complexity of the issues we face over the next few decades are much greater than they have been in the past. The planet has evolved into a sick patient with multiple symptoms that needs new, creative, common sense prescriptions that can work quickly to remedy its ills."

I knew those candid words were going to rattle a few people in the audience, but I thought she delivered the message well.

She continued, "I know that supplying our way out of our energy issues has worked in the past, but looking ahead that strategy will only be a part of the overall solution—only a small part if we're smart about it—because there is little merit in becoming addicted to more energy, whatever the source, if that can be avoided.

"As Japan, Denmark, Switzerland, and even California have shown, governments can do much to encourage society to reduce energy appetite. However, these are exceptions; there is a tendency by most nations and their policymakers to focus on the wrong end of the telescope. Waiting for new technologies to miraculously appear on the supply side, or just focusing all efforts in one segment—the electrical power sector, say—will limit the leverage needed to end energy obesity locally, nationally, or globally.

"Entrepreneurial activity and a culture of technological innovation both inside and outside the energy industry are vital components for getting creative and breaking the First Principle. Corporations need to steer beyond old-school thinking as well. I'm calling on high-tech companies in Silicon Valley, and other global technology centers known for their creativity and innovation, to think more broadly about how they can help reduce energy obesity. It's true that high-tech entrepreneurs in California and beyond began turning their attention to better solar panels, biofuels, and so on around the middle of the last decade. We certainly need those devices and energy sources, and they will be put to good use over time. But a harsher assessment suggests incremental innovations on old processes are insufficient in the context of the shake-up society needs today. Instead of trying to innovate on electric typewriters and posted letters, it's time to be thinking in terms of word processors and e-mail. We've seen what those innovations can do for productivity, efficiency, and connectivity. Looking ahead into the not so distant future, such quantum leaps are what are needed to change the energy paradigm in a meaningful way.

"Surely we can reach well beyond energy technologies to reduce our energy demand. America, for instance, has long been a world leader in high-tech communication innovations. Analogously, Silicon Valley is the new Saudi Arabia. However, as I've pointed out, globalization and the Internet are beginning to inspire high-tech innovation hubs all over the world. In terms of leveraging information technology to reduce energy demand, we may have many Saudi Arabias in the future.

"I can't tell you as prophetically as Arthur C. Clark did in 1966 about all the changes that we're going to see in the future. But I do know that we can break sharply from the past. Creativity from modern-day Edisons and Fords will move us to the next stage—especially as entrepreneurs start to recognize the enormity of the opportunity. Breaking the First Principle of Energy Consumption cracks open markets that coalesced 6,000 years ago!"

With those bold words everyone remained attentive as the walls came alive with traffic jams, strip malls, congested airplanes on runways, overhead views of suburban sprawl, night shots of lit-up office towers, and other broad images of modern, bustling society. Then the motif shifted to computers being assembled by robots, engineers working on car designs, and a sequence of factory shots making everything from air conditioners to toasters and light bulbs, finally followed by a series of lightning-fast edits of hundreds of hands turning off wall switches. The screen flashed: *Solutions are Social and Technical.*

"During the twentieth century, the Western world applied tremendous resources toward building its lifestyle infrastructure. Power lines, highways, airports, shopping malls, box stores, houses, and suburbs were added at an astonishing rate. Today, from the perspectives of both lifestyle and energy addiction, this template of living has become a trap, especially in North America. We've been pushed to extreme distances from our offices and entertainment centers. The connecting arteries are clogged, making the suburb, office park, and shopping mall lifestyle often aggravating and dissatisfying. We spend absurd amounts of time in energy obese vehicles driving to work, stores, or school. Highway systems, no matter how much they expand, can't seem to alleviate the congestion. This is aggravated by the fact that our air travel is no better. Even infrequent air travelers understand how bad the situation has become. Delays and security inconveniences have become the norms at most airports.

"Isn't it time to rethink this energy obese template? Surely products, services, and new technologies that cheaply, efficiently, and appealingly alleviate these and other energy intense aggravations will generate mass-market demand? And surely we can cut back on the waste of unused energy too?

"This is why I'm telling you that the solutions to our energy-related problems lie as much in the positive reshaping of societal templates and the attitudes that go with them as much as they lie in the capable hands of our innovative scientists and engineers. The two go together, and of course those scientists and engineers that can figure out how to effect mass behavioral change within a society are also typically the ones that get very wealthy—you only need to glance at your Blackberry or look something up on Google to convince yourself of that."

When Kate mentioned Blackberry I glanced down at mine like Pavlov's dog, doing a quick check for any new e-mails before continuing to listen.

"Yet it's unfair to think that engineers and scientists can solve everything, especially if only from an energy supply viewpoint. I'm sorry to say, but too many policymakers and individuals believe so. Everyone must shoulder some responsibility. And politicians must have the backbone to address the people they represent with creativity, candor, and vision about what's really needed. It's called leadership. Instead of offering tired platitudes and old-school rhetoric about energy and climate change that most people have become desensitized to, we need exciting vision and attainable goals that we can buy into. As with the supply side, we need to ask ourselves why are we so focused on seeking solutions that perpetuate the demands of an old model of living? Are we really so afraid to look in the mirror and change? We alter our lifestyles and habits reactively, often without noticing, so why not proactively with intent?" Kate paused to let the audience digest the questions.

I thought Kate really hit home with the mental provocations. I looked down at my Blackberry again. I received good news in an e-mail from my son telling me that he would to be able to join us for dinner. That's great, I thought, as I put the addictive gadget away. And just in time too, because the spectacle of the screens began to illuminate again. A few typical *Inconvenient Truth*-type glacier photos appeared at the left, clips of the war in Iraq showed up center stage, and massive cranes at the Hong Kong International Terminals loading cargo containers took the right. The motifs seemed to be environment, geopolitics, and economy. But there was more coming: all sorts of scenes with the common thread of energy consumption, technology, everyday lifestyles . . . actually my brain found it hard to digest so many disparate scenes. Thankfully, the subtext and our speaker offered clarity just in time: *Think and Act Holistically.*

"As I mentioned, this conference is a great step toward thinking broadly about energy-related problems. To date, our thinking has been far too narrow and simplistic about a problem set that is very wide in scope. And there are other dimensions that we need to think about holistically, too.

"Social, political, economic, and environmental forces are critical ingredients for instigating and accelerating the adoption of technologies that make new ways of life possible if not necessary. Here, too, we are seeing an alignment of trends. To break the First Principle conclusively, a combination of clear-eyed foresight, sound policies, sustained motivation, opportunistic adoption of new products, and grassroots change among the citizenry is needed. It starts with vision. Like putting a man on the moon, there has to be a deliberate harnessing of resources and determination to achieve something extraordinary. Again, leadership is a required ingredient since the attention of bureaucracies, businesses, and millions of people must be focused on the goal. At the same time, the voices of leaders cannot be overly mired by ballyhoo. In the United States, when in 2008 oil prices soared, there were calls for a new Manhattan Project to focus on technologies that would make America energy independent. But a single project or an isolated technology or a quixotic one-dimensional goal like total energy independence will not generate a realistic solution set. A high impact and realistic goal like ending energy obesity—one that's actually proven to be possible—requires a mix of all-encompassing approaches.

"As such, the policies that governments implement must be holistic in nature. Piecemeal policies and efforts won't work. Legislation or regulation that focuses only on car efficiency or renewable portfolio standards for electricity are steps in the right direction, but we cannot forget that energy consumption spans every corner of society. We have shown over and over that cutting back in one area can lead to disheartening splurges in another. All-encompassing programs like Japan's Top Runner show the leverage that meaningful, complete end use considerations can provide. We also need our policies to be dynamic, setting the bar higher and higher over time, because we know our energy appetite has the tendency to grow and technology is always evolving.

"I believe that the technologies of Conservation 2.0 will help us mitigate energy appetite going forward because they will give us heightened awareness of energy consumption. In addition, the networking and telepresence technologies of virtualization will promote healthy new habits because they improve the quality of our lives, make us more productive, and increase our comforts. But in order to achieve the long-term commitment of good policy, a consistency of messages among successive leadership groups and active support from grassroots organizations are necessary. I think it will help if our language changes. As the U.S. Department of Agriculture encouraged awareness of nutritious eating habits by introducing the Food Pyramid, and environmentalists developed our consciousness of CO_2 emissions with the notion of the carbon footprint, so speaking the language of energy appetite—ending obesity, developing healthy habits, avoiding rebound effects, and choosing good carbs over bad—will instill these intricate concepts as a mind-set that is easy to relate to and (hopefully!) easier to tackle.

"On the supply side, governments must regain a sense of realpolitik in their thinking about long-term energy needs. Energy is a strategic commodity, something that was acutely understood after World War I. Today, we talk about energy in bellicose terms but we do not think strategically and long-term about our investments. The horizon line must be truly forward-looking, not the next election or budget cycle. And our investments must be multipronged. Rather than focusing overly on one fuel like oil, energy security comes from a diversified diet with flexible fuel choice, just like an investment portfolio that has a mix of secure and high-yield options to mitigate risk.

"You may think that I'm only directing this core principle at policymakers. But it's also directed to business leaders and individuals, who have the power to question, sway, and even demand that their leaders think bigger picture and longer term. At the highest level it's about everyone 'buying in' to the greater good and having leaders lead them there. If that kind of culture sounds corny, I only need remind you again of Denmark, Switzerland, Japan, and even California; these are examples where citizens of progressive societies have bought into, if not demanded of their leaders, the idea of controlling energy appetite for the pursuit of the greater good."

A final multimedia round rattled my senses. To the left: smart meters, power lines, wind turbines, and liquefied natural gas terminals. To the right: people engaged in using high-tech gadgetry and software that have shaped society in the past 20 or so years.

"The most important principle is left to last," she said as the words, *Go Where the Leverage Is*, came at me from center stage.

After a moment's deliberate silence our speaker let down her otherwise assertive tone and began speaking more softly, sincerely. "I am really looking forward to tomorrow's breakout sessions on leveraging the asymmetry principle.

"You were given the materials to read up on, so you know the type of multiplicative power this solution set presents. Surely, this is our greatest opportunity. Honestly looking at how much source energy goes unused in the support of our lifestyles leaves one uncertain whether to laugh or cry.

"Through efficiency gains we can put more energy to work, or even better figure out how to dispense with unnecessary work and realize dramatic, multiplicative benefits.

"In an extension to my opening comments on time, it's important to recognize that the scale and rate of growth in global energy consumption is not synchronized with the rate of innovation and adoption of energy systems. However, I know that by exploiting this simple, high-leverage principle, we can get back in sync quickly, and also appreciably reduce our energy appetites and break the First Principle of Energy Consumption once and for all.

"Indeed, this last point I'm making is a corollary of all of the others, especially in thinking about how to tackle the scale issue without adding more and more supply at the source. Policymakers must channel more effort into areas where maximum leverage exists. The asymmetry principal calls out for the necessity of such efforts.

"Like any dieter, we need to set goals. A 20 percent reduction in energy appetite for WealthyWorld countries is not unrealistic given how much waste there is in the system—and now we have the technical means to inexpensively measure and monitor. It just requires entrepreneurial and visionary thinking. Over the past two centuries, we have introduced all sorts of devices that have meaningfully changed the way we live, work, and play. What other devices, already available to us now, can leverage the asymmetry principle such that we improve our standard of living, yet actually reduce our energy demand? Edison and Ford would have relished the challenge, no doubt. So I leave that with you today as a thought experiment and encourage you to submit your ideas over the week. We'll collect and judge them in time for the closing ceremonies. Hopefully, that will be a fun, creative, and productive use of everyone's collective brainpower.

"I have only a few minutes left. In other words, I'm running out of time. To that end, let me return to the theme of time with which I started this presentation.

"Time was once a very public and social concern. In the medieval age, town leaders often pooled their resources and contracted with engineers to construct giant clocks atop spires in their central squares. This gave everyone in town a common understanding of time, and helped to coordinate events, meetings, and plans, catalyzing economic growth in the process.

"Today, time is a commonly agreed upon measure. We no longer wonder whether time in one town or country is the same in another. We no longer have to go to a main square to see what time it is. In fact, we can hardly avoid a minute-by-minute awareness of time. Time has gone from a social concern to a personal concern (where wearing and winding a watch was a matter of personal responsibility) to something we no longer need to be conscientious about. We can find accurate time on our watch, our cell phone, or our computers, and time counters are found within many of our electronics devices. Time has become embedded in our lives. One of my own favorite accessories is a self-winding wristwatch. I love that I don't need to be conscientious about winding it up. The natural motion of my arm keeps my watch constantly wound and precise, a technology that must be one of the most energy efficient in history.

"The point is that we've made time easy and natural. We've gone from needing to marshal economic, social, and scientific resources to build accurate town clocks to taking time utterly for granted. One day, we'll look back on our efforts to reduce energy appetite and cut the incredible amounts of energy waste, and wonder at the primitivism of the struggle. When that day comes, energy challenges will no longer be a matter for global gatherings. Indeed, a meeting such as the one convening today will be as anachronistic as the Prime Meridian Conference of 1884 seems to us now. Instead of worrying anxiously and frequently about energy appetite, we will be aided by automatic devices and processes to moderate our energy use. By then, our energy-intense lives will have been soothed by a new template for work, comfort, and entertainment.

"That's when we'll know we have finally broken the First Principle. I have no doubt that other symposiums tackling equaly grave or compelling matters will still be necessary. But the energy consumption that underpins our lives will be free from the threats of diminished supply, geopolitical tension, and environmental degradation.

Looking pleased that her speech was well received, she took a confident step forward, "Thank you. And my best wishes for a vigorous and productive week together."

I, like everyone else applauded her keynote, which ended right on time at 6:30 P.M. The plenary sessions and networking would follow over the next four days. Many papers would be presented, ideas debated, and resolutions agreed upon. It was satisfying and exciting to think about the work ahead. For now I was tired. Our keynote speaker disappeared into the wall.

I rose to leave my home office, a gentle chime confirming that I was about to leave the room. The lights around me started dimming and my wall-sized telepresence screens faded to black. I walked down the hall and into our dining room in time to join my family for dinner. My son, who was attending university on the East Coast, would be joining us at the dinner table, something he did every Sunday. The spot he occupied for years was hooked up to a paper-thin monitor that some entrepreneur made easily attachable to a chair back. My son asked me what I'd thought of the opening ceremonies at the symposium. It turned out his class had also sat in on the lecture. But soon the family conversation turned to the new 3D gaming system that was being marketed in advance of Christmas. I made a joke about my old Telstar Pong game, and how much times had changed.

And that's the thing: Change is the hardest part of the energy struggle we're engaged in now. But lives and lifestyles adapt. Technology becomes embedded in the way we live, work, and play. And then we rarely think about those changes anymore.

Notes

Chapter 1: After the Banquet

1. Brinkley, *Wheels for the Road*.
2. Ibid.
3. Rear Admiral Hyman G. Rickover, U.S. Navy, Delivery at a Banquet of the Annual Scientific Assembly of the Minnesota State Medical Association, St. Paul, Minnesota, May 14, 1957.

Chapter 2: Whetting the Energy Appetite

1. From "In 1892" by Matt C. Woodward (Willis Woodward Co., 1890), *Thomas Edison and Modern America*, 128.
2. *Scientific American*, 1899.
3. Kyvig, *Daily Life in the United States: 1920–1940*, 28.
4. Ford, *My Life and Work*.
5. Brinkley, *Wheels for the Road,* 100.
6. Kyvig, *Daily Life in the United States: 1920–1940*, 28–29.
7. http://www.tatamotors.com/

Chapter 4: The World's Factory

1. http://www.chinaembassycanada.org/, June 21, 2007.
2. Pomeranz, *The Great Divergence*.
3. Hessler, *China: Inside the Dragon*.
4. Ibid., 144.
5. Note that Hong Kong's unadjusted, raw energy appetite is 35 BPY, as was shown in Figure 3.7.
6. Hardin, *The Tragedy of the Commons*, 1244.

Chapter 5: Breaking Our Energy Diet

1. Bradsher, *China's Central Bank Is Short of Capital*.
2. Maslow, Abraham H., A Theory of Human Motivation, *Psychological Review*, Vol. 50, p. 370.
3. *Time*, "Detroit's Gamble to Get Rolling Again," February 10, 1975, 49.
4. Copulos, Milton R., *The High Cost of the 55 MPH Speed Limit*. The Heritage Foundation, September 9, 1986.
5. Comfort, Darlene J., The Abasand Fiasco, 12.
6. Lorenz, *The Atomic Age Enters a New Dawn*.

Chapter 6: Price and Value

1. Wilde, Oscar, *Lady Windermere's Fan,* Act III-6.
2. Hagens, *The Energy Return of (Industrial) Solar*.

Chapter 7: Eating Our Efficiencies

1. http://cityroom.blogs.nytimes.com/2007/11/20/rockefeller-tree-is-green-but-is-it-green
2. U.K. Energy Research Centre, *The Rebound Effect*.
3. http://www.washingtonpost.com/wp-dyn/content/article/2008/07/15/AR2008071501259.html.
4. Solveig and Taoyuan, *Coal Cleaning*.

Chapter 8: Complex Carbons

1. Grossman and Krueger, "Environmental Impact of a North American Free Trade Agreement." A revised and expanded version of this paper, entitled, "Economic Growth and the Environment," was published in the *Quarterly Journal of Economics* 110, no. 2, (1995): 353–77.

2. http://sequestration.mit.edu/pdf/EST_web_article.pdf

3. Energy Information Administration, "Emissions of Greenhouse Gases in the United States 2007."

Chapter 9: The Maddening Allure of the First Principle

1. Richard Nixon's Fifth State of the Union Address, 1974. http://www.thisnation.com/library/sotu/1974rn.html.

2. http://www.pbs.org/wgbh/amex/carter/filmmore/ps_crisis.html.

3. Remarks delivered at the White House, Monday, January 26, 2009.

4. Speech to the Associated Press' annual meeting, April 30, 2001.

Chapter 10: The Asymmetry Principle

1. Heidegger, *The Question Concerning Technology and Other Essays.*

2. Jehl, *Menlo Park Reminiscences, Volume Two*, 859.

3. U.S. Energy Information Administration, 2006.

4. http://www.eia.doe.gov/kids/energyfacts/saving/efficiency/savingenergy.html.

5. Using data from the U.S. Energy Information Administration, in 2007 the average fuel mix for electrical power generation in the United States is 49 percent coal, 20 percent natural gas, 19 percent nuclear, 7 percent hydro, 2 percent petroleum, and 2 percent renewables.

6. Van Anglen, *Simplify Simplify and Other Quotations from Henry David Thoreau.*

Chapter 11: Beyond Nostalgia

1. Satellite technology, of course, was a subject Clarke understood well. In 1945, he proposed in a letter to the editor of *Wireless World* magazine that V2 rocket technology be adopted for other uses as a communication tool. As he wrote: "An 'artificial satellite' at the correct distance from the earth would make one revolution every 24 hours; i.e., it would remain stationary above the same spot and would be within optical range of nearly half the earth's surface. Three repeater stations, 120 degrees apart in the correct orbit, could give television and microwave coverage to the entire planet." The distance Clarke proposed for stationary satellites used to be referred to as the Clarke Orbit.

2. Clarke, Arthur C., *Everybody in Instant Touch.*

3. Davidow, *Marketing High Technology: An Insider's View*.

Chapter 12: Conservation 2.0

1. The "Owl" and the "Wattson" are two other devices that translate energy and price data into a combination of digital information and ambient information.

2. http://www.ubiq.com/hypertext/weiser/calmtech/calmtech

3. http://www.wired.com/techbiz/people/magazine/15-08/st_thompson

4. Fitzgerald, *Finding and Fixing a Home's Power Hogs*.

5. Assuming that the average phantom load is 7.0 percent and half is mitigated. According to the U.S. Energy Information Administration, the average home consume 936 kWh per month, so a 3.5% saving at the socket translates to 393 kWh per year. Running this number back through the average U.S. electrical power fuel mix of 48.5% coal or 21.5% natural gas, and applying the average inefficiencies and conversions within each system leads to the volumes calculated.

Chapter 13: Dissolving Distance

1. Marchand, *Advertising the American Dream: Making Way for Modernity 1920–1940*, 3.

2. http://www.nytimes.com/2008/12/01/technology/internet/01facebook.html.

3. Ibid.

4. http://nymag.com/news/features/27341/

5. http://www.washingtonpost.com/wp-dyn/content/article/2008/12/02/AR2008120202527.html.

6. http://movies.nytimes.com/2008/01/23/movies/23band.html?scp=4&sq=U23D&st=cse

7. Drucker, *The Dawn of E-Life*.

8. Hamel, *Leading the Revolution*, 163.

9. U.S. Department of Transportation, Federal Highway Administration, Highway Statistics 2000, Washington, D.C., 2001. Available at: http://www.fhwa.dot.gov/ohim/hs00/pdf/mf21.pdf. See tables MV-1 and MV-9.

Chapter 14: A Low-Carb, Highly-Scalable Diet

1. The Federal Reserve Board, Testimony of Allan Greenspan Before the Committee on Energy and Commerce, U.S. House of Representatives, Natural Gas Supply and Demand Issues, June 10, 2003.

2. http://www.naturalgas.org/environment/naturalgas.

3. Assuming that a new, combined cycle gas-fired power generator with 55 percent conversion efficiency replaces a fleet average coal-fired power plant at 28 percent (refer back to Figure 10.2).

Chapter 15: The Energy Health Craze

1. International Energy Agency, "Energy Policies of IEA Countries: Japan 2008 Review."

2. Abboud, *Power Play: How Denmark Paved the Way to Energy Independence.*

3. U.S. Energy Information Administration (EIA), "International Energy Annual 2005: World Total Net Electricity Consumption."

4. Ibid.

Epilogue: The 2012 Tri-Issue Energy Symposium

1. Blaise, *Time Lord: Sir Sandford Fleming and the Creation of Standard Time*, 32.

2. Ibid., 18.

Glossary

Asymmetry principle   The lopsided relationship between how much raw energy is available at the primary source—for example, at an oil well—and the small fraction of energy that is actually put to useful work at the consuming end. The principle states that a unit of energy saved at the consumer level amplifies into multiple units of energy saved at the source. In effect, the asymmetry principle exposes the high levels of inefficiency in society's energy systems and highlights the tremendous leverage offered by efficiency gains and conservation in mitigating source energy consumption.

Asymmetry diagram   A step-like diagram that illustrates the asymmetry principle, by chaining and displaying energy losses from source energy to end use work.

Avatar   A virtual representation of oneself in a computer game or virtual world.

Backfire   What happens when efficiency gains in an energy system directly and indirectly result in an *increase* in source energy consumption. In other words, a condition where rebound effects exceed 100%.

Bandwidth The volume of digital information that a network or telecommunication system can transmit in a unit of time. Commonly expressed in bits per second (bps).

Barrel of oil equivalent (BOE) The equivalent amount of energy that is contained in one 42 gallon barrel of oil. A BOE, like a British Thermal Unit (Btu), or gigajoule (GJ), or a Kilowatt hour (kWh) is a standard unit of energy that all other energy units can be converted into. For example, one good-quality U.S. ton of thermal coal (12,300 btu/pound) contains the same amount of energy as 3.9 barrels of oil; therefore, one ton of coal can be said to contain 3.9 BOE. A 2 Megawatt wind turbine running full out for 24 hours will produce the same amount of energy as is contained in 26.1 barrels of oil equivalent, or 26.1 BOE.

BOE See Barrel of oil equivalent.

BOE/d The number of BOEs of energy supplied or consumed in one day.

BPY A standard unit of personal energy appetite, or the amount of total energy (in BOEs) that one person in a society consumes in one year. BPY is a shortened acronym for the more cumbersome descriptor, BOE per Person per Year.

Break point innovation A compelling innovation that enters the market quickly and transforms society in a way that significantly alters energy consumption. Cars and light bulbs are classic examples. This book argues that societies need to be looking for break point innovations that change the way citizens live, work, and play such that energy consumption growth trends are reversed without compromising standard of living.

Calorie A standard unit of energy that was used predominantly by physicists in the nineteenth century to measure heat. There are various definitions depending on experimental conditions. Generally, a calorie is the amount of energy required to raise the temperature of one gram of water by one degree Centigrade. Calories used by physicists should not be confused with food calories. There are 1.46 billion calories of energy that can potentially be put to work in a barrel of oil.

Commons A common geographic area with a limited resource that is typically occupied by self-interested parties that must learn to ration the resource or face dire consequences. A term made famous by American ecologist Garrett Hardin in a paper he published in the journal *Science* in 1968.

Compelling In the context of this book, compelling is used to describe products and systems that are irresistible in their utility and are therefore readily adopted by society.

Conservation and Conservation 1.0 In the context of this book, conservation is the act of reducing energy appetite by seeking ways to reduce unnecessary energy consumption. In other words, making decisions to turn things like light bulbs off. Specifically, Conservation 1.0 refers to mitigating energy consumption through uncomfortable reduction in standard of living or change in lifestyle.

Conservation 2.0 The next generation of conservation, beyond Conservation 1.0, where personal energy consumption can be reduced through intelligent automation, new high-tech innovations that alter the way we live, work, and play, and by evolving into less-energy intense societal templates.

Conventional gas Natural gas that is found and produced using conventional vertical well bores in relatively porous geologic formations.

Conversion device A device that converts energy from one form into another. For example, a light bulb converts electrical energy into light and heat. A generator converts rotating mechanical energy into electrical energy. An internal combustion engine ultimately converts the chemical energy in gasoline into rotating mechanical energy.

Efficiency The ratio of how much useful work is produced out of an energy conversion device relative to how much energy went in. Efficiency can be measured at the point of one energy conversion device, like a light bulb, or between a series of conversions across an entire system. For example, a conventional light bulb is no more than 10 percent efficient at converting the input electricity into usable light; the remaining 90 percent is 'wasted' as heat.

Energy appetite The rate of energy consumption in a country or region.

Energy appetite (adjusted) The rate of energy consumption in a country or region that has been adjusted to account for the net amount energy that is being "offshored" to other jurisdictions.

Energy appetite (personal)   The rate of energy consumption of an individual, expressed in this book in BPY. For a country in any particular year, this is calculated by taking the total amount of energy consumed in that year (all primary sources normalized to BOE/year) and then divided by the population at that time.

Energy appetite (raw)   The rate of energy consumption in a country or region unadjusted for any offshoring or other effects.

Energy break point   A relatively discrete point in time when the way that a society consumes its energy, and the way that it is supplied its energy, starts to change significantly. Energy break points have historically been accompanied by significant change in a country or region's energy diet. A break point is typically catalyzed by a series of forces—for example, environmental, geopolitical, military, economic—that often converge to a point of crisis, and are usually accompanied by reactive government policy implementations.

Energy diet   The composition of primary energy sources in a country or region's total energy mix. For example, the United States energy diet in 2008 consisted of 37.3 percent oil, 22.8 percent coal, 24.0 percent natural gas, 8.5 percent nuclear, 2.5 percent hydroelectric, and 4.9 percent renewables (which is mostly burning wood).

Energy menu   In a region or country, the energy menu constitutes all the available source energy options. A region's energy diet often differs from what is on the menu.

Energy obesity   A condition where a large energy appetite (typically greater than 40 BPY) and "unhealthy" energy diet makes a region or country especially vulnerable to the ill effects of energy crises. Mitigating energy obesity is a proactive form of rebalancing, in advance of unwanted energy break points.

Energy physique   The social, geographic, demographic, and economic circumstances of a country or region that broadly define its energy appetite and energy diet. A society's energy physique can evolve over time, though once it has gone through its industrialization phase its physique, or energy template, becomes more rigid and difficult to change.

Energy template   See Energy physique.

EROEI   The acronym for Energy Return on Energy Invested, pronounced "E-Roy." A ratio that measures the efficacy of making source energy available for societal use. Put another way, EROEI is a measurement of how much energy it takes to make energy available. For example, it takes the equivalent energy contained in one cubic foot of natural gas to find, develop, and produce 20 cubic feet for societal use. Therefore, the EROEI for natural gas is 20:1. The higher the EROEI, the better. On the other hand, an EROEI less than 1:1 is dire, because it indicates that society is consuming more than one unit of energy to deliver a new one.

First Principle of Energy Consumption Also referred to as just the First Principle. A 6,000 year-old relationship that correlates personal wealth and well-being directly with energy consumption. Simply put, more wealth (and therefore standard of living) equals more energy use and vice versa.

Food calorie A food calorie, or dietary calorie, is a unit used by nutritionists to measure the amount of energy in food that is available for digestion. Quantitatively, it's the amount of energy required to raise the temperature of one kilogram of water by one degree Centigrade. Therefore, one food calorie is equal to 1,000 "physics" calories.

GDP Gross Domestic Product; a standard measure of economic activity measured in dollars per year. The GDP growth is the rate at which GDP increases.

Hypocaust A 2,100 year-old Roman innovation for heating homes and buildings. Heat from fire stoked in a chamber was channeled under stone floors for heating living space in the winter. The hypocaust was the harbinger of underfloor heating.

Industrialization phase A phase in the evolution of a country where it transitions from a dominantly agrarian mode of life to an industrial one. The industrialization phase is accompanied by mechanization (building of infrastructure and adoption of machines) and mobilization (building of roads and adoption of cars).

Manufactured gas Combustible gas, similar to natural gas, that was made from coal in a toxic process. Manufactured gas was a significant source of primary energy in the nineteenth century.

Nature's gas The name given to conventional natural gas produced from wells drilled into subsurface geology after it began to substitute for manufactured gas.

OECD countries Established in 1961, the OECD is a Paris-based organization that "brings together the governments of countries committed to democracy and the market economy." The Organization for Economic Cooperation and Development is a club of 30 already-industrialized, developed countries that among many other things, collects financial and economic data from around the world for the purposes of fighting poverty and building prosperity.

Offshored energy As in offshoring of energy. The amount of energy that is embedded in goods that have been manufactured abroad, but consumed domestically. Repatriating offshored energy gives a more accurate measure of personal energy appetite. For example, the energy used to manufacture goods made in China and exported to the United States should be repatriated to the buyers living in the United States.

Primary energy Similar to source energy. The five primary energy sources that constitute over 98 percent of the world's energy diet are: coal, oil, natural gas, nuclear, and hydro.

Rebalancing The process of changing a region or country's energy appetite and diet to ensure future growth and prosperity. A rebalancing phase is the time period that comes after an energy break point, when a country or region's energy diet and appetite must change to new environmental, political, and economic realities.

Rebound effect An societal outcome where efficiency gains in an energy system do not translate into a decrease of source energy consumption. For example, greater steam engine efficiencies in the 19th century led to an accelerating demand for steam engines, thereby actually increasing the overall demand for coal. A 100% rebound effect is when efficiency gains are completely offset by greater energy use, a condition termed "backfire."

Smart grid Systems that are starting to be adopted by power utilities to monitor, manage, and optimally control the distribution of electrical power to consumers. Smart grid systems incorporate two-way communications and advanced sensors. A key component of smart grids is the transmission of information about the electrical power that is being distributed, especially price.

Smart home A home that can take advantage of smart grid technologies. As well, homes that are automated (to various degrees of sophistication) to intelligently manage energy consumption. In its most sophisticated form, a smart home can "learn" the habits of its inhabitants and optimize energy consumption to minimize waste.

Societal template   A rigid template of living (and resultant energy appetite and diet) that forms after a country or region's energy physique matures.

Source energy   The primary sources of energy that are used by society. Coal, crude oil, natural gas, uranium, and flowing water (hydro) are the five major sources of energy. The wind, the sun, geothermal energy from the earth, and biomass from organic matter are also source energies.

Standard of living   Qualitatively, standard of living is our level of perceived comfort and well-being. Quantitatively, there are several metrics that can be used. In this book, average standard of living for individuals in a country, in any one year, is measured by dividing real GDP by population.

Telepresence   The experience of feeling in the presence of others without physically being in the same location. The convergence of new virtualization technologies is dramatically improving telepresence experiences. Cisco is an example of a company that is now offering customers full-featured commercial Telepresence systems.

Unconventional gas   Natural gas that originates from geologic sources that is typically produced from "tight," low-porosity reservoirs. Liberating such gas requires innovative drilling and well completion techniques that are different from the conventional realm. The tremendous potential of vast new unconventional gas reserves is just beginning to be realized.

Utility   An economic term, mostly qualitative, that captures the total satisfaction derived from consuming a good or service.

Wanting World   Countries that are striving to give their citizens the standard of living comparable to that of WealthyWorld.

Wealthy World   Countries that have already gone through their industrialization phase and have achieved among the highest standards of living in the world. In general, WealthyWorld countries overlap with those in the OECD.

Work   The amount of useful energy that is turned out by an energy conversion device for the benefit of a consumer. For example, the work produced by a blow dryer is heat for drying hair. A light bulb produces work in the form of light for seeing better in dark or dim surroundings.

Virtualization The process of turning an individual's physical presence and circumstances into a virtual one that can be transmitted to, and experienced by, other individuals in remote locations. Virtualization can be near-to-real, as in telepresence, or quasi-real, as in the use of avatars in virtual worlds.

Virtual World A computer-based simulation for people to interact with others via digital representations of themselves; for example, avatars.

Bibliography

Books

Ahlbrandt, Thomas S. *AAPG Memoir 86: Global Resource Estimates From Total Petroleum Systems*. Tulsa, OK: American Association of Petroleum Geologists, 2005.

Allen, Frederick Lewis. *The Big Change: America Transforms Itself 1900–1950*. New York: Harper & Brothers Publishers, 1952.

Anderson, Judy, and Curtis D. Anderson. *Electric and Hybrid Cars: A History*. Jefferson, NC: McFarland & Company, 2005.

Anthony, Bird. *Antique Automobiles*. London: George Allen & Unwin, 1967.

Ausubel, Jesse H., and Hedy E. Sladovich. *Technology and Environment*. Washington, D.C.: National Academy Press, 1989.

Ausubel, Jesse H., and Dale H. Langford. *Technological Trajectories and the Human Environment*. Washington, D.C.: National Academy Press, 1997.

Axelrod, Robert. *The Evolution of Cooperation*. New York: Basic Books, 1984.

Billington, David P. *The Innovators: The Engineering Pioneers Who Made America Modern*. New York: John Wiley & Sons, 1996.

Blaise, Clark. *Time Lord: Sir Sandford Fleming and the Creation of Standard Time*. New York: Random House, 2000.

Boyle, Godfrey. *Renewable Energy: Power for a Sustainable Future, Second Edition.* New York: Oxford University Press, 2004.

Bradford, Travis. *Solar Revolution: The Economic Transformation of the Global Energy Industry.* Cambridge, MA: MIT Press, 2006.

Bright, Arthur A. Jr. *The Electric-Lamp Industry: Technological Change and Economic Development from 1800 to 1947.* New York: The MacMillan Company, 1949.

Brinkley, Douglas. *Wheels for the Road: Henry Ford, His Company, and a Century of Progress.* New York: Viking, 2003.

Burrows, Edwin G., and Mike Wallace. *Gotham: A History of New York City to 1898.* New York: Oxford University Press, 1999.

Cardwell, Donald. *The Norton History of Technology.* New York: WW. Norton & Company, 1995.

Carson, Iain, and Vijay V. Vaitheeswaran. *Zoom: The Global Race to Fuel the Car of the Future.* New York: Twelve, 2007.

Catton, William R. Jr. *Overshoot: The Ecological Basis of Revolutionary Change.* Urbana, IL: University of Illinois Press, 1980.

Childress, David H., and Nikola Tesla. *The Fantastic Inventions of Nikola Tesla.* Stelle IL: Adventures Unlimited, 1993.

Clymer, Floyd. *Henry's Wonderful Model T: 1908–1927.* New York: McGraw-Hill Book Company, 1955.

Comfort, Darlene J. *The Abasand Fiasco.* Edmonton, Canada: Friesen Printers, 1980.

Collins, Theresa M., and Lisa Gitelman. *Thomas Edison and Modern America: A Brief History with Documents.* Boston: Bedford/St. Martins, 2002.

Conot, Robert. *Thomas A. Edison: A Streak of Luck.* New York: De Capo Press, 1979.

Crosby, Alfred W. *Children of the Sun: A History of Humanity's Unappeasable Appetite for Energy.* New York: W. W. Norton, 2006.

Dahl, Carol, A. *International Energy Markets.* Tulsa, OK: PennWell, 2004.

Davidow, William H. *Marketing High Technology: An Insider's View.* New York: The Free Press, 1986.

Diamond, Jared. *Collapse: How Societies Choose to Fail or Succeed.* New York: Viking, 2005.

Dickinson, H. W. *A Short History of the Steam Engine.* Cambridge: Cambridge University Press, 1938.

Drucker, Peter F. *Post-Capitalist Society.* New York: HarperBusiness, 1993.

———. *Technology, Management and Society.* New York: Harper Colophon Books, 1970.

Duany, Andres, Elizabeth Plater-Zyberk, and Jeff Speck. *Suburban Nation: The Rise of Sprawl and the Decline of the American Dream*. New York: North Point Press, 2000.

Ellerman, Denny A., Barbara K. Buchner, and Carlo Carraro. *Allocation in the European Emissions Trading Scheme*. Cambridge: Cambridge University Press, 2007.

Eveleigh, David J. *Candle Lighting*. Princes Risborough, U.K.: Shire Publications Lts., 2003.

Ford, Henry. *My Life and Work*. Sioux Falls, SD: NuVision Publications LLC, 2007.

Foster, Richard N. *Innovation: The Attacker's Advantage*. New York: Summit Books, 1986.

Friedel, Robert, and Paul Israel. *Edison's Electric Light: Biography of an Invention*. New Brunswick, NJ: Rutgers University Press, 1987.

Golley, John. *Genesis of the Jet: Frank Whittle and the Invention of the Jet Engine*. Shrewsbury, U.K.: Airlife Publishing, 1996.

Halberstam, David. *The Reckoning*. New York: Avon Books, 1986.

Hamel, Gary. *Leading the Revolution: How to Thrive in Turbulent Times by Making Innovation a Way of Life*. Cambridge, MA: Harvard Business School Press, 2002.

Heidegger, Martin. *The Question Concerning Technology and Other Essays*. New York: Harper Perennial, 1982.

Hounshell, David A. *From the American System to Mass Production, 1800–1932*. Baltimore, MD: Johns Hopkins University Press, 1984.

Hospitalier, E. *The Modern Applications of Electricity*. London: Kegan Paul, Trench & Co., 1882.

Hughes, Thomas P. *Networks of Power: Electrification in Western Society, 1880–1930*. Baltimore, MD: Johns Hopkins University Press, 1993.

Ihde, Don. *Philosophy of Technology: An Introduction*. New York: Paragon House, 1993.

International Energy Agency. *Energy Policies of IEA Countries: Japan 2008 Review*. Paris: OECD/IEA, 2008.

———. *Mind the Gap: Quantifying Principal-Agent Problems in Energy Efficiency*. Paris: OECD/IEA, 2007.

———. *Tracking Industrial Energy Efficiency and CO_2 Emissions*. Paris: OECD/IEA, 2007.

———. *World Energy Outlook, 2007: China and India Insights*. Paris: OECD/IEA, 2007.

Israel, Paul B., Keith A. Nier, and Louis Carlat. *The Papers of Thomas A. Edison: The Wizard of Menlo Park: Volume 4, 1878*. Baltimore, MD: Johns Hopkins University Press, 1998.

James, Peter, and N. Thorpe. *Ancient Inventions*. New York: Ballantine Books, 1994.

Jehl, Francis. *Menlo Park Reminiscences, Volumes One to Three*. Dearborn, MI: The Edison Institute, 1938.

Krupp, Fred, and Miriam Horn. *Earth: The Sequel: The Race to Reinvent Energy and Stop Global Warming*. Environmental Defense Fund. New York: W.W. Norton & Co., 2008.

Kyvig, David E. *Daily Life in the United States: 1920–1940*. Chicago, IL: Ivan R. Dee, 2002.

Leach, William. *Land of Desire: Merchants, Power and the Rise of a New American Culture*. New York: Vintage, 1993.

Marchand, Roland. *Advertising the American Dream—Making Way for Modernity 1920–1940*. Berkeley, CA: University of California Press, 1986.

Millard, Andre. *Edison and the Business of Innovation*. Baltimore, MD: John Hopkins University Press, 1990.

Moore, Geoffery A. *Crossing the Chasm: Marketing and Selling High-Tech Products to Mainstream Customers*. New York: HarperBusiness, 2002.

Mumford, Lewis. *The Culture of Cities*. New York: Harcourt Brace Jovanovich, 1938.

Nye, David E. *Consuming Power: A Social History of American Energies*. Cambridge, MA: MIT Press, 2001.

———. *Electrifying America: Social Meanings of a New Technology*. Cambridge, MA: MIT Press, 1992.

Pomeranz, Kenneth. *The Great Divergence: China, Europe and the Making of the Modern World Economy*. Princeton, NJ: Princeton University Press, 2000.

Porter, Alan L., A. Thomas Roper, Thomas W. Mason, Frederick A. Rossini, and Jerry Banks. *Forecasting and Management of Technology*. New York: John Wiley & Sons, 1991.

Ratcliffe, Samantha. *Horse Transport in London*. Brimscombe Port, U.K.: Tempus Publishing, 2005.

Schumpeter, Joseph A. *Capitalism, Socialism and Democracy*. New York: HarperPerrenial, 1975.

Shidle, Norman G. *Motor Vehicles and Their Engines*. New York: D. Van Nostrand Company, 1941.

Spence, Jonathan D. *The Search for Modern China*. New York: W.W. Norton & Company, 1990.

St. Louis Exposition of the Association of Edison Illuminating Companies, *Edisonia: A Brief History of the Early Edison Electric Lighting System*. New York: Edison Light and Power, 1904.

Stross, Randall. *The Wizard of Menlo Park: How Thomas Alva Edison Invented the Modern World*. New York: Random House, 2007.

Swan, Kenneth R. *Sir Joseph Swan and the Invention of the Incandescent Electric Lamp*. London: Longmans, Green and Co., 1946.

Tainter, Joseph A. *The Collapse of Complex Societies*. Cambridge: Cambridge University Press, 1988.

Tertzakian, Peter. *A Thousand Barrels a Second: The Coming Oil Break Point and the Challenges Facing an Energy Dependent World*. New York: McGraw-Hill, 2006.

Tilton, Rafael. *Henry Ford*. Farmington Hills, MI: Lucent Books, 2003.

Toffler, Alvin. *Future Shock*. New York: Random House, 1970.

United States Department of Energy. *Energy Security: A Report to the President of the United States*. Washington, D.C.: USDOE, 1987.

Utterback, James M. *Mastering the Dynamics of Innovation*. Boston, MA: Harvard Business School Press, 1996.

Vaitheeswaran, Vijay V. *Power to the People*. New York: Farrar, Straus and Giroux, 2003.

Van Anglen, K. P. *Simplify Simplify and Other Quotations from Henry David Thoreau*. New York: Columbia University Press, 1996.

Walker, Rob. *Buying In: The Secret Dialogue Between What We Buy and Who We Are*. New York: Random House, 2008.

Warren, Louis S. *American Environmental History*. Malden, MA: Blackwell Publishing, 2003.

Watts, Steven. *The People's Tycoon: Henry Ford and the American Century*. New York: Alfred A. Knopf, 2005.

Weitz, C. E. *Electric Illumination*. Scranton, PA: International Textbook Company, 1938.

Winchester, Simon. *The Man Who Loved China*. New York: HarperCollins Publishers, 2008.

Articles

Abboud, L. "Power Play: How Denmark Paved the Way to Energy Independence—Thirty-Year Plan Uses Wind, Taxes, Pig Fat; Consumers Pay More." *Wall Street Journal*, April 16, 2007.

Armagnac, Alden P., "New Pipe Lines Point to Gas Heating Era." *Popular Science*, August, 1930, p. 23.

Bai, Matt. "Home–Office Politics." *New York Times*, November 4, 2007.

Boorstin, Daniel J. "Television: More Deeply Than We Suspect, it has Changed All of Us." *Life*, September 10, 1971.

Bradsher, Keith. "China's Central Bank Is Short of Capital." www.nytimes.com, September 4, 2008.

Buckleitner, Warren. "So Young, and So Gadgeted." *New York Times*, June 12, 2008.

Bush, Vannevar. "As We May Think." *Atlantic Monthly*, July, 1945.

Clarke, Arthur C. "Everybody in Instant Touch." *Life*, September 25, 1964.

Clifford, Stephanie. "Billboards That Look Back." *New York Times*, May 31, 2008.

Coase, R. H. "The Problem of Social Cost." *Journal of Law and Economics* 3 (October 1960): 1–44.

Corbett, Sara. "Can the Cellphone Help End Global Poverty?" *New York Times Magazine*, April 13, 2008.

Davis, Lisa Selin. "The Green House as Classroom." *New York Times*, December 20, 2007.

Delong, J. Bradford. "Creative Destruction's Reconstruction: Joseph Schumpeter." *The Chronicle Review*, December 7, 2007.

Drucker, Peter F. "Beyond the Information Revolution." *Atlantic Monthly*, October 1999.

———. "The Dawn of E-Life." *Atlantic Monthly*, September 20, 1999.

Energy Information Administration. "Emissions of Greenhouse Gases in the United States 2007." EIA Publication, December 2008.

Faltermeyer, Edmund, K. "The Coming Battle for the Color-TV Market." *Fortune*, January, 1966.

Fitzgerald, Michael. "Cloud Computing: So You Don't Have to Stand Still." *New York Times*, May 25, 2008.

Fitzgerald, Michael. "Finding and Fixing a Home's Power Hogs." *New York Times*, Sunday, July 27, 2008.

Flaccus, Gillian. "Disney revives 'House of the Future.'" *Associated Press*, February 13, 2008.

Florio, Mike. "Coming Soon, NFL Games in 3D?" www.ProFootballTalk.com, April 7, 2008.

Friedman, Thomas L. "If I.T. Merged With E.T." *New York Times*, October 31, 2007.

Fuchgott, Roy. "Navigating With Feedback from Fellow Drivers." *New York Times*, October 18, 2007.

Gertner Jon. "Capitalism to the Rescue." *New York Times Magazine*, October 3, 2008

Gladwell, Malcolm. "In the Air." *The New Yorker*, May 12, 2008.

Gross, Daniel. "An American Prius?" slate.com, September 22, 2007.

Grossman, Gene M., and Alan B. Krueger. "Environmental Impact of a North American Free Trade Agreement." National Bureau of Economic Research, Working Paper no. 3914. Cambridge, MA: NBER, 1991.

Guynn, Jessica. "Google Unveils its Green Dreams." *Los Angeles Times*, November 28, 2007.

Hagens, N. "The Energy Return of (Industrial) Solar—Passive Solar, PV, Wind and Hydro." www.thoildrum.com, April 2008.

Hammerschlag, Roel. "Ethanol's Energy Return on Investment: A Survey of the Literature 1990–Present." *Environmental Science Technology* 40 (2006): 1744–50.

Hardin, Garrett. "The Tragedy of the Commons." *Science, New Series* 162 (3859): Dec. 13, 1968, p 1243–1248.

Heffernan, Virginia. "Personalize This." *New York Times*, June 1, 2008.

Heller, Aron. "Israel Pushes Electric in a Big Way." *Associated Press*, January 21, 2008.

Hessler, Peter. "China: Inside the Dragon." *National Geographic*, May 2008.

Kincaid, Jason. "Android's SugarTrip Takes A New Approach To Dodging Street Traffic." www.techcrunch.com, October 20, 2008.

Koerner, Brendan I. "Are the Yankees Bad for the Environment?" www.slate.com, October 9, 2007.

Kolbert, Elizabeth. "Running on Fumes." *The New Yorker*, November 5, 2007.

Krisher, Tom. "GM Researching Driverless Cars." www.MSNBC.com, January 6, 2008.

Lavelle, Marianne. "Putting Your Home on an Energy Diet." *US News & World Report*, April 17, 2008.

Lepore, Jill. "Our Own Devices." *The New Yorker*, May 12, 2008.

Life, "Television: A Special Section." September 10, 1971.

Lloyd, Bob. "The Commons Revisited: The Tragedy Continues." *Energy Policy* 35 (2007): 5806–18.

Lohr, Steve. "A Social Order Shaped by Technology and Traffic." *New York Times*, December 20, 2007.

Lorenz, Andreas. "The Atomic Age Enters a New Dawn." www.spiegel.de. July 11, 2008.

Markoff, John. "Mashups Are Breaking the Mold at Microsoft." *New York Times*, February 10, 2008.

———. "The Team That Put the Net in Orbit." *New York Times*, December 9, 2007.

———. "Two Views of Innovation, Colliding in Washington." *New York Times*, January 13, 2008.

Markoff, John and Saul Hansell. "Hiding in Plain Sight, Google Seeks More Power." *New York Times*, June 14, 2006.

Maslow, A. H. "A Theory of Human Motivation." *Psychological Review* 50 (1943): 370–96.

Portfolio.com, "Google and GE In Energy Tie-Up," September 17, 2008.

Rae-Dupree, Janet. "Da Vinci, Retrofitted for the Modern Age." *New York Times*, June 1, 2008.

Rakoff, David, "The Future Knocks Again." *New York Times*, July 10, 2008.

Rosenberg, Scott. "Trapped in the Grid." www.salon.com., January 24, 2008.

Rosenthal, Elisabeth. "Trying to Build a Greener Britain, Home by Home." *New York Times*, July 20, 2008.

Scientific American, "Electricity," November 19, 1910, p. 395.

Schiesel, Seth. "O.K., Avatar, Work With Me." *New York Times*, May 15, 2008.

———. "Resistance Is Futile."*New York Times*, May 25, 2008.

Solveig, G., and W. Taoyuan. "Coal Cleaning: A Viable Strategy for Reduced Carbon Emissions and Improved Environment in China?" Statistics Norway, Discussion Paper no. 356, October 2003.

Squatriglia, Chuck. "Gasoline Is Here to Stay, But It's Greener Than Ever." *Wired Magazine*, January 10, 2008.

Stark, Betsy. "The Future of the Workplace: No Office, Headquarters in Cyberspace." *ABC News*, August 27, 2007. http://abcnew.go.com/WN/story?id=3521725.

The Economist, "Buy Our Stuff, Save the Planet," May 22, 2008.

———, "Cutting the Cord," April 26, 2007.

———, "Fridges of the World, Unite!" April 15, 2008.

———, "In Search of the Perfect Battery," March 6, 2008.

———, "Marconi's Brainwave," April 26, 2007.

———, "Not on Our Roads," May 1, 2008.

———, "Power from the People," February 7, 2008.

————, "Power Plays," March 6, 2008.

————, "Revving Up," October 11, 2007.

————, "Sharing What Matters," June 7, 2007.

————, "Something New Under the Sun," October 11, 2007.

————, "Stretchy Electronics," January 1, 2008.

————, "The Age of Mass Innovation," October 11, 2007.

————, "The Drive for Low Emissions," May 31, 2007.

————, "The Hidden Revolution," April 26, 2007.

————, "When Everything Connects," April 2007.

————, "World of Dealcraft," December 6, 2007.

Tierney, John. "The Future Is Now? Pretty Soon, at Least." *New York Times*, June 3, 2008.

U.K. Energy Research Centre. "The Rebound Effect: An Assessment of the Evidence for Economy-wide Energy Savings From Improved Energy Efficiency." U.K. Energy Research Centre (UKERC), October, 2007.

U.S. Department of Labor. "Consumer Expenditures in 2005." U.S. Bureau of Labor Statistics, Report 998, February 2007.

U.S. Energy Information Administration (EIA). "International Energy Annual 2005: World Total Net Electricity Consumption."

Vogelstein, Fred. "The Untold Story: How the iPhone Blew Up the Wireless Industry." *Wired Magazine*, Issue 16:02, February 2008.

Zachary, G. Pascal. "The Risk of Innovation: Will Anyone Embrace It?" *New York Times*, January 20, 2008.

Zapotosky, Matt. "Teleworkers Say It's A Gas-Gas-Gas Saver." *Washington Post*, July 27, 2008.

About the Author

Peter Tertzakian, best-selling author of *A Thousand Barrels a Second: The Coming Oil Break Point and the Challenges Facing an Energy Dependent World*, is Chief Energy Economist at ARC Financial Corp.

His background in geophysics, finance, and economics, combined with his entrepreneurial spirit, helped him rise from the trenches of hands-on oil exploration fieldwork to become an internationally recognized authority in energy matters. An amateur collector of antique lighting devices, Peter's passion and expertise is in studying how energy use evolves in societies.

Often seen and heard through media outlets around the world, Peter's been a featured guest on many high-profile radio and television shows, including *The Daily Show with Jon Stewart*. He also writes a weekly column and is a sought after public speaker.

Index